Elisabeth
SLADEN

the
autobiography

with
Jeff Hudson

10 9 8 7 6 5 4 3 2 1
2016 2015 2014 2013 2012

Typeset in Fournier MT Std Regular by
SX Composing DTP, Rayleigh, Essex

and bound in Great Britain by CPI Group (UK) Ltd, CR0

entertainment

First published in 2011 by
Aurum Press Ltd
7 Greenland Street
London NW1 0ND
www.aurumpress.co.uk

This paperback edition first published in 2012 by Aurum Press Ltd

ISBN 978 1 84513 826 4

Printed   4 YY

Typeset in Fournier MT Std Regular by

Acknowledgements

There are so many people to thank from us as a family as well as on Mum's behalf.

Top of the list is Pat and the Davis family for being there through everything and for being the best friend Mum could have wished for.

Also Andrew Beech, for being the original Sladen roadie; Alan Langley for conventions and beyond; Roger Carey Associates; and the whole *Sarah Jane Adventures* team – with special mention to Anj, Danny, Tom, Julie Gardner, Phil Collinson, the gorgeous Nikki Wilson, Phil Ford, Brian Minchin, Matthew Bouch, Emma Bailey, Stewart Meachem, Gary Russell, Graeme Harper, Joss Agnew, Ashley Way, Michael Kerrigan, Charles Martin, Alice Troughton, all the wonderful writers and the very hard-working crew! Not forgetting everyone in the new *Doctor Who* team, particularly Ed Russell for his amazing *feat* . . .

Very special mention to the late Barry Letts who was much loved and who, of course, created Sarah Jane, and also to the much loved and cherished Russell T Davies for bringing Sarah Jane out of her attic.

Friends past and present, especially Liz and the Bowyers, Jane and Dave, the Lonnens, the Badgers, the Plumleys, the Benthams, Barbara and Chris and all those unmentioned but who know who you are.

A very special mention to Sam Harrison and everyone at Aurum Press, and Jeff Hudson, Mum's co-writer, for all their hours and dedication in creating a fitting tribute and a great read.

A huge thank you to all the children, young and old, who loved watching Mum and who have shared their thoughts and best wishes with us.

Finally, I'd like to thank my Mum, Elisabeth Miller – not Sladen – who will not be shared with anyone and whom I miss and love very much.

Sadie Miller
London, September 2011

Contents

Foreword

It Was Always The Doctor And Sarah

2005. My first day on a new job.

A long table scattered with scripts, water bottles and paper name plates stretched the whole length of the room. What felt like hundreds of people milled around expectantly, chatting, checking BlackBerries, casting sideways glances as I tried to keep breathing and affect an air of insouciant calm. I took my place in front of my little paper sign and glanced around the table. And there, just across from me and down to my left, a face from my childhood leapt out from among the throng.

Sarah Jane Smith was quietly leafing through a script and composing herself for the afternoon ahead. Perhaps she was sipping a glass of water, maybe chatting to her neighbour, I don't remember now – all I remember is the sense that in that moment someone familiar, someone comforting and someone slightly magical had come to make sure everything was going to be all right.

If Sarah was here, there was nothing to worry about. Later that afternoon she would be calling me Doctor. The little eight-year-old in my head (who was frankly reeling at the fact that I was in that room at all) was soothed, and of course *thrilled*, that the Doctor's one true assistant was there to look out for him.

Of course later I would get to know Lis and realise she was just as nervous as me that day, but in that moment she represented all that made me want the job in the first place. It was her voice that transported me. In one line she catapulted me back to Saturday tea times, the little catch in her voice as she confronted the latest intergalactic horror. The jeopardy was always palpable; everything seemed so real, almost raw. Everything Sarah did was alive and true. Lis's absolute conviction in playing that role brought the worlds of *Doctor Who* to vivid, irrefutable life. There was no danger that a cheap set or a less than convincing rubber mask would puncture the magic when Lis was there, believing in everything around her with such passionate certitude.

And here she was, just the same: the same conviction, the same passion for it. She was utterly consummate. And of course, she looked the same. Everybody would say it, but Elisabeth Sladen never seemed to age, either in looks or spirit. As an actor you're not supposed to get star-struck; it isn't the done thing to be in awe of someone you are working with. It wouldn't be very helpful if you couldn't look your co-star in the eye when you're supposed to be playing their boss, or their lover. It's a professional necessity that you can at least *pretend* to be easy in the company of your colleagues. I would have to admit to a handful of instances where such professionalism has failed me though, and that afternoon, when I finally met Lis, was one of them.

Reading through the script was easy. I was doing scenes with Sarah Jane Smith, I'd played them out a million times in the playground as a kid, but actually meeting Elisabeth Sladen, who used to be on posters on my bedroom wall, and having to talk to her as an *adult*. It was too much. Except, of course, she was everything I could hope she would be. Charming, diffident, conscientious, giggly, determined, straightforward, a little crazy and enormously warm. She inspired absolute devotion in everyone who worked with her. Through her largesse and openness I very quickly moved from adoring fan to genuine devotee. I would quiz her for stories about Jon Pertwee and Tom Baker, and after a while she'd oblige, but always with absolute grace and generosity. She would never bore anyone with actorly anecdotes – she had way too much class – but if you could tease some out of her, they were always delicious.

That day around that long conference table was the beginning of a fantastic journey for me. For Lis it was the continuation of a much longer one (albeit the beginning of a glorious new chapter for Sarah Jane Smith). Those scenes in the episode 'School Reunion' where the Doctor sees Sarah again after all that time were some of the most thrilling I had on *Doctor Who*. It was the realisation of a childhood fantasy I never imagined I would entertain. It could only have been with Elisabeth. It was *always* the Doctor and Sarah.

I loved my time on *Doctor Who*. I had the huge privilege of working with a host of remarkable, gifted and often highly prestigious actors. My own travelling companions – Billie, Freema and Catherine – were second to none, but the experience just wouldn't have been the same if my TARDIS hadn't been graced by the lady who lit up my childhood and helped me fall in love with it all in the first place.

As a child I was delighted to know Sarah Jane Smith.

As an adult I was privileged to know Elisabeth Sladen.

David Tennant
September 2011

Prologue

I Wouldn't Have Missed It For The World

IT SHOULD have been the happiest day of my life.

Sweeping up to the front door in a vintage white Rolls, a vision in ivory, from the flower in my hair to the heels on my feet; this was the moment I'd been waiting for all my life.

I entered the hall and saw him waiting: the man of my dreams. I stared into his eyes and the world melted away. Nothing else mattered. Not our guests — neighbours, an old editor, my hairdresser and accountant — or my trusty dog hidden under the table. Not even my son, who had given me away. Those people were my past. My future was standing next to me. In a few minutes it would all be over and we would be together. Forever.

Finally, the wedding music stopped and the ceremony began. The registrar's words drifted past like clouds; she could have been saying anything. I wished she'd hurry up.

Just a few more seconds . . .

The formalities continued: 'If any person can show just cause or impediment why they may not be joined together, let them speak now or forever hold their peace.' *Nearly there,* I thought, *just a few more moments.*

And then the skinny man in the blue suit ruined everything with four simple words.

'Stop this wedding — *now!*'

* * *

'And cut!'

Thank God for that. I could finally breathe. A prop it might have been, but my beautiful frock was as uncompromisingly tight as a real wedding dress. After all, no one wants to look anything short of their best on their special day – even if it is only make believe.

It was May 2009. We were shooting *The Wedding of Sarah Jane Smith* and the skinny man in the blue suit, none other than David Tennant, had just blown the doors off our show. It was an incredible entrance, so passionate, so electric and so above and beyond anything we might have expected considering he was coming to us direct from filming his last moments as the Tenth Doctor. You knew he could smell the freedom, almost touch the fresh pastures. But first . . . Seriously, no one on *The Sarah Jane Adventures* would have been surprised if he'd turned in a more low-key performance. To be honest, we were just grateful he'd actually turned up at all. But David – and the Doctor – always delivers (even when he almost certainly didn't want to be there, but more of that later).

Back in my trailer, after an amazing first day with our guest star, I had to pinch myself. Was it really more than thirty years since I had first stepped into the TARDIS – and into the living rooms of millions of viewers? It seemed like yesterday, but that's time travel for you. In fact, even though I'd said goodbye to relative dimensions in space in 1976, my character, Sarah Jane Smith, seemed to have lived on in the memories and hearts of so many fans. I don't know why she was so popular, but the letters from new generations of audiences never dried up, not when I left *Doctor Who*, not even when the show was finally taken off air in 1989. People always cared about Sarah, and no one more so than the wonderful Russell T Davies, who not only brought her back in 2006 but also created an entire show for her.

My show.

And here was David Tennant starring in it. You really do have to check it's not a dream sometimes. I wasn't in David's show. He was in mine. *Mine!* *The Sarah Jane Adventures*, for goodness' sake.

At the point Russell had rung to ask if I'd return for David's first series, I was actually retired. I had certainly left the Doctor long behind, especially so far as television was concerned. But Russell wanted me back and, as soon as I'd spent one moment in his company and experienced his enthusiasm and — let's face it — his genius, I wanted me to come back as well.

And here we were, three years later. Little Sarah Jane Smith, wide-eyed, obstreperous Sarah Jane Smith had gone from pretending to be her Aunt Lavinia — RIP, Auntie — to leading her own band of junior alien-battlers — and topping the viewing figures for BBC1's children's programming in the process. Who saw that coming when I was shuffle-step-changing as a teenage dancer? Who saw that around the corner when I was sweeping the stage at the Liverpool Playhouse in the hope of winning a line or two? Or when I was the non-speaking attendant in *Twelfth Night*, the figure of Alan Ayckbourn's mocking in Scarborough, or Elsie Tanner's whipping girl in *Coronation Street*? Who looked at young Lis Sladen, starving and cold in Clapham in the early 1970s, and predicted the fever pitch that would accompany her appearances at conventions the world over so many decades later?

Doctor Who has given me so much. Not just me, in fact. International adoration of Sarah Jane and the show has taken me and my family all over the world. Like a lot of wonderful actors, my husband, Brian Miller, has appeared in *Doctor Who* several times (as well as in *The Sarah Jane Adventures*) — no thanks to me, mind — while Sadie, our daughter, also starred with me in the *Sarah Jane Smith* audio plays. Even before that, Sadie had her own fan club, thanks to her mother's association with Sarah Jane. She's been signing autographs for as long as she could hold a pen and receiving fan mail for even longer. Seriously, what other programme in the world could have given her that?

So, why does it happen? What makes *Doctor Who* so special? You have to start with the story of course, and the characters, and then there's the writing, and the effects, and so, so much more. Honestly, though, I think the main difference is the fans.

When you've been carried over the heads of thousands of cheering Americans at an LA convention – despite having not been in the show for half a decade – you realise you're in the presence of truly passionate people. It's like that all over the world – *Who* fans pop up in the most unlikely places. In fact, I'm sure I only got invited to audition for *Peak Practice* because the producer had been such a fan as a boy!

Over the years, thanks to *Who*, I've met hundreds of wonderful people, worked with many of them and, sadly, said goodbye, ahead of time, to some. Jon Pertwee, John Nathan-Turner and, of course, the wonderful Barry Letts (without whom . . .), truly memorable pals, one and all.

It hasn't always been easy, of course, for three years' work in the 1970s do not a career make. At times it's been a struggle. On other occasions I've fallen into jobs without looking. There's never been a plan, I'm proud of that; never been a strategy to achieve this by then. And yet here I am, in 2011, star of my own show and with new fans arriving from all points of the globe every minute of the day. I may not always have loved it, I may not at times have even liked my character, but one thing I do know. As Sarah says to David's Doctor at the end of her comeback *School Reunion* episode: 'I wouldn't have missed it for the world.'

Chapter One

'S' Is For 'Star'

JON PERTWEE, like the Doctor he portrayed, was very much what you would call a 'man's man'. He got off on gadgets, fast cars and physical challenges – anything that got the adrenaline pumping.

I don't think it was any coincidence that Jon's time on *Doctor Who* saw the introduction of Bessie, his beloved canary-yellow roadster, the space-age Whomobile and all manner of car, speedboat and helicopter chases. And whereas his predecessors usually took flight at the first sign of fisticuffs, how many of Jon's fans were left disappointed if an episode didn't feature a swift demonstration of his trademark fictional martial art, 'Venusian Aikido'?

As the new girl on the *Doctor Who* set in 1973 I have to admit to initially being intimidated by Jon's off-screen macho bravura. I'm sure part of him would be horrified to hear that but, if I'm honest, I think another part wouldn't have wanted it any other way. He loved an audience: he was a born performer.

One day Jon was regaling us with tales of his new-found passion for sailing. Any chance he got, he would disappear down to the south coast to take on the elements. None of it appealed to me, although he was always entertaining to listen to. But then he happened to mention where he was sailing in Devon that weekend and my ears pricked up.

'Jon, did you say Salcombe?'

'That's right, Lissie. Do you know it?'

'Know it?' I said. 'My father's family used to own half of it!'

Jon fixed me with those piercing eyes for a few seconds then burst out laughing.

'Don't be silly, darling. You're from Liverpool.'

And that was the end of it.

It didn't matter how many times over the years I told him that my family had once owned the Salcombe Hotel, where Jon actually stayed, or how accurately I described the little ferry that carried him across to the other side of the water.

'No, no, darling. That's impossible.'

I don't know whether he thought I was pulling his leg or just deluded, but it was all true.

My father, Tom Sladen, was born in Salcombe in 1900. His mother came from Hallsands, another Devon village that was famously annihilated by a tidal wave – it just doesn't exist any more – and his dad was Captain Thomas Sladen. Sometimes Dad and my grandmother were allowed on Grandpa's ship, which was called *The Lonsdale*. I owe my life to that ship, actually. The whole family does. *The Lonsdale* was docked in San Francisco harbour in 1906 when California was devastated by a huge earthquake. Thousands died. It must have been awful. Grandpa watched it all, helpless, from *The Lonsdale*. For a few terrifying hours that ship was the safest place in the whole state. My grandparents named their house after *The Lonsdale* as well.

Speaking of names, as well as the hotel and lots of surrounding land, my grandparents also owned the little ferry boat that you hopped on to get across to Salcombe Sands. The name plaque on the side of the boat, which read 'Clara Heath', probably wouldn't have meant much to Jon or most other daytrippers, but it meant everything to me. Dad's mum was called Clara Heath and my full name is actually Elisabeth Clara Heath-Sladen – although Dad never used the Heath part. The first time I was old enough to read the sign on that boat I thought I would burst with pride.

I would love to be able to say the Sladen name is alive and well in Salcombe but the story of our family fortune is a sadly familiar one. Dad had three uncles: Fred, Tom and Frank. Frank was a local sporting hero who captained the local cricket and football teams during the war, but when I met him, as a little girl, he'd gambled everything away and was living in a hovel.

The only Sladens with anything left by the time I was born were Dad's parents, who still had their big house. Grandpa always used to tell him, 'When I'm gone, Tom, this will be yours.'

I think Dad was a born adventurer. When the First World War began he was only fourteen, four years younger than the minimum age to be sent to the front line. Two years later, however, he turned up at the army recruitment office claiming to be eighteen. I don't know what he was thinking but after some basic training he was sent off to fight. I've still got some shell cases he smuggled back.

I don't think it turned into the adventure Dad was expecting. He once showed me a picture of five young lads in smart military uniforms, all smiling as if they didn't have a care in the world. It only took me a second to spot Dad among them.

'I was the only one who came back, Lis,' he said, tears in his eyes.

And that was the last word he ever spoke on the subject.

Dad was still a teenager when the Great War ended, and he needed a profession. You can't be born in Salcombe and not love the sea, so he signed up to work for the Cunard shipping line. Unfortunately his first posting wasn't to be in Devon – it was in Liverpool. For a young lad who had never been out of Devon before the War, Merseyside must have seemed like the other end of the world.

But that was where he met my mother.

There were all sorts of film connections in Mum's life although she never had any interest in amateur dramatics – she preferred dancing and tennis. Apparently there were gasps at her christening, when the vicar baptised her 'Gladys Trainer' because everyone had been expecting him to say 'Mary'. Mum always blamed the last-minute switch on her mother's love of the actress Gladys Cooper – although I don't think she was famous when Mum was christened, so we'll never know.

It was another actress who became associated with Mum as she grew up. To her friends she was the 'Vilma Banky' of Liverpool. Vilma was a silent film star from Hungary and everyone said Mum really looked like her. She was about my height, with dark hair and green hazel eyes. Oh, and the most beautiful nose. I wish I had it!

Funnily enough, one of Mum's boyfriends said he wanted to take her off to America but she didn't believe him. Eventually she read he had opened a film studio in Hollywood. I've still got pictures of the pair of them in his old car.

In the end Hollywood came to Mum instead. Whenever the old 1930s movie star Charles Coburn used to call at their neighbour's house in Huskisson Street, Mum would pop round to talk to him. He hadn't worked with Marilyn Monroe in *Gentlemen Prefer Blondes* by then, but there was already an Oscar on his mantelpiece. Charles was a great character and Mum adored listening to him (the company of talented raconteurs is definitely a passion we share). Later, once her brothers started travelling to the United States, they would come back with tales of all the American films and fill her head with visions of supermarkets that were so big you had to push a trolley around them!

By the time Mum and Dad were dating, Dad was being posted all over the world. One of the first people to be sent trading to the Gold Coast in 1920, he absolutely delighted in every moment of it. Every so often family members or friends would return from visiting Lagos and bring new reports of Dad's antics.

'Your Tommy's as bald as a billiard ball and brown as a nut.'

'Your boyfriend's riding motorbikes through the jungle!'

Dad was about five foot eight, with piercing blue eyes and, when he allowed it to grow, blond curly hair. He was kind of square to look at, quite a powerful-looking build. I've never seen anyone tan like him. It must have been his time overseas because he always said, 'You can never have too much sun or too hot a curry.' How I tried to prove him wrong with the curry, but I never succeeded.

After years of to-ing and fro-ing from exotic climes, in 1930 Dad returned to Liverpool to marry my mother. It wasn't a white wedding. Mum's mum had recently died and she didn't feel up to making a fuss. I think Dad always regretted that he didn't get to see Mum in the full veil and sweeping train because he wanted only the best for her. They had a six-month honeymoon instead, travelling the high seas on the Cunard line.

Upon their return, Dad decided it was time to put down some roots in the area, so he gave up his Cunard job and became a bookmaker. He'd always loved sport, like his Uncle Fred, and in particular the horses. I think profits were good for a few years but a bad run of favourites winning and the oncoming recession pushed him out of business. I'm sure he thought he would just get another job, but finding work during the Depression of the 1930s was impossible.

Dad was unemployed for five years but he stayed busy. 'He kept the house beautifully,' Mum recalled. 'He always set the table, our shoes were always gleaming – the shiniest on the street – and he could pack a suitcase like no one else!'

Even though Dad was due to inherit his father's large house one day, five years without a wage coming would have been impossible without the money Mum managed to bring home from her little job. A lot of women were forced to turn to cleaning or other physical work during the 1930s and Dad would have been horrified had his wife been forced to go down that road. But when Mum heard that Bon Marché, the big department store on Basnett Street, was looking for hat models she and her sister Dolly ('Doll') ran along. I've still got pictures of them posing in all the milliner's finery. It was the ideal job for her and that store is still there, although today it's called John Lewis.

Dad finally found work as an accounts clerk at the Automatic Telephone Manufacturing Company in Edge Lane, where he remained until he was sixty-five. Retirement didn't suit him, though, and he worked for another ten years at Thomas Cook, where he was in charge of the currency. Unlike me, he was brilliant with figures.

When the Second World War started, Dad was at the Automatic. Too old to be conscripted this time, he became a member of the Home Guard. He would do a full day at Edge Lane then go straight out on the night watch. Mum hated it – 'You never knew if he was going to come home.'

Liverpool was a prime target for the Luftwaffe's bombs during the War because of its importance to British shipping and manufacturing, but Devon also attracted attention from marauding Messerschmitts trying to stop ships in the Estuary. Grandpa was killed in one of the attacks.

When Grandma had died a few years earlier, Grandpa decided to rent out the big house. 'I don't need all this space,' he told Dad. 'But it's yours and Gladys's whenever you want.' His brother Fred's old cleaner, Nell, and her husband had become good friends so Grandpa moved in with them and let out the house. I think his last years were very happy but nobody foresaw what would happen after he was killed.

Dad arrived in Salcombe to attend to the funeral and later to sort out the family's financial matters. When it came to acquiring the paperwork for the house, however, he hit a snag.

'Your father sold the house to us,' Nell told him.

He bloody didn't, and Dad knew it.

'I'll need to see some paperwork for that, Nell,' he said.

'There's nothing left. Everything burned during the bombs.'

And that was that. Mum was livid. She knew that if Dad had called lawyers in the family would have kept *The Lonsdale* but he didn't want the fight. I don't think he wanted his last memory of Salcombe to be ruined by squabbling over money so he just walked away.

Even though Dad was too old to be conscripted for the Second World War, Mum still had five brothers who enlisted. Four went to sea and one joined the army. Every day while they were away, Mum and Doll used to go down to the Pierhead in Liverpool for news.

When I was little, my mum was still quite jumpy about the War.

Odd little things, like a car backfiring, would set her off down memory lane. To me, it all seemed like eons ago but the older I get, the more I appreciate how close I was to being caught up in all of it.

I was born on 1 February 1946. That's right, 1946. My daughter Sadie has a wicked sense of humour and she is forever laughing at articles that list my birth as 1948. 'Here's another one, Mum. Someone else who hasn't done their homework.' I think my agent was asked for my age once in 1970 and he gave the wrong answer and that's the year that has appeared in every piece of print ever since. So you can see how thorough journalists can be sometimes.

My husband, Brian, really was a war baby, though – which Sadie reckons explains why he will never leave a scrap of food on his plate. 'Dad never saw a banana until he was twenty – he's making up for lost time.'

Mum was forty-four when I came along, and Dad two years older, which probably explains why I stayed an only child, like Dad.

Mum had planned all along to call me after her mother but when a neighbour heard her intention she said, 'Well, you can't have your mum in there and not Tom's. It's not right.' So that's why I became Elisabeth Clara. I wish that bloody woman had never opened her mouth – Liverpool neighbours can be very influential like that – because there was a picture of a cow called Clara on the wall at school, so of course that is what I was called. 'Clara the Cow' – that was me.

As for why Mum chose to spell my name with an 'S' and not a 'Z' like her mother's, when anyone asked she just said:

'The "S" is for "star".'

She reminded everyone of that when she first saw me on television.

If I was a star then Mum was sunshine. She was just lovely. Every childhood memory I have of her is wonderful. Mum and Auntie Doll loved dancing as The Dolly Sisters, which was always fun to watch. And her baking days were legendary on Auckland Road, where we lived. Once every couple of weeks Mum would just devote the entire day to baking. I'd be out playing in the street and someone would say, 'Glad's baking.' We had a houseful on those days.

Every weekend we would all gather with Mum's brothers' and sister's families. As the youngest child I was always made such a fuss of wherever I went. I thought life was always going to be like that!

* * *

I looked forward to bedtimes when I would have Mum all to myself. She loved to read poetry to me, or sing lullabies, which years later I found myself relaying to Sadie – although I wish my voice was half as good as Mum's. (So does Victor Spinetti – but more of that later.)

Our house on Auckland Road had four bedrooms and I had the smallest, the box room at the front. When I was older, that room would be plastered with posters of Elvis. He was my heartthrob. I always wrote on my schoolbooks: Elvis Presley, Errol Flynn and – someone who you'd never think was a heartthrob at all, with his very pockmarked face – the Australian actor, Ray Barrett. I think he was in *Emergency – Ward 10* and, of course, an early *Doctor Who*, although I never saw that. A strange mix, I know. But my posters were Elvis, just totally and utterly Elvis. You're not supposed to say this being from Liverpool but I never really liked The Beatles. They were never my cup of tea. It was The Kinks that I liked listening to. They were quintessentially English and Ray Davies wrote such timeless songs, like 'Waterloo Sunset'. He was a poet really.

One of the other bedrooms was usually inhabited by one of Mum's brothers, Bill, when he was between commissions on ocean liners. He was always bringing me back little presents from his travels. Unfortunately, they were usually bottles of exotic alcohol!

'Here you go, Lis, have a swig of that.'

When guests came to the house I would offer them the drinks

and Uncle Bill was always shocked I still had any left. I guess a sailor's life is very different. Actually I never really drank until I was thirty.

Any spare moments were spent playing with my friends in the street. We'd all invent games or sometimes put on little dance shows. I worshipped Danny Kaye in the film *Hans Christian Andersen,* so I'd have all the kids singing and dancing up and down to 'Wonderful Copenhagen'.

Children weren't under such scrutiny then. I remember one of our neighbours, Mrs McLean, running along the road and calling out, 'Have you seen our Susan? Has anyone seen her?'

We shook our heads. Susan hadn't been playing with us.

'Well,' Mrs McLean said, 'wherever she is she'll be extremely popular because she has her sweet rations!'

When I think of stories like that it's only then that I realise how hard life for my parents and everyone in Britain must have been at the time. Rationing continued for five or six years after the War, but I never remember having to queue for things like some people do, or missing out on anything.

Travelling with my older cousins on the train, across the Mersey, to the seaside town of Hoylake was a regular treat. You knew you were getting closer when you saw the sand on the grass. Usually we'd take sandwiches and spend the whole day playing by the water. In the school holidays we practically lived at Hoylake because Dad would come with us every day. When we weren't there we'd go to Auntie Doll's house whenever there was good weather because they had a garden instead of a yard like us. I loved staying over there with my cousins as well – it felt like such an adventure being away from home.

And it seemed I was perfectly capable of having adventures anywhere. At the end of our road lived Mrs Derry, a colourful old Barbara Cartland sort of character. Everything about her was very pink, very chiffon, and she always wore hats with ribbons. It was as if she was always dressed for four o'clock high tea – completely inappropriate for walking around during the day.

Mrs Derry, like a lot of people, kept chickens in her backyard, but unlike everyone else she used to take hers for a walk! She bought a little cat lead and fixed a collar onto a particularly plump bird and every day you'd see the pair of them pecking their way up to the bus shelter and back. Obviously I was fascinated by this and soon began turning up on Mrs Derry's doorstep at chicken-walking time, begging to be allowed to hold the lead. It felt like such fun to a five-year-old, even when I had to wait for it to poop.

Later on Mrs Derry's son, Derek, came to live with her and all of a sudden my poultry-walking days were over. He drove a flashy red sports car and wanted somewhere to park it, so he persuaded his mother to get rid of her chickens and build a garage. It was the oddest one I've ever seen, with battlements on the roof, like on a castle, and just to make sure no one went near his beloved car, he kept a damn big Alsatian up there as well. I don't think imagination was his strongest point because of course the dog was called Rex. I hated that dog – it always lolloped over to the side of the garage, barking its head off if you strayed near. In the end I had to walk a different route back from school.

My fear of large Alsatians aside, I think I was pretty tomboyish. Another neighbour's son, David, was about twenty and one day he came home on a brand new motorbike. It was the most impressive thing our group of six-year-olds had ever seen. After doing a few noisy revs and showing off how loud it could be, David said, 'Anyone fancy a ride?'

And of course I put up my hand.

While my little friends screamed at me to stop, I climbed up behind my neighbour and said, 'Let's go!' It didn't occur to me that I was barely big enough to reach round him properly or that I didn't have a helmet.

The noise was amazing and as we shot forwards I hugged David for dear life. We just drove around the block, about six roads up, six roads back, and it was great. I loved every moment. When we pulled back into Auckland Road, though, there was a reception committee waiting in the shape of my mother. And boy she looked angry.

I can't remember ever being told off like that. Normally I was such an obedient child that I don't think Mum knew what to say either.

I had obviously inherited a bit of my dad's adventurous streak. In fact, while on holiday recently, just getting my breath before filming on the fourth – and fifth! – series of *The Sarah Jane Adventures*, I found myself thinking about a few old battle scars that were a result of my love of speed when I was young. When I was fifteen I used to walk home from school and fantasise about owning this stunning red Raleigh racing bike that was in the window of the bike shop on the corner of Smithdown Road. Every day I lusted over it, and every day I asked Mum and Dad if I could have it.

'Bikes are very expensive, Elisabeth,' Dad would say. 'Maybe one day.'

And then, not long after Christmas 1961, I walked past the shop and my heart sank.

The bike – *my* bike – had gone.

I was inconsolable that night and even looking at the other bikes the next day didn't cheer me up. But of course my sixteenth birthday was just around the corner and on the morning of 1 February, Mum and Dad led me into the yard and there, gleaming in the morning sun, was the red Raleigh.

I would spend every afternoon after school whizzing around the area. Then one weekend a group of us went blackberrying in the fields. For me, finding the fruit was only half the fun – bombing down muddy hills as fast as I could was what I was there for. It was such a great day – and then the inevitable happened. I was flying down a hill when I thought, *I'm not going to make that bend*. I braked as hard as I could but as I turned, the front wheel clipped a small kerb and I flew clean off. Luckily it was high, thick grass that I tumbled onto, so I just skidded along a raised verge for a few yards. As I lay on my back, gasping for breath, I realised, *At least I had a soft landing*.

But then the pain hit me.

I went to stand up and couldn't – my right leg felt like it was on fire. My calf was livid red, like a square slab of fresh meat on a butcher's block.

The grass I'd landed on had grown over rusty barbed wire. I'd actually had a lucky escape but boy it didn't feel like it. I can still see the scars of the twenty-one stitches today.

On the bright side, I discovered that if I stretched my scar for a minute or two it would turn bright red. So on the days I didn't fancy sports it was just a case of limping along to the tyrannical games teacher and saying, 'Sorry, Mrs Potts, but I don't think I can walk well enough to take part today.'

And she fell for it every time.

Mum was just as gullible. Once I'd shown her my raw scar she immediately wrote to the school: 'Elisabeth's leg has gone septic again. She won't be able to attend her mock exams today.' Which of course was exactly what I was hoping for!

* * *

It says a lot for my early acting ability, I like to think, that I got away with my tall tales. But I should have been quite good at it by then considering I'd been training for a dozen or so years.

When I was four my mother enrolled me in a local dancing school. Dancing had always given her such pleasure and she thought it would be a nice thing for me to do with my little friends. Nobody at that time saw it as the first step towards a career in performing.

When Mum picked me up after my first class I was gushing.

'I love it, Mum. I want to go every day!'

'We'll see about that. For now let's start with Saturdays, shall we?'

After that I couldn't wait for weekends to come around so I could run along Bold Street, where Shelagh Elliott-Clarke ran her dance school.

'SEC', as we called her, had been in Liverpool all her life, acting and dancing. She lived in one of the grand old houses on Rodney Street, which also doubled as the venue for her drama classes. A big, round lady with Beaujoi, a yappy little dog always at her heels, she was in her fifties when I met her. For such a large woman, to this day I have never seen anyone dance so lightly on their feet. She was such an inspiration. I owe her a great deal although she scared the hell out of me, she really did. I think she terrified everyone. One glance from her and you'd be quivering like jelly for the rest of the day. Woe betide anyone summoned to her office for misbehaving or, even worse, not trying hard enough in a class. You'd stand there, white with fear, while she let you have both barrels, her ever-present cigarette waving theatrically around. Somehow, however long the ash extended, it never seemed to fall off.

It was the tradition in those days to enter competitions at local festivals where you would recite or perform a little piece and judges would hand out marks. I can still remember my first performance at one of these, as Gretel, at five years old. For this I wore a blue skirt with white spots on and a velvet jacket. I remember going up to the little girl playing my brother and saying, in my loudest voice, 'Wake up, Hansel, wake up. The little dickie birds are coming!' I can't even recall scripts from this year so I'm amazed I can still dredge that one up!

Just thinking about that show gives me tingles because I can still recall the exact feeling of 'This is magic.' I was only five years old but I knew at that moment that performing was something I wanted to do for the rest of my life.

Soon afterwards I began attending Friday acting classes after school as well. SEC's school had a really strong reputation in those days. She wasn't interested in producing dozens of identikit performers, one after another, like other drama schools tend to do. She used to encourage you to be yourself, which I think is actually quite rare.

I tended to focus most of my acting on whatever performances SEC was putting on and didn't even bother auditioning for school productions, but in my last year at Mosspits Lane junior school I won the part of Alice in *Through the Looking-Glass*, which I think is much more interesting and dark than *Wonderland*. Years later I played the dormouse in *Alice in Wonderland* in a BBC production for the incomparable Barry Letts.

The headmaster at Mosspits was Mr Calman, an amazing teacher. In fact I saw him on a television programme about twenty years ago. He'd just been parachuted into one of those troubled schools to sort it out. That gives you an idea of how good he was. You didn't mess with him, but by God he was supportive.

Mr Calman was in charge of the school production and he would rehearse us over and over until everyone knew their lines – like professionals. It paid off. We had a week of excellent shows. Finally it was Saturday night, the last performance of the year, and the end of a particularly hot day. Because of the weather I'd had more than enough ice cream. In fact, by the time the curtain went up I was not feeling in the best of health, so I told Miss Lyons, the headmistress, I couldn't do it.

'Of course you can, dear. Try not to think about it.'

Somehow I managed to get to the interval. Then as soon as I came offstage Miss Lyons rushed me outside for some fresh air, which I really needed. But then she ruined it by pulling out a hanky soaked in lavender scent.

'This will help you,' she said.

But I knew it wouldn't.

The second half was easier than the first and I was actually beginning to enjoy myself. We were about twenty minutes from the end and I remember a scene with the Red Queen and the White Queen sitting next to me. I don't know how it happened, but as I turned to speak to the Red Queen I somehow got a whiff of lavender and that was it.

I threw up – all over the Red Queen.

The next thing I knew, Mr Calman was lifting me up and carrying me through the shocked choir. It was so awful, so embarrassing. Even backstage the only thing I could hear was the same whispered gasp rushing around the auditorium: 'Elisabeth Sladen has been sick on Edwina Cohen! Elisabeth Sladen has been sick on Edwina Cohen!'

You'll probably be more familiar with Edwina's later married name of 'Currie'. We've never spoken about the incident but perhaps that helped give her the thick skin she needed for a life in politics.

I pretty much retired from school productions after that. The attitude at my secondary school didn't help. I'd only been at Aigburth Vale High School for Girls a few weeks when we had our first careers session. The teacher rattled off a few suitable – to her mind – job titles, then went round the class asking for our aspirations. I'm sure she thought she was being quite progressive by even encouraging us to think about a profession. When she got to me, I said, 'I would just like to perform.'

She decided I was a lost cause there and then, shook her head and moved on to the next girl.

Right, I thought, *if that's your opinion, you're not going to get me*.

Once I'd made the decision to devote myself to SEC, life at Aigburth Vale – or 'Eggy Jail' as we called it – was never going to be fun. Even so, I think the place was too big for me. I felt lost among the hundreds of grammar school girls filling its giant corridors and large classrooms. There didn't seem to be anyone there like Mr Calman who made you feel special, or simply not another nameless pupil, and so I kept my head down, trying my best to get through the day unnoticed. I think the cheekiest thing I ever did was join in with some of the other girls when they waved at the lads at the Tizer factory across the road.

The one teacher who did show an interest in me was our elocution mistress, although I don't think I was as nice to her as I could have been. I wish I could recall her name. She used to come in and make us say things like 'Claire has fair hair and Mary's hair is brown' and we'd all just parrot it back in our best Cilla Black Scouse accent and giggle at her exasperation. The silly thing is this was the one lesson that would actually have benefited my dream of acting. In order to break into the British media in those days you needed to speak the Queen's English. No trace of a regional accent. It wasn't like today where you sometimes think it's the ones with

Received Pronunciation who might struggle. But the reason I messed around in those lessons was because I felt that I didn't have an accent to begin with. My cousins and uncles may have spoken with a pure Liverpudlian lilt, but my father had never lost his southern vowel sounds and Mum spoke the Queen's English as well as anyone, and so that is how I sounded.

At the time, however, it seemed the grammar school curriculum was hell-bent on removing all trace of Scouse from our voices and I guess it worked – and not just on me. After all, how many people watching *Doctor Who* around the world would ever have guessed that both Tom Baker and I hailed from the same city as The Beatles?

Thinking about it, the biggest influence on my voice didn't come from a teacher at all. In the final year, when we should have been revising for exams, girls were allowed to take their books up into an attic room at a house separate to the school. Some pupils worked diligently but generally we played poker for drawing pins and gossiped. The thing I most looked forward to was using the room's old record player. There was only one album up there, which happened to be a performance of T.S. Eliot's *Murder in the Cathedral*, but I would just play it again and again, absolutely mesmerised by Robert Donat's mellifluous, rich voice – I even found myself trying to copy his enunciation and intonations. I must have mentioned this in an interview once, because a fan very sweetly presented me with a copy of this recording, years later.

The desire not to be at Eggy Jail manifested itself in my results, I think. I liked history, because my dad had given me an interest in it, and I loved English, but otherwise resented my time there and I'm amazed I managed to pass the six O-levels that I did. In contrast, it seemed there was always something exciting happening over at SEC, never more so than when the Royal Ballet came to town.

Every Christmas the company arrived at the Crane Theatre and invited girls from SEC to audition for roles in their new production. They weren't exactly casting for Clara in the Sugar Plum Fairy outfit – although, as I shared the name, I dreamed that one day the role would be mine – but what young girl wouldn't explode with excitement at the chance to dress in a beautiful frock and dance around the Christmas tree? Imagine my twelve-year-old face when SEC unveiled my costume.

'The Great King Rat needs his little mice, Elisabeth,' she smiled, handing over a brown suit. 'It's a very important part.'

Every year it was the same story. I'd queue up for one of the glamorous dresses and be given a tail and big ears instead. Always the bloody mouse!

I think I took part five years in a row. There was nothing like that excitement in the weeks building up to it, especially in my first year. I was genuinely shocked that I was still expected to go to school during the day, though.

'But I'm dancing with the Royal Ballet tonight, Mum!'

I remember her smiling face waiting at the gate when I came out on performance night. She had my costume and dancing shoes all ready for me and some sandwiches because I'd be missing tea. I was too nervous to eat a single crumb.

It was such a different experience performing on the huge stage at the Crane Theatre rather than in our dance studio at Bold Street. In fact it was so big that I once got completely lost. There were so many legs kicking and flicking, and pirouetting and pliéing, I couldn't even see where the audience was!

The older I became, the more I began to socialise less with local school friends and more with the girls from SEC. I couldn't have been happier than on a Saturday, going to Rodney Street, having a spot of lunch with the adorable Lizzie Gay – later we were both bridesmaids at each other's weddings – then dancing or performing in competitions in places like Crosby in the afternoon.

Between spending time with friends like Lizzie and all my rehearsals, I didn't have much time for boys – certainly not as much time as other girls at Eggy Jail seemed to have. My first boyfriend, though, was a friend of Lizzie's called Dave Owen. He was so nice, and destined for a life in uniform, I thought. We used to go ice skating together and had a lot of fun but I think I was a bit mean to him, really. It was nothing personal, I just preferred to spend my time at SEC. If either of us had been told then that the next time we would meet would be on my way to an oil rig, we wouldn't have believed it – but that was still to come.

* * *

In the 1960s you were allowed to leave school, before your exams, at fifteen, and a lot of my friends did. I couldn't wait for the end of term so I could sign up for full-time classes with SEC, but my parents had other ideas. They wanted me to stay on in the sixth form and then possibly go on to university. Somehow we managed to come to a compromise.

'Just stay on for one more year, Lissie,' Dad reasoned. 'If you still want to dance and act at the end of that, then OK.'

So that's what I did, but the year dragged by. The highlight was being able to spend my six weeks of holidays at a special 'summer camp' that SEC was running. We had some amazing teachers. I remember Susan Hampshire's mother coming along to take some lessons, and once she even brought Susan herself along. She'd just been in *Espresso Bongo* or *Wonderful Life*, I think, so we were all excited. Anne Robinson, from *The Weakest Link*, was another summer student. It was such a vibrant time.

And, of course, being around SEC for more than just one or two sessions a week allowed us to listen to so many more of her fantastic stories about working with the stars from the Liverpool Playhouse. The more I heard, the more I dreamed of performing there. That's where people like Michael Redgrave were, of course, and we were all shocked to discover she'd gone out with him for a while.

Somehow I got through my lower sixth year and, aged sixteen, I signed up for three full-time years with Shelagh Elliott Clarke – and I couldn't have been happier.

Despite what I'd told my careers mistress, I'd never really dreamed of acting for a living. I was just a child – the idea of doing anything for an actual wage hadn't passed across my radar. I just knew it was how I wanted to spend every minute of my day – and finally, for the first time, I could do just that.

Despite her gruff exterior, SEC was born to encourage. Her mantra – which we all had to chant in unison before exams – was 'Personality is the key to success' and she really drove us to develop our natural abilities. Nothing pleased her more than investing time and love into a student and seeing that student flourish. She was always pushing us to enter competitions and grasp any opportunity. And that is how I found myself appearing on *Search for a Star*.

I don't think I've ever told anyone this before. *Search for a Star* was a national television talent show hosted by a DJ called Keith Fordyce. SEC found out that they were hosting auditions in Liverpool so she sent me along. Other people were singing and dancing as their audition pieces – so what did I do?

Portia's speech from *Julius Caesar*!

I mumbled my way through it and Keith was very nice, actually. When I left, I didn't expect to hear from them again, though. Then a few days later a letter arrived. I'd qualified to appear on the television show! I don't know how – I must have been a bit different, I suppose. All the same, I cringe to think that they saw me as the token novelty act.

The recording was at a studio in Teddington, so far west as to barely be in London. Just as well I wasn't there to sightsee! I think one of my friends came with me – I didn't tell my parents – and I was so nervous. All the other contestants looked so calm and confident. They were obviously the product of many years at drama school whereas I'd just signed up.

The lights went down and my name was called. I delivered my speech once again in my best Robert Donat-inspired tones, then left the stage.

Thank God that's over, I thought. *I never want to go through that again*.

But I had to! Keith Fordyce called me back onto stage at the end of the show to say the public had voted me through. Then I heard those dreaded words: 'Can you come back next week?'

Seven days later, I was back at Teddington.

Unfortunately the show that week was being filmed halfway across London in White City!

I don't know how long I spent wandering around before I realised my mistake. This time I was on my own and I suddenly became aware that I didn't have a clue where I was. For a girl from Liverpool, travelling from Teddington to BBC Television Centre in White City was like trying to get to the moon.

Panicking, I began to run back towards the train station. I think I must have darted across a road without looking because suddenly I heard a squeal of brakes and looked up to see a flashy red sports car skidding to a halt next to me.

That was a close call. I remember staring at the driver, half expecting old Mrs Derry's son, Derek, to climb out. But as the car pulled away I realised it wasn't him. It was the *Carry On* star, Jim Dale!

Somehow I found my way to White City and managed to perform, although this time I didn't win. In fact you've never seen anyone happier to lose. I couldn't wait to get back to Rodney Street – and tell everyone about my brush with near-death and near-celebrity.

Another of Shelagh Elliott-Clarke's ideas for me was a lot more successful – and once again it involved London. My first year was coming to an end and I showed enough promise, she said, for her to recommend me to London's Youth Theatre during the summer holidays.

'London?' Mum said. 'You can't go to London on your own! Where will you live?'

The practicalities hadn't occurred to me, and I didn't care. I can't believe I managed to persuade my parents to let me go, but a few weeks later we arrived at the Scala Theatre for the welcoming meeting. Once Mum and Dad were convinced it was a respectable company they got chatting with another couple and my accommodation was arranged. Their daughter was going to stay at the YWCA in Queensway – and so was I.

'That way you can both keep an eye on each other,' Mum said. 'It will be better living with someone you know.'

The YWCA had one bathroom for a dorm of about ten people. It certainly wasn't what I was used to, but the chance to work in a London theatre – actually acting on the *London stage* – was worth any sacrifice. For the entire summer I was a part of the Scala Company and I'd never been happier.

The first play we worked on was *Hamlet*, with Simon Ward in the lead. I spent most of my first day at rehearsals amazed at how fantastic he looked, striding around with such pale skin and dark glasses. I'd never seen anything like it – he was like a rock star. Jeremy Rowe was in it as well, and Neil Stacy, Michael Cadman and Hywel Bennett – all of them famous television actors in the 1970s, if they weren't already. Michael Croft directed and boy didn't I know it. Every half hour he'd be waving at me, 'Girly, girly – fetch me something from the fridge.'

I only had a small part (as a court lady) but we all have to start somewhere. In fact, my fellow courtier was none other than Helen Mirren, who was stunningly beautiful. Actually there was a secret Company poll and apparently I was voted most likely of the two of us to reach the heights as an actress. I don't remember how well Helen took it at the time, but as she polishes her Oscar every now and then, I'm sure she doesn't let it trouble her!

I wasn't the only one from SEC who passed the auditions, however. Our only boy, from a class of a dozen, had been selected for the Youth Theatre as well. These days Bill Kenwright is better known as the owner of Everton Football Club and one of the country's leading impresarios, but he was an actor first. I think he played Second Sailor in *Hamlet*.

My mum and his were actually quite close and I had tea at their house a few times. Years later I bumped into Mrs Kenwright on the Smithdown Road on a trip back to Liverpool and she told me what Bill was up to. I don't know why but I just blurted out, 'I'm doing *Doctor Who* now – he can't afford me anymore!' Although I was only joking, I don't think she found it funny. Nearly thirty years later I worked for him in panto, so I don't think he held it against me.

After *Hamlet* we did *Julius Caesar* and as well as being part of the crowd every night, I was also understudy for Portia. Who would have imagined my *Search for a Star* party piece could be so useful?

I returned to London for the Youth Theatre the following summer as well. With a year's training from SEC behind me, I auditioned for Hermia in *A Midsummer Night's Dream*, but Diana Quick got the part. Kenneth Cranham was Bottom and I ended up being one of the bloody fairies! I wouldn't mind but it was Mustardseed – I didn't even like his name.

Most of the time SEC taught us personally, but every so often she would invite guests to give us further inspiration. One day she said, 'Girls, we have a treat today. Tony Colegate from the Liverpool Playhouse is going to take a lesson.'

Tony was assistant director at the time but he was such a talented actor too, although he never really enjoyed it. The only Irishman I ever met who didn't have an accent, he was clever, quite hypnotising to listen to, and very powerful when it came to putting his ideas across. I dreamed of working with someone who was as passionate and talented as him. How often had I walked past the Playhouse and stared longingly at the posters of people like Tony Hopkins? That was where I wanted to be.

Of course, being a filmstar would have been fine as well.

When SEC announced that a film crew were seeking extras for a few days, my friends Jackie and Alex and I ran down to sign up. The film was *Ferry Cross the Mersey* starring Gerry and the Pacemakers – I think it was their attempt to do a Beatles-type movie. All I knew was, it was my chance to be seen by an audience of millions.

In the end, I was so embarrassed by the final result that I've never told anyone about it. You certainly won't find it mentioned on my CV! Our contribution involved going down to the Mersey Ferry and riding it back and forth all day to Beddington, so we were in the background while the main actors wandered around the ship.

Anyone would have been happy with a pound a day for that. Then the moment came for our close-up. I had on my Mary Quant dress and I thought I looked the business. The three of us couldn't wait to see it at the cinema.

Well, thank God DVDs didn't exist in those days! The finished scene was horrendous – or rather, *I* was horrendous. At that moment I realised how little I knew about movie acting. My hair was all over the place, my smile fake on film and as for my weight – you really do look two stone heavier onscreen. I remember sitting in the cinema with Alex and Jackie and we cried. I nearly gave up acting there and then.

If anything, though, it simply focused my desire to work harder on my stagecraft. In summer 1964 I joined the Hillbark Players for their open-air production of *Much Ado About Nothing* – a risky undertaking in the Wirral, even in July. We played outdoors at Hillbark House. Entrances and exits were behind bushes and from the house. I wore a yellow frock as Hero and the local papers said I was 'charming and sincere' and 'engaging'. There were a couple of boys who I kept in touch with; they'd come and sleep on our floor in Liverpool sometimes. One wanted to be an artist. I quite liked him, and my Elvis posters came down and his paintings went up in their place – for a while.

My hard work was noticed at school. SEC came over one day, and said, 'There's a place going for an assistant stage manager at the Liverpool Playhouse – I think you should go for it.'

Talk about a bolt from the blue.

'But what about my lessons, what about my acting?'

'My dear Lissie, you will learn more in a year at the Playhouse than a lifetime in this studio.'

Encouraging as ever. And it made sense, but there was a caveat. 'There's just one thing. It's a post for a student – if they find out you've been to drama school you'll not get in because they'll have to pay you more!'

I was nervous enough auditioning for David Scase, the Playhouse's famous director, but keeping that little secret made me a bundle of nerves. I must have said something right, though. A couple of days later Shelagh found me before class.

'I've just had a phone call from the Playhouse. Congratulations, my dear, they want you.'

Now I just had to convince my parents. It had been hard enough to persuade them to let me go to dance school in the first place – and now I wanted to quit halfway through and join a theatre.

'Are you sure, Lissie?' Mum kept saying. 'Are you really sure it's what you want to do?'

'Mum, for the chance of acting at the Liverpool Playhouse I would happily wash that stage every night on my knees,' I said.

I'm such a bloody idiot – that's exactly what they had me doing!

Chapter Two

Here She Comes, Sarah Heartburn

THE LIVERPOOL Playhouse, on Williamson Square, is a beautiful, majestic old building that was built as a music hall in the 1860s. It's where Noël Coward first worked with Gertrude Lawrence as child actors and where London's Old Vic relocated during the War. I wasn't aware of this rich history as a youngster, of course. All I knew, every time I walked past its tall, imposing stone columns, or occasionally if I was lucky enough to see a play in its luxurious auditorium, was that the people inside that building were lucky enough to be doing the thing that I most wanted to do for the rest of my life.

But now I had my chance.

I've still got the letter from David Scase, the artistic director: 'We're delighted to welcome you to the Liverpool Playhouse Repertory Company.' As I made my way to the theatre in August 1965, I clutched it tightly just in case anyone needed proof that I deserved to be there. Reaching Brythen Street, I stopped. There was the sign marked 'Stage Door'. A shiver ran through me. Stepping through that door would be like stepping into Narnia – my life would never be the same again.

I thought of the dozens of productions I'd seen there, all the stars who had stepped through this door before me. It was such a magical company at the time: Cynthia Grenville, Lynda Marchal – who became Lynda La Plante – Tony Hopkins, future husband and wife Malcolm Read and Helena de Crespo, and Jean Boht. I used to watch them all. And Patrick Stewart, he was marvellous, although bald even then. I remember going to see him as Oberon in *A Midsummer Night's Dream* – it only cost a few coppers for a seat up in the gods – and I don't think people recognised him when he came on because he was wearing a wig. Normally the fact he became bald so prematurely meant he got all the meaty, older man parts, but this time they actually wanted him to appear younger.

Here I was, a few years later, about to follow in their footsteps. It didn't matter that I was only a student, I was still part of the same company to count my hero Robert Donat, Rachel Kempson, Rex Harrison and Michael Redgrave among its alumni.

I took a deep breath and went in.

The best job in the world can be ruined if you're working with the wrong people – fortunately, right from day one, the backstage crew at the Playhouse were superb. David Scase went out of his way to make me comfortable but I was thrilled to meet once again his deputy, Tony Colgate. He'd been such an inspiration during his lesson at SEC – I couldn't wait to work with him. Jenny Smith was the stage manager and my boss. Her assistant, Sally Crowgey, was extremely glamorous, always very high heels, low zip and lots of makeup. She was lumbered with showing me the ropes, and fortunately she'd been there long enough not to worry about someone else coming along trying to do her job. Ivor Dykes was a great character, a lighting guy who was terrified of heights. If you went anywhere near his ladder when he was up in the gods he soon let you know about it! His assistant, Michael, didn't have the same problem. He was very sweet. Finally on that first day, I met Christopher Bullock, my stage director. Even now I only remember him one way: six foot two of absolute authority. You didn't mess with Chris – or his brother, I heard – but right from the word go he was nothing but caring and paternal towards me. One of the first things he said was, 'Now, Lis, we don't want any involvement with these actors, do we? They'll all try to hit on you, you know.'

Hit on me? I thought. I was quite a bit bigger then, not fat but what people in Liverpool at the time called 'bonnie'. 'Isn't your Elisabeth looking bonnie, Mrs Sladen?' I was always hearing.

Compared to all the skinny actresses I was working with, I couldn't imagine anyone looking at me twice. Anyway, boys were off the agenda – I was there to learn.

I had an amazing first week and then I thought my world was going to fall in. Kay, the company manager, approached me one morning. 'So,' she said, 'you're from a drama school.'

God, I'd forgotten about that.

I felt the tears welling. 'Does that mean you're going to throw me out?'

Kay just sighed. 'No, it just means we have to pay you £4 a week instead.'

So I'd only been there a week and already I was getting a raise, but it wasn't the best of starts.

Now I don't think there is a piece of paper big enough to list every aspect of the role of ASM. I had to sweep the stage, look after the props, manage the 'book', operate sound effects and generally run the backstage area in Jenny's absence. In other words, it was a bit – *no, a lot* – of everything. But, do you know what? I couldn't have been happier! To find myself so immersed in a real live theatre was a dream come true. And to be given a wage for it when I would happily have worked for free was unbelievable.

They really got their money's worth. I arrived at nine in the morning and, on a show night, left with everyone else around eleven o'clock – often straight to the nearest pub (in my case for a sparkling water) to unwind. The day I joined they were just beginning work on a production of *Seidman & Son* starring David Kossoff and I was given immediate responsibility for the show's props. Any cushions or teapots or guns or rugs that were to be used in a scene, I had to put there and make sure they stayed there. If an actor needed to enter stage left with a book, I had to give him that book. And if he came off-stage with a cigarette lighter, then I whipped it from him and made sure it was ready the following night. I seemed to spend the whole evening chasing one cast member after another – 'Have you got your personals? Where are your personals?' The pressure was tremendous.

And the buck stopped here. As Jenny reminded me, if I didn't do it, it didn't happen.

Opening night came and I had never been so nervous. Mum and Dad were in the audience and even though they couldn't see me, I'd told them everything I was doing. As I sent the various plates and hats and other bits and pieces onto the stage I could imagine Mum applauding them as though I was up there myself. A week into the run and the adrenaline began to wear off. I loved it, but boy was I tired! I remember Kossoff passing me, almost on my knees, on his way to the stage. 'Ah, dear,' he said in his rich accent, 'Vot's a nice girl like you doing in a job like this?'

There were two other main roles for the ASM apart from props. The next one I was given was working the panetrope – basically an old-fashioned sound-effects machine. If a telephone needed to ring, that was me. Whenever there was a doorbell, that was me. It was all pretty straightforward – or so I thought. In rehearsal I had to play a track of a car supposedly reversing into its garage. Basically, you just press 'play' on the machine and turn the volume up, but I did it so fast it sounded like the car had exploded.

'No jerky movements,' Jenny said. 'Nice and smooth.'

Well, that night it was certainly smooth. It took about five hours for that car to park!

My other job was the hardest and most important – and the one I was best at. It was called being 'on the book', because essentially you had to sit with a copy of the script and make sure everything happened when it was scheduled. The work started in rehearsal when you had to write down notes about the actors' movements, counting their paces, and noticing every detail – I suppose it's the equivalent of taking Polaroids for consistency in films. Two pages before every sound effect, lighting cue or stage entrance, you would put a mark in the script to give you some warning. Then on the night you'd sit at the side, looking for cues, and go, 'Standby, Mr Cowdrey, your call' when it was two pages from his entrance. Then there would be another call, and a little bell to press. Or if it wasn't an actor I'd be saying, 'Cue electrics' or 'Cue lights'. The book is the oil in the machine – I really enjoyed it.

But of course it was acting I really wanted to do. The second play of the season came and went. When the third was announced, *The Long and the Short and the Tall*, there was no part for me. I didn't expect there to be, but it was still a shame.

For the new play, as well as the usual company, Tony Colegate had cast two of his favourite actors of the day: Steven Berkoff and a guy from Birmingham, Brian Miller. Tony had worked with them both before and only had great things to say.

Rehearsal day arrived and the cast began assembling. I was there early as usual – the lot of the ASM. Suddenly, though, the door in the giant soundproof screen opened and my head was filled with different thoughts entirely.

Brian Miller had stepped backstage and my mouth literally fell open. I don't know what it was. He was wearing a tweed jacket with leather elbows and jeans. And he had very red golden hair. I couldn't take my eyes off him.

Well, that's just great, I thought, annoyed at my own instincts.

I remember arriving home early a few nights later while Mum was still cooking dinner. I just walked in and said, 'I've met the man I'm going to marry.'

I don't think she even looked up.

'Don't be ridiculous. You're far too young.'

And maybe I was. But when it strikes, it strikes and I knew instantly. After everything Chris Bullock had warned, despite all my best intentions, this guy walks into the room and – *bang* – that's it.

It's a fact of theatre that you're thrown together for long periods at a time. That's why Chris had said to be careful – convenience and proximity can be confused for love. But Brian and I found ourselves chatting for longer and longer. One of my jobs was to wash the tea things, and I noticed he started coming for a cuppa every time I filled the sink. One day he said, very casually, 'By the way, do you want to go for a drink tonight?'

'No,' I said. I'm sure I should have dressed it up a bit, made an excuse. 'I can't tonight' – something like that. But if Brian was daunted, he didn't let it show.

'Oh well,' he breezed, perfectly nonchalantly. 'Another night then.'

And that's sort of how we left it. I wasn't really sure if he was just sniffing around the fresh faces or whether he was thinking what I was thinking. But the next time he asked I said, 'Yes.' We didn't really do any formal dating as such – we didn't have the time. There were plenty of lunches together and lots of conversations at work and snatched moments in the pub with the rest of the team, but for a while that was it.

I really liked the way Brian went about things. He was quite diffident, off-hand I suppose, but so cheeky when he could get away with it – very funny and charming. Yet he wouldn't suffer fools. Nobody tried to mess with him. He drew a line, which I liked.

But I wasn't sure where we stood and when the whole cast of *The Long and the Short and the Tall* went out to perform the play at a festival in Florence for a week (the Playhouse booked The Seekers to fill the gap) I thought, *Well, I'm sure he'll find some nice Italian while he is there. Then I'll know if I'm wasting my time.*

It turned out Brian had spent most of his spare time away from everyone else in museums, galleries and cinemas. And he'd brought me a present! At first I thought it was just a bag of nice sweets. I was staggered to discover it was a beautiful bracelet.

Ah, I thought, *I've got you now!*

I was so excited I rushed off to show Sally, the other ASM. She happened to be looking for me so we virtually bumped into each other.

'There you are, Lis!' she said. 'Look what Brian Miller has bought me!'

It was the same bloody bracelet.

I was in a bit of a foul mood for a while after that, mainly annoyed at myself for being so naïve, so when Warren Clarke – famous to modern generations from *Dalziel and Pascoe* – who had joined the company, asked me out we went to the cinema together, which was nice. It was a John Wayne film, I think. (The details you remember as you get older!) But then I heard from one of the other girls that a chap had asked Brian if he was serious about me and he'd said, 'Yes.'

Well, he's got a funny way of showing it, I thought. But gradually we spent more and more time together and, without either of us really saying anything, soon we were a couple. There weren't any bold gestures, no dramatic speeches. It just happened.

To be honest, I don't think we would have had time for anything more flashily romantic. Those early weeks of being smitten coincided with my busiest time as ASM, so if I wasn't at the theatre, I was either on my way there or back.

The problem was that, because we were a company, each new play was put on by us. You didn't have a completely different crew coming in when the production finished. So, no sooner had *The Long and the Short and the Tall* got up and running than rehearsals started on the next one, and it wasn't just the actors who suffered. Every night, after *The Long and the Short and the Tall* closed, it was my job to sweep the sand from the stage – it was set in the jungle – strip all the markings and set it out for the following afternoon's run-through. Then as soon as that was finished, and I'd done all the notes for the book, it was up with those marks and on with the evening performance. Incredibly tiring but I was still having the time of my life, in a job I loved and watching a man who I was beginning to feel the same way about every day.

Although Tony had hired Brian for *The Long and the Short and the Tall*, it was actually the next production, *Twelfth Night*, that he had really wanted him for. Brian was already an incredible actor, even then. He was five years older than me, had had his place at the Birmingham School of Drama paid for by the local council and had been working successfully as a full-time actor for a few years. In fact, he had worked with Tony at the Playhouse two years before, while I was still at drama school, in a Beckett production. Bernard Hepton was director of productions and, coincidentally,

Jon Pertwee told me that Hepton was the best actor he'd ever seen on stage. However it was Brian who had caught our director's eye. He was only in his early twenties but already he had that ability to play any age. In the 'Scottish Play' at Watford he once doubled as Seaward, the young lad, and the 70-year-old porter at the gate. With versatility like that Tony thought he would be the perfect Malvolio, traditionally an older man's role.

More importantly for me, I was given a part as well. *Me*! Walking out onto the Liverpool Playhouse stage with Brian, Lynda Marchal, Warren Clarke and the rest. Marjorie Yates was playing Viola, Lynda was Olivia and I played her maid – I'm not even sure there's normally a part for a maid, I think it's usually a male attendant, but Tony wanted to give me a chance. Such a thoughtful man and he directed it so intelligently. It's the only production I've ever known where the scene taunting Malvolio doesn't have the actors bobbing up and down behind a hedge as usual. Instead they were part of the audience so everyone could see what was going on. You connected; you could see everything. I think Dickie Marks, the set designer, had to take a lot of the credit for that.

Despite my years with Shelagh Elliott-Clarke, and even appearing on television and in a film, nothing prepared me for the opening of *Twelfth Night*. Once again Mum and Dad were in the audience and I know they were proud as punch. I didn't have many lines but even so, they went clean out of my head the second the curtain was up and I could see from the side the packed auditorium, with its deep stalls, circle and upper tier. It was a familiar view but usually I stayed at my post, watching everything from the ASM's desk. Tonight, though, I would be stepping out there.

It was all over in a blur, of course, word perfect in the end, and soon enough we were celebrating at one of the nearby pubs that used to stay open and cook for us. I couldn't have been happier.

Brian was just as fabulous as Tony had hoped, but he was a monster to share a stage with. I had to come on and say something to Olivia, while Malvolio was in the room. It was only our second performance and just as I entered the stage I heard him say, under his breath, 'Here she comes, Sarah Heartburn.'

It was so naughty!

He would do things like that to me all the time. Every night it was something else, just to see if I would start giggling. So, what did he say when I told him to stop?

'It's for your own good – you should learn some control!'

There was another classic Brian moment a few months later which still makes me laugh – just as it did at the time, even though I got into a lot of trouble. I was playing a dead body in Friedrich Dürrenmatt's *The Physicists*, which isn't a great part – in fact it's a pretty dull play – but it meant I could still do the book as well. That would have been fine except Scase, the bugger, decided he wanted to have the curtain up so the audience could see the murder scene when they took their seats. That's all very well, but it knocked half an hour off my meal every night because I had to eat, then tear around getting everything set on the stage, get dressed in the dead nurse's outfit and lie on the stage behind the sofa. Horrible! Just lying there, stock-still, with my legs sticking out from behind this sofa for half an hour, listening to the audience oohing and aahing about what was about to happen when all I could think about was, 'Have I set this? Have I set that? Is the clock in the right place? Did I put the lamp out properly?' Pure torture.

The only plus side was I was carted off soon after the show started. But who was playing the doctor? *Brian.* He gets bored during good plays, so he was going crazy in this one. Every night he'd vary his lines a little bit, or do something a tad different to keep it fresh for everyone. We'd been doing it two weeks, just one week to go, and he came on as usual to take my pulse.

Now, the line he was meant to say, was 'Respiration – nil.'

But this night, he added quietly, 'Aston Villa – 2.'

I could have killed him! Everyone could see this corpse twitching with laughter and they had no idea why.

* * *

Once I'd had a taste of performing, of course, I just wanted more. The problem was, I was so useful to Jenny that she was loath to release me for bigger parts.

'No one does the book as well as you,' she said. 'We couldn't do it without you.'

The only way I would ever get out of it, I realised, was if I started making mistakes. But sorely tempted though I was, I could never have jeopardised the production.

Not intentionally, anyway.

But unintentionally, a few nights later, I achieved the same result. I had all my notes – mostly memorised – and all the bells and buzzers at my fingertips: cue for lights, cue for curtain, red for standby, green for go . . . Over the other side of the stage Fred was on the curtain waiting for my cue. I pressed the red light for standby, as usual, and then a few minutes later, when everyone was in place, hit green. Up went the curtain and on with the show.

Now, Fred was a man of fixed habits and, like me, he was pretty bored of the show by then. So after the interval he would raise the curtain then disappear to the pub for an hour or so until he was needed to bring it down again. This night would have been exactly the same except while I watched the crew set up during the break for the second act, I found myself wondering, *What would happen if the curtain went up now?*

Well, we soon found out. We needed about a minute to clear the props people off the stage so I hit the 'standby' button. Or so I thought.

Over in Fred's area a green light – for go – started flashing so he did what he always did: pulled the curtain up, then vanished out the back door. We were such a tight, slick outfit by then that Fred didn't even look at the stage – he just trusted me to tell him what to do. So he didn't witness the surprised looks on the audience's faces when they saw half a dozen men and women, including a furious-looking Sally, still shifting furniture around, completely caught out by the premature curtain-up.

Panicking, I started hitting the 'curtain down' light but Fred had already cleared off to the pub.

Oh Christ, I thought, *what now?*

Then I heard frantic footsteps under the stage and sighed with relief as Chris Bullock appeared by the curtain ropes, swinging on them with all his might. Sally came storming over and let me have both barrels. A minute later a panting Chris appeared in the doorway.

Here we go, I thought. *Get your coat, Sladen.*

But Chris just shook his head, smiled and said, 'Who is my favourite ASM?'

Accidents happen, he knew that. Funnily enough, I got out of doing the book a lot more after that, though.

* * *

The very last play we did at the Playhouse, in April 1966, was *Mirandolina*. Tony was the raconteur, the front man in it, with David Scase directing. Brian and I played the two little lovers, Berto and Brigida. It was a big moment for me, and I've still got a splendid picture of us kissing.

With the Playhouse due to close for refurbishment, Tony asked some of us if we'd like to take some plays under him to St Helens' Theatre Royal. There was Brian, Jimmy Hazeldine (who later starred in *The Omega Factor* and *London's Burning*), me, Geoff Brightman, and a few others. We would all meet up in the car and go to St Helens, do the play, then travel back along the motorway at night. It was all a bit gruelling but we must have done about four or five plays. My performance in one of them, *Pajama Tops*, drew kind words from the local paper, which pleased Mum no end. There can't have been many neighbours who didn't have 'the amorous maid, splendidly portrayed by Elisabeth Sladen' quoted at them when they visited.

At the time I was still living with my parents, so most of my wages were spent on clothes and treats. I don't think it occurred to me to save anything. Brian was in digs with Mrs Burns in

Faulkner Street – she was the theatrical landlady who everyone used. Every time I popped in, I would see Lynn Redgrave and people like that. Warren Clarke stayed there as well, I think. It really was the place to go.

There was only so much of this commuting I could take, so when the opportunity to do a summer season in Lytham St Annes came along, I grabbed it. Duncan Weldon, who had been Kossoff's manager, was starting a rep company in St Annes and there was a space for me – as an actress! Not an ASM, or a dogsbody. There'd be no shifting costumes or making tea. I was so happy I didn't even care that it was going to be the workload from hell.

Liverpool had been three-weekly cycles – that is, we had a new play every three weeks. But St Annes was weekly. Weekly! God, it was hard. Trying to juggle the show you're doing with the one you're rehearsing at the same time every seven days was a nightmare. Somehow we got through it and every night I would go skipping home to see if I had a letter waiting from Brian. He was working at the Malvern Festival and we wrote to each other every day. Occasionally, on a Sunday when there were no shows, we'd bomb down to visit each other.

Looking back, going to St Annes was the moment I left home. It didn't feel like it, though. There were no big goodbyes, no sense that I was growing up. There was no plan, no great target that I had to achieve by a certain age. I was just following the next job. *That's what actors do, isn't it?*

I shared lodgings with Sheila Irwin, who had been in the year above at Miss Clarke's, so it was nice to see her. Our ASM came from Liverpool as well, so it was happy families for a while, especially when my mother came up for a few days after she'd been ill.

I learned an awful lot. The stage was so thin, like a piece of Sellotape. You had to move along sideways; there was no depth to it at all. That took a bit of thinking about. I also discovered some plays didn't give their characters much to do. The more experienced actors seemed to deal with this by grabbing a prop. So whenever I didn't know what to do with my part, I'd find a banana and stand there playing with that for a while. Probably a bit phallic, thinking about it, but it's an extremely effective tool when you're bored on stage – and you can always eat it. I used the same trick in *Doctor Who* as well. In fact, they used the same theatre for *Who*, which was odd.

Two different plays a fortnight was a treadmill, but the end was in sight. When Duncan said to me one day, 'Lis, how would you like the lead in the last play of the season?', I was so happy I didn't wonder what the catch was. Because with Duncan, there's always a catch . . .

I soon found out.

Mary Mary wasn't a weekly – it had a four-day turnaround. Four days! And it was a two-hander, which meant that I would have half of all the lines and the stage time.

My co-star, Paul Webster, who went on to work with the RSC and with whom I still keep in touch today, was a lot of fun but the play was impossible. I remember walking on stage for the third and final act, putting my key in the door, opening it to come on stage, and thinking, *I don't know a damn word*. By then it was too late – I was in front of the audience. Paul was the perfect pro, however. He carried me until the curtain, working with the odd crumb I could recall.

Your memory goes when you're tired, but that wasn't the only problem. I was so hungry as well. It wasn't until I moved to Lytham St Annes and had to pay for my own lodgings that I realised how hard it is to get by on theatrical wages – by then up to about eight pounds a week. I couldn't afford much food and the weight fell off me. When you're busy you don't always notice your tummy rumbling and there are only so many bananas you can weave into a show. Afterwards I'd stagger home, famished, to empty cupboards.

Shelagh Elliott-Clarke's had taught me so much about acting but they hadn't prepared me for the truth – that you don't earn enough to have three meals a day, even when you're the lead.

It will be all right when I finish here and I'm with Brian, I thought. How wrong could I be?

* * *

Brian and I have never been ones for planning – I don't think you can be when you're an actor. We sort of go with the flow and see what happens. So when he finished at Malvern, with no other options, he took a room in our friend Terry Lodge's house in Clapham, south London. (Terry, like Brian, was another actor from the Midlands.) A few weeks later, I joined him. It was just like when I'd left home – no fuss, no big romantic gestures, just Brian and me living together as a couple for the first time.

The room was big, but bare, and there was no running water in the house. If you needed the loo or a wash, the tap and toilet were outside. But it was cheap – and cheap was what we needed. With neither of us working, just getting by was hard. I lost even more weight because I used to skip meals so Brian could grab something, not that he ever knew. I'd say, 'Oh, I don't fancy this roll – you have it.'

Looking back, you wonder why neither of us got a proper job – although I don't know what on earth we'd have been qualified for. But just when I thought we'd made a mistake moving to London, our fairy godmother, Tony Colegate, stepped in. He'd been appointed director at the Manchester Library Theatre and wanted Brian to go up and join the company. At the same time Jenny Smith, our stage manager at Liverpool, offered me an ASM job in Farnham. I didn't think twice even though I might not get on stage. It was the opposite end of the country to Brian but it was work. That's all I thought about, that's all that mattered.

And at least I'd be able to eat.

I wasn't at Farnham long before Tony called again, this time inviting me up to join them in Manchester. I wasn't fooled – he mainly wanted me to be his ASM.

'But there'll be parts as well, I promise.'

He didn't have to ask twice. The chance of being back in the

Northwest with Brian was irresistible, even if I was back on the book again.

The first play at Manchester was a panto, *The Thwarting of Baron Boligrew*, in December 1966. Brian had one of the leads, Obadiah Bobblenob, Terry Lodge, our landlord, was the storyteller and I was listed as one of the 'Poor and Needy'. I had to go on stage in rags, a hood over my head, and pretend to tie something. It was a funny little piece.

I remember David Jackson coming down one day to talk about doing *Antony and Cleopatra*. David had been at Liverpool with Brian. He was a big, big bloke and obviously very heavy. I was talking about him afterwards with Linda Polan and she said, 'Oh, I knew Jacks when he fell through his first flat.' (Linda later appeared with me in *K-9 and Company* and a couple of other things. It's funny how these things go round.)

I remember I was in my peasant's outfit when Jackson wandered by with Tony. He took one look at me and said, 'They don't pay the staff very much these days, do they?'

Actually Brian and I were both on the Library's top pay of eighteen pounds a week, which for doing what we loved was a fortune. After the horrors of St Annes I even managed to save about ten pounds a week. Working such long hours, all day long and into the night, didn't leave much time to spend anything anyway. If it hadn't been for a couple of places that stayed open for us I would have saved every penny. My favourite, Tommy Duck's on Barbirolli Square, used to wait until the actors had arrived after eleven then lock us in. It felt so naughty and, I admit, it was a nice boost for the ego that they went to such trouble for us. But then trouble wasn't exactly a stranger to Duck's. The owner, Tommy Duckworth, was an ex-wrestler, I think. If only half the rumours about him were true then he was quite a handful, but he bent over backwards for us and was a real character. You just had to look at the ceiling with its ladies' knickers pinned to it to realise that.

George Best had his club at the same time, so we went there as well.

It was such a fun time. Tony was a great raconteur – he'd tell us all about working with Joan Littlewood and even persuaded her to come and have a chat with us. My parts got bigger and better. That season he gave me Iras in *Antony and Cleopatra*, Fran in *The Poker Session*, Deidre in *How's the World Treating You?* and Leanthe in *Love and a Bottle* (played 'with charm', according to one review). Then, after the summer break, I got the big one. Tony wanted to do *Othello* – and he wanted me to play Desdemona. What an honour! I don't think I appreciated how lucky I was, even when the reviews came in ('Elisabeth Sladen's final scene with Emila (Linda Polan) was a little gem' – *The Observer*). If I'm honest, I was more delighted that Brian was playing Iago.

Another big play for me was *The Promise*. It was a gloomy affair, set during the German occupation of Russia in 1942. I played Lika and Brian and Paul Webster were Marat and Leonodik. Our characters were just trying to survive – my raggedy trousers were held up by a tie, not a belt; it was that sort of look. So when they find a can of food, of course, they fall upon it.

It was Brian's job to open this thing – it was Fray Bentos corned beef – and then mash it up for us to share. One night his hand slipped and raked against the tin's sharp edge. It was as if he'd cut his jugular. Blood just spurted out – all down his arm and over the corned beef. I thought, *He'll have to go off to get that looked at*, but he didn't flinch. He looked at the tin, then at me and said, 'Well, it's only me.'

Couldn't you have thought of a different line? I wondered.

But he had to be the consummate professional, didn't he? So there we were, eating the bloody stuff and trying not to vomit.

Of course, the bleeding didn't stop, so I remember taking the tie off my trousers and winding it around his hand to stem the flow. I was not happy. Brian had gone with it so I followed, but when we came offstage I said to the stage manager, 'You make damn sure that tin is opened properly in future!'

* * *

I shared a dressing room with Sara Kestelman, Jeanie Boht and Maria Aitken, who'd also both come over from Liverpool. Jean had got to know David Scase because she was an amateur operatic performer, but she was a natural comic. The pictures of her in my scrapbooks are hysterical. Maria, on the other hand, was like a creature from another planet. When she first turned up we said, 'What do we call you?'

'Maria – as in Black.'

She used to saunter in, wrapped in expensive furs, and just drop them wherever she stood. Jeanie and I would dive down, scoop them up and dust them off. We couldn't bear such exquisite things getting dirty but Maria didn't seem to mind – or notice. Maybe people had always picked things up for her. She was a sweet girl but coasting on a different plane to the rest of us.

My mum and dad, bless them, used to come over on the train to see every single play (eight a season) and every weekend I would go home with Brian. The station was very near Manchester Library Theatre – it's not there any more – and we'd wait for the final curtain on a Saturday before flying out the door. If we missed the 10.30 it was hours until the next one. Of course, we'd both be in full stage slap and it took most of the journey to get it all off. God knows what the other passengers thought.

It was worth the effort just to walk into Mum's house and smell her cooking. Wonderful memories! She used to send me back with a big cake every week – that was our little treat.

Living with Brian in Whalley Range might have been inconvenient as far as seeing my family went, but it opened up other opportunities. Manchester was a thrilling place to be in the 1960s. So much of acting and the media is based in London these days that it's hard to imagine a time when the capital didn't dominate so much. It was still the centre of theatreland, of course, but other cities were a lot more important then. Leeds had a strong radio scene under Alfred Bradley and Alan Ayckbourn, and there was a buzz about Granada TV because Jack Rosenthal and the Stables Theatre Company had begun doing great work there for the drama department. I hadn't been at the Library long when I began to hear of work going there. Warren Clarke got his first TV role in *Coronation Street*, as a lad called Barry, and every other day someone else would be popping over to film this or that. You could just jump on a train when you weren't busy and record for a day then get back to your own bed. Granada loved that because they didn't have to pay you subsistence.

A lot of actors today can't wait to get onto television. And then when they get there, telly is just a stepping stone to film, which is then a way of getting to Hollywood. Theatre seems to have been left behind slightly. That's why it was so impressive to see David Tennant take on *Hamlet* while he was still the Tenth Doctor. An RSC old boy, he didn't want to forget his roots.

Obviously I'm known today for my work on television but at the time telly wasn't a road I particularly wanted to go down. My only ambition was to work, and so far the theatre had been very good to me. But when Margaret Crawford, the delightful Granada casting director, rang and offered me a day's filming on a Sunday – my day off – I leapt at it. Why act six days a week when you can work all seven? Just remembering that makes me feel tired – I'd do anything for a day off now!

The programme was an ITV *Playhouse* episode starring Patrick Wymark. (Patrick had been considered as a replacement for William Hartnell on *Who* at one point, so, once again, there are the connections.)

I don't know if it was the arrogance of youth or plain naïvety but I turned up at the Granada drama department without a care in the world. I knew I could act. I knew theatre production inside out. And I'd been filmed on *Search for a Star*, even if I was too nervous at the time to take much of it in.

Whatever you throw at me, I'm ready.

Or so I thought.

'Can I see a script?' I asked the director.

'You won't be needing one of those.'

Welcome to the wonderful world of TV.

I got into my costume and the director introduced me to Patrick and John Wood.

'John's your boyfriend, Patrick's your father-in-law. Now just stand there.'

And that was it. No script, no lines, and no discussion about characterisation. I was plonked in front of the camera, the director called 'Action!' and Patrick Wymark started screaming three inches from my face.

It was a joke, it really was. I didn't have a clue what to do. I didn't know if I should look scared or defiant or amused or angry. I didn't know anything about the character or how she should react or what on earth her father-in-law was mad about. I wasn't sure what expressions I should be giving. There was no direction at all.

All I knew was I couldn't wait to get back to the Library, back to proper acting.

I swore I'd never set foot in Granada's studios again. Then Margaret Crawford rang back. They'd been delighted with me. I've no idea why. 'We've got a speaking role in another *Playhouse* episode,' she said. 'Will you do it?'

Go back to that place? It was acting. Of course I would do it.

This one was called *If Only the Trains Come*, based on the Chekhov story *Ward Six*, and I played a hotel maid. This time I had some lines – and a script! Barry Davis was a very pleasant director, so refreshing after my last experience, and it starred Bernard Archard, who of course was so crucial in the *Doctor Who* story *Pyramids of Mars* later.

I don't think I even told my parents about the first play. This one, on the other hand, they really looked forward to watching. I'm sure if you blinked you'd have missed me but, bless them, they said it was a triumph.

But I wouldn't know – I was on stage when it was broadcast. I remember friends and neighbours telling me that I must have been so sad to miss it. I had to laugh. Coming from theatre, you get used to never seeing your own performances.

I learned so much at the Library under Tony and got some nice reviews as well. All the broadsheets sent their critics up so every opening night we had people like Michael Billington, Keith Nurse and Robin Thornber with their pens poised. The *Telegraph* said I had 'some highly effective moments' as Mary Warren in *The Crucible*; the *Guardian* said of my part in *Mother Courage*: 'Elisabeth Sladen, as usual, puts everything into the rewarding role of the dumb Kattrin', while Simon Hoggart, writing even back then for *The Times*, reviewed *The Plough and the Stars* by saying, 'Of a remarkable cast, the best is Elisabeth Sladen'. Mum and Dad were prouder than I was but I kept everything in my audition book to show prospective employers. It never hurts to have nice crits.

Tony was such a marvellous friend and important figure in our lives that it made perfect sense when Brian asked him to be the best man at our wedding on 8 June 1968. We'd been engaged for a year by then. I don't think it surprised anyone when we decided to make our relationship formal. There was no song and dance. Brian did the old-fashioned thing and asked Dad for my hand, which was the easy part. He then had to find the ring that I'd already identified – sort of. I love Jane Fonda, and when I saw her in a film called *La Ronde*, wearing this fabulous aquamarine band with two diamonds, I said, 'That's the ring I want.' Poor Brian spent days looking for the right one.

We were such a tight-knit company at Manchester. I think if you asked any of us we'd all agree it was the happiest time of our lives. Warren Clarke had joined us from Liverpool as well and he was so funny – you'll always have a good time with him around. He actually got married a few days before us, to Gail, a sweet little girl, and of course we all went along to the wedding and a week later they attended ours. We were like family.

All the arrangements for the wedding were done on our weekend visits to Liverpool. I realise now that I must have loved playing Desdemona so much my wedding dress looked just like hers. It would have been cheaper to use the same one!

Typical Brian refused to wear tails, which my parents didn't like at all. Everyone else was in their finery and he strolled up in a normal pin-striped two-piece. He said, 'No, I'm having this suit and that's the end of it.' I thought he looked lovely, though.

For my entrance song, we went back to another important play in our lives. *Twelfth Night* was where Brian and I had first met on stage, so we chose the clown's song, 'O, Mistress Mine, Where Are You Roaming?' and hired the choir to sing it. A couple of nights before the wedding, the vicar rang my mother. He said, 'You can't have that song.'

'Why ever not?'

'The words are rather suggestive – and this is a holy occasion.'

Mum wasn't having any of that.

'Well, we've paid for the choir now – they'll just have to hum it!'

So that's what they did. I couldn't help smiling as I came down the aisle, on Dad's arm, accompanied by my young second cousin, Jane Palmer as she was then, on one side, and my old Saturday drama friend from when we were both five, Lizzie Gay, on the other.

The reception was at Dovedale Towers in Penny Lane. Afterwards we all went back to the house. Uncle Bill was still living there and he and a cousin had festooned the place with this exquisite display of *petits fours* and flowers. It was so moving to see everyone crammed into that house for us. We've got a grainy old piece of film somewhere that shows guests hanging out of windows and one of them, an actor friend Ray Lonnen, stumbling around the road pretending to be drunk. We showed it to Sadie a while ago. She was horrified!

The photos are pretty funny as well. There's one woman in every shot and nobody has a clue who she is – I think she must have been a professional wedding crasher. No one noticed on the day. I suppose that's how she got away with it.

For our honeymoon we flew by Pan Am to New York. This was before the era of budget airlines, although we were certainly watching the pennies. Anywhere that was free, we went: the Guggenheim, Central Park, walking all over the place. The day after we were in the Park, some neo-Nazi guy went on the rampage with a gun. I think he killed two people before the police got him. That must have been horrific but even after that we never felt unsafe – although in my case that was more naïvety than anything else. Sometimes, though, I wonder if Brian just liked walking on the wild side. We saw quite a bit of off-off-Broadway, and I remember him one day suggesting we see a show in Harlem. When I tell people this now they're amazed we dared to go there. White faces in the late 1960s weren't exactly encouraged, it seems. I didn't have a clue but you can bet Brian bloody well did. I'm sure he found it hilarious watching Little Miss Innocent stroll about, oblivious to everything. If we did get any harsh looks, I certainly didn't notice.

The first time I noticed anything really out of the ordinary was when the play began. Everyone on stage was black. Everyone in the audience was black. And then there was us. It didn't matter but, unless I'm working, I always prefer blending in to standing out and until the curtain went up, I swear I could feel every pair of eyes trained on us.

The play was an audience-participation number and I hate audience participation with a vengeance. I can't stand it. We did a show like it at Manchester and as soon as you'd get people up on stage they'd start talking to you.

'Oh, I loved you as Desdemona last week.'

'I saw your mother in the supermarket. She's very proud.'

It's as if the second they reach the stage, they forget there's a show on.

I remembered this in Harlem when they invited everyone up on stage. Though I tried to hide against my seat, as I've said, it was pretty hard in that audience not to stand out.

'Oh God, I'm not doing that,' I said, shrinking as far as I could into the seat.

'You have to,' Brian said, 'or else they'll think you're racist.'

Reluctantly I dragged myself up into the aisle. A minute later I'm up on stage dancing and generally making an arse of myself. I looked round a few steps later and saw Brian still rooted in his seat. I could have throttled him. Of course I don't know if he could make out the swear words I mouthed at him, but he looked to be having a great time.

* * *

Before we knew it, we were back in Manchester with a season to finish at the Library.

Knuckling down to work on *Mother Courage* was quite tricky after all the excitement of getting married. It didn't help that it was such hard work. The stage at the Library rakes quite severely and Jeanie Boht and I had to manoeuvre this large wagon around the scenery. It was so heavy that one lapse of concentration and it was rolling me straight into the audience.

We were on our second day of technical rehearsals and Jeanie and I had just kept it out of Row A.

'This is ridiculous,' she said. 'We'll have to scrap the scenery.'

The look on Dickie Marks' face! No one else would have dared to speak to him like that. I certainly wouldn't. But Jean was a character. And she got her way.

We weren't far into rehearsals when I noticed Tony hadn't come in to work. Someone told me he had gone to hospital with colitis. I had no idea he was even ill. And I certainly didn't realise just how severe it was – he'd seemed in good form at the wedding. It was a sombre cast that went on stage that night.

John Blackmore, Tony's assistant, had to take over. At rehearsal a few days later I was sitting inside the wagon that had caused so many problems. There's a part in the play where Kattrin has to stay there for quite a while, so I was looking around at the back of the stage. Because it was just a rehearsal, the great big dock doors at the back, where this thing would be wheeled away to the storage area, were still open. Tony preferred it like that – it meant he could pop in from his office and see how we were getting on.

I still had a few minutes to wait when I looked up and there was the familiar sight of Tony walking past, tapping his fingers on his brown briefcase as usual. He gave me a smile so I waved back. It was so good to see him up and about.

The next day I turned up for work and found Jeanie and John Blackmore in the dressing room looking very down. I decided to leave them to it and went off to get some tea. Before I got there, Mr Colley, the theatre manager, called us all into the auditorium.

What's this about?

Everyone shuffled in and Colley cleared his throat.

'Now,' he said, 'as I'm sure you all know, Tony died in hospital last night.'

I froze. 'Died last night'? That was impossible – he'd been at work in the afternoon. I'd seen him, we'd waved.

People were crying but I was in too much shock. Apparently Tony hadn't left hospital since being admitted after the wedding yet I'd seen him with my own eyes. I know it was Tony. I know that's exactly who I saw and now I know he was saying goodbye.

Not everyone believes me. Some people think I dozed off in the wagon and dreamt it. I got the same thing later during similar events at Wookey Hole when we were filming *Revenge of the Cybermen*.

But God, I wish I'd spoken to Tony. I owed him so much – we all did.

Chapter Three

How Do You Keep Your Shoes So White?

O NE OF the nicer moments while I was in Manchester came when a chap introduced himself as the agent Todd Joseph, of Joseph and Wagg. He liked what he'd seen and said he'd be interested in representing me.

'But only when you move to London. I can't do anything for you while you're up here.'

'What if I don't want to move to London?'

'You will. And when you do, give me a call.'

What a cheek, I thought. *Why would I leave Manchester?*

In fact, why did I need an agent at all? I was doing all right, thank you very much. When we hadn't been disappearing at weekends to plan our wedding or film at Granada, Brian and I had taken the occasional trip over to Leeds to record for the BBC's *Northern Drift* strand. I loved radio. It was great work, and easy to fit in around downtime at Manchester, so ideal for a little extra income. No book, no makeup, no costumes nor any rehearsal really, just acting, script in hand. It's so liberating, and that's why I was keen to work with Jon Pertwee on the *Doctor Who* radio plays later, and why I love reading the Sarah Jane audio books: you can be anyone you want on radio.

Our producer at Leeds was Alan Ayckbourn, who was still starting out as a playwright. When he was appointed director of productions for the summer season at the Library Theatre in Scarborough, I thought we wouldn't see him again, but he invited Brian and me up to join the company. The timing couldn't have been better – with Manchester closed until autumn – so off we went.

There were three plays in rep. *The Dynamic Death-Defying Leap of Timothy Satupon the Great* and *A Little Stiff Built Chap* were funny little things, but the big one, the one everyone really cared about, was *How the Other Half Loves*. This was Alan's first play since *The Sparrow* so there was a lot riding on it for him. Not that you'd have guessed from his behaviour. We were performing the second play at night and we'd started on rehearsals for *How the Other Half Loves* during the afternoons. For some reason Alan only gave us the first act to work on. A few days later he handed out the second. We had a week until opening and eventually someone said, 'Alan, have you got copies of the final act?'

'Oh,' he said, 'I haven't written that yet. I work better under pressure!'

Alan reminds me of a gnome at the bottom of the garden when he works. He is very insular, always thinking, always taking notes under the table. You know he is studying you, catching everything. I came in once wearing a nice new dress and Alan said, 'That would be perfect for Mrs Featherstone' – this ridiculous, mousey character. I still wasn't a drinker at the time and so whenever we went out together I'd ask for a tonic water. 'Just a tonic water, please' became a bit of a catchphrase for the company, but I didn't realise how much so until I saw the final draft of *How the Other Half Loves* and Mrs F was given my line! I know Alan must have had a good old laugh about it but I could have poked him in the eye.

That wasn't the last laugh he had at my expense either. I had to wear this big fat-suit for one of the plays and all I had to do in this scene was put an apron on. That was all. But I dropped it and because of the costume I took an age to pick it up again. You try picking something up when you suddenly can't see your own feet. It was a complete accident, but Alan thought that was the funniest thing he'd ever seen.

Laughs were never far away when Alan was around – even when the joke was on him. He's a very sweet, very generous man and the

first time we all went for a drink at the pub, he said, 'I'll get these.'
While he was rooting around in his pocket for his wallet all these
crumpled old bits of paper fell onto the floor. They were cheques
he hadn't cashed!

When it came to directing his own work, Alan was like a
machine. He never looked at the script – even when he'd finished
it – but he knew instantly if you'd deviated. There's such a rhythm
to his writing that if you'd said an 'and' instead of a 'but' he could
just feel it.

When Jeremy Franklin, the guy playing my husband in *How the
Other Half*, slipped a disc, there was no understudy. Because Alan
knew the script so intimately he said he'd do it. He used to be an
actor but even so I think he was a bit shaken by the ordeal.

As he walked offstage he muttered, 'Who the bloody hell wrote
this!'

* * *

Scarborough is a very healthy place, full of old people climbing its
hills, and both my own and Brian's parents came up to stay.
Working there, though, had the opposite effect on one's blood
pressure. The theatre really was in a library, and it was in the
round, so everything was terribly compact and you were exposed
to the audience on all sides. There was just one room for all the
actors to change in, with the curtain down the middle – girls one
side, boys the other. It felt like being back in school again.
Brilliant. But Alan's sitting-room dramas always have a lot of
door action and this stage just wasn't built for it – especially if
you're carrying a tray of tea props, another staple of his plays.
One exit from the stage took you straight into the dressing room,
which was the 'safe' side. But if you had to go out the other door,
this led straight into the vestibule. If you were running out and
someone was returning from the toilet, there was always that
moment where they tried to talk to you. More than once I flung
the door open just as an audience member was coming in. There
were teacups everywhere.

I loved working with Alan, especially on *How the Other Half Loves*, because I was playing a complete menopausal bitch. A bit of a stretch for a 23-year-old, but what fun, and something I could really get my teeth into, even if I did have to wear a daft blonde wig. The funny thing is, now I really am like that character no one will give me those parts – I'm stuck with Sarah Jane!

When I heard the show was to transfer to the West End the next summer, I didn't hold my breath that I would keep my part, even though the *Guardian* reviewer said I 'flourished as the cut-glass Fiona'. Obviously Alan was planning to take on an actress closer in age to Fiona for the London run. But Brian, the jammy bugger, had been perfect as William Featherstone and so he was invited back, with Elizabeth Ashton as Mary Featherstone. I couldn't wait to see it, especially when I heard that Robert Morley had the lead. Morley was a big box-office draw at the time, but he was known for shaping scripts to suit him. It might start as an Ayckbourn play but it would finish as a Morley one, I was sure of that.

'Ands' and 'buts' will be the least of Alan's worries by the time Morley's finished, I thought.

* * *

While Brian toured the show prior to the move to London, I moved back to Manchester. But instead of heading to the Library in St Peter's Square as usual, I went to a different address.

Coronation Street.

The producer was looking for a new barmaid for the Flying Horse pub and had seen me at the Library. She was also meant to be Len Fairclough's young new girlfriend, because they wanted to spruce his character up a bit. I didn't hold out much hope. I thought, *Well, age is on my side but I'm not exactly built like your classic barmaid, am I?* But they liked me and I was invited down for six weeks' work to play Anita Reynolds.

These days *Corrie* is an institution as much for its longevity as anything else. But even at ten years old, it was already firmly established. Walking onto the set that first day I was made very aware of the fact that I was an outsider. I went to sit down in the green room and someone said, 'Not in that chair, chuck, it's Albert's.'

'Albert's?'

'Albert Tatlock's.'

Oh God, I thought, *they call each other by their character name!*

No joke. They were deadly serious. The cast were treated like royalty by Granada and at four o'clock on the dot, the tea trolley arrived. It was pure silver service for *Corrie* – the canteen was for other people.

This was the era of Pat Phoenix. She was the Queen Bee and so proprietorial. Her character on the show, Elsie Tanner, was married to Alan Howard and she was dating the actor, Alan Browning, in real life as well. Who knows what they called each other at home. I felt so sorry for him – she wouldn't let him leave her side, he was so hen-pecked.

I can't say Pat was a favourite of mine. She came up to me one day and looked at my shiny white Mary Quant shoes (yes, I had to supply my own shoes). 'Anita, love,' she said. 'How do you keep your shoes so white?'

Bloody 'Anita'!

But in six weeks she never said another word to me.

I wasn't really a *Corrie* watcher because it was always on while I was onstage, but I knew that Peter Adamson, who played Len, was the big star at the time. There weren't so many celebrities back then so the major ones got a lot more coverage in the papers. In fact, he'd just confessed to being an alcoholic and going to AA, which the producers were spitting chips about. Peter confided in me a lot. He was really charming, and he got on well with Brian too. They're both from Birmingham and they remembered the same cinema, and Peter remembered the shows that Brian was in when he was touring. When I left Peter bought both Brian and me presents.

Years later, when a Sunday newspaper accused Peter of assaulting young girls in a swimming pool – for which he was found not guilty in court – I just couldn't equate it with the kind, thoughtful gentleman I knew. He had no airs or graces and the beautiful way he cared for his disabled wife was amazing.

The other person who went out of her way to make me feel welcome was Eileen Derbyshire, who still plays Emily Bishop – or Nugent as she was then – today. I was totally out of my depth, not having done much telly, but she was very maternal and ready with advice, a cuddle or just a smile. I think some of the younger regulars were getting a bit carried away with the fashionable drink and drugs scene at the time, because they were all on good, regular money, and Eileen was one of those trying to keep everyone on the straight and narrow.

You read how some characters are hired for a few episodes and are still with the show decades later. That was never going to be the case with me. I knew from the start that it was six episodes, end of story. I just had to get in, overhaul Len's character, then get out again, which suited me fine.

Coming from a theatre background it's easy to think you know it all, especially when you're going into a soap, a genre which has never had the highest reputation. Actually I really struggled to get up to speed. In fact, without the lessons learned on *Coronation Street*, I think my career might have been very different. I understood theatre: you could be fairly free with movement and the other actors would respond. But on television, everything is blocked out. You've got a camera that can only accommodate certain angles without shooting off and showing backstage, so there's a level of precision that I wasn't expecting. On the other hand, theatre audiences can look wherever they like, so you always have to be on form. With telly, a director tells viewers exactly where to look, how long for, and by using close-ups or long-range shots, how intimate we should feel with the scene. The old hands always knew when they were in shot or not and you'd see them relax once the camera moved away, but I didn't have a clue, especially when I was just background in the Flying Horse. I'd be pulling pints, polishing glasses non-stop, just in case. Those pint pots had never been so clean.

One of the other things I had to get used to on *Corrie* was the makeup. All stage actors do their own, unless you're in something like *Cats* where it's a bit full-on. You know how to get the most out of your face in the theatre lights, but on *Coronation Street* they knew best. So they sat us all down in a line and did a job lot at once.

'But I know how to make myself up,' I complained.

'Not for telly you don't, dear,' came the reply.

Even so, I only needed to see how they did me once to be able to replicate it myself.

On the plus side, whereas a decent theatre run would pay around £20 a week, television usually earned you about five times that. So for a while I had a nice little income. What with Brian touring the country too we had quite a bit coming in, so we both took driving lessons and bought a second-hand Ford Anglia for fifty quid. Eventually one of the doors had to be held on by rope so after a while Brian purchased an old Saab, which had the gears on the steering wheel, like a Formula One car. I couldn't get on with it at all, which means all these years later I'm not very roadworthy. I have to do a fair bit of driving on *The Sarah Jane Adventures*, which is always an interesting day on the shoot. I'm really good at going forward and turning but they won't let me reverse. 'Don't let her back up!' It terrifies them. And God help any passengers I have to carry!

Having the car meant that wherever Brian was in the country he could bomb up the A roads to find me after his Saturday night show, then charge back down again the following evening. It was so fantastic to see him but I worried about him being too tired to drive.

I wasn't the only one.

Eventually I got a note from Peter Bridge – the adorable impresario whose money was funding the West End run and the tour – saying, 'Could you please stop your husband driving. We're really worried something will happen to him and he won't be there for the performance!'

I agreed with him, of course, but Brian was furious. 'They're not going to tell me when I can see my wife!' I'm sure he visited twice as often after that – and made a point of getting back closer and closer to curtain up on the Monday.

I think if you're commissioned for half a dozen episodes on *Coronation Street* or *EastEnders* or one of the other soaps these days, you can pretty much expect a whole load of press and your pick of spin-off opportunities. It seems you only need to have half an hour in the Rovers Return these days to qualify for a feature in *OK!* or *Hello!* magazine. But I actually hated having my publicity photos taken to promote Anita's arrival and I cringed when I saw my quotes in the local papers. My parents, of course, were thrilled. It meant a lot more to them, I think, that I was in the biggest show in Britain, and Dad framed one of the Granada shots on the lounge wall in pride of place so you could see it when you stepped through the door.

Maybe if I had had an agent I might have capitalised on my brief brush with national fame and got more well-paid telly work, but it just didn't occur to me. Fifteen million viewers had seen me in their homes but you don't worry about that at the time. I certainly didn't think I was a celebrity, even though my mum kept telling me that such-and-such had seen me and so-and-so said to pass on their regards; it was just another job. In fact, no sooner had I finished than I was looking for my next one.

* * *

David Scase had taken over from Tony Colegate at Manchester so I did a few more plays with him. Then, come summer, Alan Ayckbourn invited me back to Scarborough. This time we did *Wife Swapping – Italian Style* (I was Flamina), *The Shy Gasman*, and that year's new Ayckbourn original, *The Story So Far (Family Circles)*, in which I played Jenny. Some things aren't so good when you return to them – and I've certainly experienced that feeling in my career – but this wasn't one of those times.

Bob Monkhouse was up there with a different company. He was

a great film fan and always carried a projector and reels of old movies around with him. There wasn't much to do by way of entertainment in Scarborough, so every Saturday after work we used to join forces with his company and Bob would put on a film for us. It was such a nice thing for him to do – he was a very considerate man.

Alan was extremely considerate as well, although one of his grand gestures I could have done without. Hull has a maximum security prison and he offered the company's services as a treat for the inmates. Obviously this had to be on a Sunday, which was the only day we weren't already working, but it meant Brian could come and watch. This wasn't one of my finest moments. I'd decided my character should have a little dog, a bit like the fashion today, so I spent a lot of the play with my arm up this fake pooch's posterior, making it nod like Rod Hull working Emu. But worse than that, I was dressed in a 'mein hostess' style low-cut dress! We were told only the best behaved prisoners were allowed to see us, but even so, I didn't like the look of some of them as they filed into the hall. Brian being Brian, he just pulled up a chair in the middle of them. I could see him chatting to one guy and afterwards I asked him what he'd been talking about.

'I asked him what he was in for.'

'What did he say?'

'He'd murdered his wife.'

'Oh.'

It wasn't our first time in prison. When Brian and I were doing *The Promise* at Manchester – with our tins of Fray Bentos – someone had the brilliant idea to take it into Strangeways. Somehow that was even worse . It's such a depressing play, all those starving Russians, and even as we were ploughing through it I was thinking, *These poor buggers are miserable enough without watching this! Can't we give them a bit of can-can instead?*

After Scarborough, I wasn't short of work offers in the North and in hindsight this was another opportunity to capitalise on my name up there. But once Brian had opened at the Lyric in London, it made sense to move down to be with him, especially since the reviews had come in and it was obvious he was in a hit that could run and run. Our old Manchester and St Helens friend Jimmy Hazeldine had already given Brian use of the sofa in his Hammersmith flat, and when I arrived to join him no one raised an eyebrow. (I think most actors with a sofa or a spare bit of floor will always offer it to a fellow thesp – you never know when you'll be the one asking.) Once we'd got our bearings, we took a flat in Ealing after visiting our friend, Chris Raphael and his wife Pam, who lived there. We've stayed in the area ever since – even Sarah Jane lives there now!

There was a tremendous fanfare around the opening of *How the Other Half Loves* and Robert Morley milked it all. Poor Alan, I think, was quite shocked by it. He'd been very fortunate on *Relatively Speaking* with actors like Celia Johnson and Michael Hordern. Famous as they were, they promoted the characters. Morley promoted himself. On paper he must have seemed like an ogre.

But, my God, I loved him to bits.

The joy of the man was immense. I've never met anyone like him. Robert was truly one of those larger-than-life people, but he really was so big-hearted with it. He could have the most important person speaking to him and a child might come over and he would switch all his attention to them. Everything about the man was expansive and open-hearted and fun. He was always throwing open his country house on Sundays. Anyone could go to eat, swim, drink, you name it, and take whomever they liked. If the weather was nice, he was the one saying, 'Let's have a picnic today. I'm taking you all to lunch!'

Of course he was exactly the same onstage and that's why audiences flocked to see him. The show was Alan Ayckbourn's biggest London success because of Morley, but boy, was he a handful! Brian once returned home and said, 'Robert came on stage at the matinee in the middle of a scene he wasn't in again.' Apparently there was this big fuss coming from the wings while

Brian was onstage, then Morley burst on, mid-conversation with someone, and said, 'Ooh, you're busy, dear. I'll come back later!' And off he went again.

It's always nice to be associated with success, so Brian stayed with *How the Other Half Loves* for two years. Like so many of our decisions, we probably got that one wrong as well. In hindsight, he perhaps should have left to capitalise on his hard-earned cachet. But we don't do that, do we? It was work, well-paid work, and we thought, *Why leave something so successful?*

While Brian was busy I had plenty of time to kill. There was no way I fancied taking the Saab around London so I dived into the Tube or walked for miles every day. I spent days wandering around Covent Garden, popping in to see the ballet whenever I could. I even got a walk-on part in *Romeo and Juliet* with Fonteyn and Nureyev. I was only part of the background but it is still fresh in my mind today. Really, though, I needed work, but I hadn't been there long before I got a call from Barry Hines, who wrote the Ken Loach film, *Kes*, and was a big player at the time.

'We've got some parts that were made for you, Lis. Get the next train back to Manchester! You'll regret it if you don't.'

You're probably right, I thought, but I had to say no. I wanted to be with Brian and if I just had the first idea how to find proper work in London I'd be happy. Suddenly I remembered the agent who had come to see me in Manchester. I dug out the number and booked an appointment with Todd Joseph of Joseph and Wagg. A day later I was on their books, although in twenty years I never once saw Wagg – I don't even know if he existed.

Todd was very good to me and I had a position by the end of the week.

'It's not much,' he said, 'but if you'd come to me after *Coronation Street* . . .'

Really I should have turned it down – there's that hindsight again. I know I wasn't a name in London, but the role of understudy was a bit beneath me. The play was *The Philanthropist*, at the Mayfair Theatre, and I was to play Liz – this weird character who just sits at a party and says nothing. Not a single line so not exactly what I'd been building up to my whole career. My main job, though, was to understudy the lead: Annabel Leventon, who was replacing Jane Asher.

You meet all sorts of characters in theatre. Some you know you'll be friends with forever. Others you instinctively keep your distance from. Edward de Souza was delightful and we stayed in touch. George Cole, on the other hand, proved an odd fish. He was already a successful film and television actor, a very solid performer, but you knew right from the off that he saw the world a bit differently. He was very insular, as if he had a wall around him. His wife had a second child during the run and I congratulated him. No smile, no thanks. He just said, 'Well, it's not nice watching your wife in pain.' I thought, *OK, George, I get the message. Backing off now*.

I only planned to be in the show for a few weeks until something better came along but it ended up being six months. Six nights a week, and two afternoons, I'd just sit there, bored and depressed, as the rest of the cast performed. People said I did it very well but still I felt such a fraud. You couldn't even call it acting. I mean, I may as well have sat in the front row.

Then one Saturday, about eleven in the morning, I got the call I'd been waiting for.

'Annabel's sick – you're taking the lead today.'

God, the look of fear in George Cole's eyes when I arrived! That put me right off, I can tell you. But we got through it, matinee and evening.

I saw George a few years later when I was doing a radio play in Leeds. Martin Jenkins was directing and I played a prostitute from Liverpool in period setting. As soon as I saw George I bounded over, hand out, and said, 'Hello, George. Nice to see you again.'

For the second time in my life I saw that look of fear in his eyes.

'Oh no,' he said, shaking his head, 'you never go up to someone and say that.'

It wasn't a particularly happy job, actually. I really had a handle on my character but Martin wanted me to play it a different way – a completely different way. There's only so far you can go before you lose the voice of the part and start to sound a bit fake, and so we fell out over that.

George watched this whole argument unfold, then at the end just said, 'I would have played it your way.'

Now he tells me? So exasperating! But he'd made an effort so I thought that was an invite for a conversation. Wrong. The wall had gone back up. Such a shame as there are so many delicious stories I'm sure he could tell.

Anyway, I made the most of my run at the Mayfair. I saw the sights of London and in the evenings I'd wander over to meet Brian. We'd get the Tube back to Ealing or often Robert Morley would take everyone out for supper. It was a pleasant life, and quite a starry one because of the success of *How the Other Half Loves*, but professionally I was coasting. When *The Philanthropist* finally closed I got a few parts up in Leeds on the odd radio play, but the only other sniff in London was a brief job working on a showcase of new work at the Royal Court. I played 'The Girl' in *Pretty Boy*, the first big play from Stephen Poliakoff. That was a weird one – all that work for one night. Poliakoff used to come to rehearsals, sit cross-legged on the floor and click this biro all the time we were working. Very off-putting. Jill Mears was in it as well, who I later worked with on a *Who* audio. We got on very well and both laughed when one of the other actors, a guy who thought he was a bit grander than the rest of us, said, 'Don't worry – I usually try out a lot of different things on opening night.' *We were only doing it for one night!*

Ironically, I think my lack of work in London theatre probably shaped my television career. As far as Todd Joseph was concerned, I was a blank canvas, so he began to send me out for all sorts of telly roles. I wasn't picky at all – I just wanted to work.

The first one he lined up was for a show that had been running almost as long as *Coronation Street*. *Z-Cars* was the first police serial to show the real side of bobbies on the beat. It was meant to be everything that *Dixon of Dock Green* wasn't. The episodes were two-parters, which meant a decent bit of screen time, but best of all it was set in Merseyside.

Threshold House was where the BBC did all its casting in those days. It was an old building next to the Bush Theatre on Shepherd's Bush Green and I can still remember the thrill of walking up to the front door and seeing the words 'Threshold House – BBC Television Service' above the door. It might have been just another job but look who it was for!

The Beeb don't use that building anymore, which is a shame because the feeling inside back then was electric. Corridors warrened off all over the place and people kept popping out and shouting across to everyone else. There was an energy – I could sense it even as a visitor – and I really wanted to be a part of it.

I was there to read for a small part for that episode's director, Derek Martinus, who had just finished working on the first colour *Who* serial, *Spearhead from Space* with Jon Pertwee (not that I was aware of this at the time). We chatted for a while and I thought I'd blown my chances when Derek said, 'I'm not going to give you this part.'

That's a shame, I thought, *but I've had a nice day*.

Then he pulled out a script and threw it across the table. 'I'd like you to read for this instead.'

The bugger!

In fact the new part was actually the lead guest for two episodes, which was fantastic. I couldn't wait to get back and tell Brian – and Todd. On the way out Derek introduced me to Ron Craddock, the show's producer. I wouldn't know for a while just how serendipitous that encounter would prove to be.

My character was called Valerie, a sixteen-year-old runaway.

I thought, *I've played old women – there's no reason why I can't go younger*.

Annoyingly she was from Northumberland and not Merseyside, so my local advantage was lost. Eager to please, I went down to the BBC Library – it's not there any more, sadly – and asked if they had any tapes featuring Northumberland accents. They had one – an eighty-year-old talking about her butter-making days. It wasn't ideal, but better than nothing, so I took it away then listened and copied and listened and practised until I was perfect. It was a funny old accent, a great mix between Geordie and across the sea to the Scandinavian countries. I was pretty pleased with myself when I arrived on set but the second I opened my mouth everyone just stared.

They couldn't understand a word!

'I think you'll have to take it down a few notches,' Derek laughed.

That's not the effect I was going for.

I was always trying to do new things, suggesting different touches I could do. This is how you workshop a play, after all. After yet another bright idea Derek sighed, 'You're a real thinker aren't you? But we haven't got time for any of this.'

I'd learned a lot on *Corrie* but I was still very green where filming was concerned. The fact you shoot out of order takes a bit of getting used to, obviously, but it's something that never gets any easier. Sometimes you can film a character's death scene before they've even been introduced in a show. You don't yet have any relationship to react to. That's why the continuity people in TV are so important – always running around with Polaroids or digital cameras these days to capture how you look and where you're standing so it tallies with everything else. (Jon Pertwee really struggled with this sort of thing, so we invented a sort of shorthand for scenes – which I'll tell you about later.)

Even though the show had been running since 1962, there was none of the 'them and us' vibe that I'd got from *Corrie*. *Z-Cars* was a great working environment, actually, very friendly, like a proper company. If I'm honest, most of the cast probably enjoyed it a little *too* much – some of the regulars could have phoned in those performances. But for a new girl they all made it a lot of fun and I was sad to leave.

My next job was *Doomwatch*, a science-fiction series which was the brainchild of Gerry Davis and Kit Pedler – former *Who* writers who also happened to have created a breed of villain I would soon become very familiar with.

The Cybermen!

I don't know how to say this, but I was never a sci-fi fan – and I'm still not! But I'd heard of *Doomwatch* because Robert Powell was making a bit of a name for himself in it. I was looking forward to meeting him, but sadly he wasn't in my episode. I did meet Anthony Andrews, though.

I had a decent part in the episode *Say Knife, Fat Man*. My character, Sarah Collins, was a university girl suspected of hiding plutonium, so she was on the run from the police. The problem was, she wasn't just running – she was driving.

I'd struggled to handle our old Anglia – and the Saab was a no-no – but they wanted me to drive this large van. At night! All I had to do for the shot was drive, at speed, down a hill and stop where the soundman and the lights were but do you think I could get the hang of it? After half a dozen attempts Hugh Ross, who was in the van with me, said, 'Look, you do the pedals and I'll do the gears.'

Maybe that gave me a little too much confidence. The director called action, I slammed my foot down and we shot down that hill! We screeched to a skiddy halt inches from where the sound guy was holding the boom mic.

'Christ, Lis,' he said, 'I think my underwear's changed colour!'

Z-Cars aired in November 1971. *Doomwatch* went out in June the following year. I can't remember where I was when they were broadcast, but I know my parents were glued in front of their set. Around this time I was beginning to pick up a few little adverts as well, but you never knew when those were going to be aired, much to Dad's annoyance.

Meanwhile Brian's run in *How the Other Half Loves* was finally coming to an end. I think he was ready for it by then. Then he announced proudly, 'They're taking it to Toronto!'

Obviously I was delighted for him, if insanely jealous, and we did discuss me flying out with them but with his regular salary ending and mine being so hit and miss we really couldn't afford it. A few days later I was backstage at the Lyric when Robert Morley's distinctive tones bellowed out from his dressing room.

'Hello, my little star' – he always called me that, I don't know why! – 'I hope you're coming out to Canada with us?'

'Oh I wish, Robert,' I said, 'but I don't think we can run to it.'

'Nonsense,' he boomed. 'Brian, you have to have her out there. Lissie has to come. Production will pay!'

And off he stormed to inform poor Peter Bridge what he'd committed him to now.

Well, obviously we couldn't allow that, but Morley insisted and in the end, once we were sure Peter really didn't mind, we said yes. I was so excited. Sod's law, then, that Todd Joseph called practically the next day with more work. It was only ten days but slap-bang in the middle of the Toronto run.

Obviously I couldn't – and didn't – turn it down, especially when the job was another Z-Cars and it was such an honour to be offered that part so soon after the first. Shows very rarely do this. It messes with the implied realism of the episode a bit too much if an actor pops up playing different parts too close together. It wasn't quite so prominent as Freema Agyeman being cast as a Torchwood employee in David Tennant's first series, then coming back as the Doctor's companion, Martha, in his next, but you get the picture.

I'd never had a female director before so I was quite looking forward to working with Julia Smith, but she was some taskmaster. This was years before she created Angels or EastEnders but I could tell she was a person who would go places – and probably not quietly.

She was a name to be reckoned with even then, but she could turn on a sixpence. I was happy she'd cast me so obviously against type as Rose, one of three Liverpool scrubbers accused of shoplifting. I just loved this part and relished making myself up for it. I thought I looked gorgeous in a trashy sort of way: false eyelashes, torn stockings, skirt hitched up.

Then the note came down from Julia: 'Could you tell her to make her skin look a bit more unpleasant?'

Bugger off! I'm trying my best to look beautiful here, I thought.

I think Julia was having a relationship with one of the other actors on it, John Collin. John had a drink problem, so some days Julia would come into rehearsal and yell at us for no reason. Or so I thought, but it was because he'd annoyed her at home. I remember the first time she tore into me – just bollocked me in front of everyone because I wasn't doing exactly what she wanted – and I wanted to burst into tears. But her PA, the chap you'd call a 'First' today, came over afterwards and said, 'It's not your fault. She's having a bad day.'

The PA's name was George Gallaccio and we became really tight friends. He was a jolly, even-tempered sort, which I like, and I was delighted later on when I bumped into him again on the set of *Invasion of the Dinosaurs*. In fact, by the time Tom Baker joined *Who*, George was production manager for the show. If you needed money for something, he was the one you had to persuade.

Someone sent me a copy of this episode recently – God knows where they found it, because I thought so many of these things were lost. But there's one scene which I just love watching, of me and John Collin. There's this cream cake and all that matters to him is that he wants the cake. It's fascinating to witness. Of course it's very difficult to talk with food in your mouth but he was all over it. I'm sure this sounds disgusting, but it's a terrifically powerful scene, one of my favourites.

After the one-woman ordeal that was Julia Smith it was a relief to head for the airport and Toronto. At least I thought it would be. In fact, the plane jumped all over the place the whole way, like a toy being pawed by a kitten, and by the time we finally landed I was a nervous wreck. My fear of flying started there and then.

Toronto was a beautiful city and, just as I had done in London, I wandered all over the place, simply exploring. And with no rehearsals or any other prep during the day, Brian was able to join me. At nights I'd either watch television in the hotel or go to see another show. It was quite idyllic.

While Brian and I were happy to saunter around the local area, Robert Morley, of course, had grander plans. Morley loved gambling and thought nothing of hopping onto a plane for a day trip to the casinos of Vegas. He was always back for curtain call, sometimes only just, but imagine poor Peter Bridge's nerves every time he disappeared.

The only thing worse than losing your star is to lose the entire show, and that nearly happened, too. Morley – of course – invited the whole company for a day trip to Niagara Falls. What fun! We looked so funny, like giant penguins, smothered in black water-proofs as we darted underneath the torrents. It was so slippery and of course Morley couldn't help dashing up and down, 'Ho, ho'-ing in glee. Suddenly we'd hear a thunderous, 'Whoops, nearly went there!' But then he'd be laughing again against the deafening roar of water. I don't know how much of it was for Peter's benefit but the producer had his hands in his mouth the whole time.

'He's going over, he's going to fall. This is it. Oh my God!'

Just when Peter thought his torment was over, Morley marched us all over to the cable car which stretches across the widest part of the river. I loved it, but gosh it was a rickety ride! The wind was howling, the whirlpool below crashing spray up and we seemed to be boinging all over the place like a conker on a string. Peter looked terrified enough – until I saw Brian, completely green. I'd forgotten how much he dislikes heights. Just taking an express elevator in Toronto had been enough to floor him.

Morley did so much for us. He took us to lunch in Niagara with his friend Paul, the brother of David Tomlinson – Mr Banks from *Mary Poppins* – and it was such a pleasure to hear those old hands rattling away. The Skylon restaurant was at the top of a tower and as you ate it revolved so you could see for miles. Of course, poor Brian hated it.

We were always scratching our heads for ways to pay Morley back, but when someone is so patrician and controlling, not to mention rich, you rarely get the chance. But when we visited an old pioneer village and saw him wandering around on his own we invited him to join us for once. Ever the gentleman, he wouldn't intrude.

'Come on, Robert,' I insisted. 'Have some pie.' Eventually he agreed and we had a marvellous afternoon. It was nice to treat him.

Neither Brian nor I had anything to rush back for when the show ended and as we both love travelling we couldn't pass up the opportunity to see more of America. Brian discovered this great Greyhound deal – unlimited bus travel for three weeks for $100, or about £40 at the time – and so off we went.

Lucky we were young, that's all I can say. I always thought a Greyhound tour would be quite romantic. In fact, the Greyhound stops are invariably in the crummiest part of town, which doesn't make your introduction to new cities particularly welcoming – that's if your husband lets you see them. I quite fancied a wander around Texas but Brian let me sleep through the stop in Amarillo.

San Francisco was our intended destination. Their streetcars were so emblematic of the city, and seeing where Steve McQueen had driven in *Bullitt* was brilliant. Alcatraz Prison was another site from the movies we enjoyed, but looking across to the harbour, my smile suddenly vanished as I recalled my own family's connection with the place. I thought about how it must have been for Grandpa in 1906, staring at San Francisco from the safety of *The Lonsdale*, watching as that beautiful city was devastated by an earthquake.

Eventually we made it to LA, which, for a film fan and an actor, is the dream holiday destination. Standing there, outside the studio gates where all those stars had driven in, felt magical. Doing the studio tour just made my mouth fall open – all the glitter of the industry, all the stardust of the past, was right there. It sent a tingle through me. At moments like this you forget you're in the same industry.

* * *

Back in England it was business as usual. Brian joined another play and I did a couple of parts in police shows like *Special Branch* and *Public Eye* plus a few ads. Then Todd Joseph rang to discuss a possible lead in a new TV series and I leapt at it.

But thank God I didn't get the part.

Surprisingly, Todd hadn't found me this audition – the programme's producer, Michael Mills, had actually asked to see me. After so long feeling out of my depth in London I thought, *Maybe I am getting somewhere*.

The meeting was at the BBC, right at the top of White City where the hoi polloi aren't usually allowed. That was an honour in itself, just being invited up there instead of dashing off to Threshold House. I got on well with Mills and, if I had to put money on it, I would have thought the part was mine. It was only after I left that word arrived that I had missed out to Michele Dotrice. That was a shame, of course, especially as I'd got on so well with Mills, but he rang me personally and said there was a part in the fifth episode of the series if I wanted it.

A lot of actors, I'm sure, would have told him where to stick it if they'd been downgraded from star to walk-on part, but I said yes. Mills was nice – he was soon to be married to a beautiful actress called Valerie Leon, with whom Brian had worked on a Hai Karate aftershave advert. The work imperative in me overruled everything else. Looking back, the episode just showed me how lucky an escape I'd had.

The second I walked onto the set I picked up another one of those *Coronation Street* us-and-them vibes.

The show in question was *Some Mothers Do 'Ave 'Em* and, while Michael Crawford is pretty much a national treasure these days, working with him every day as Frank Spencer's long-suffering wife, Betty, would have driven me mad.

It was Crawford's show, there was no doubt about that. The rest of us were ballast. I was really surprised at Mills for going along with it. Right from the start he spent the whole time huddled with his star. The rest of us virtually had to direct ourselves. So while the two Michaels went over and over Crawford's lines and his stunts in the minutest detail, everyone else was abandoned on the other side of the room desperately trying to listen in to glean any nuggets of direction we could.

It was such a shame because I really could have done with some guidance. I was Judy, a greengrocer. Michael had to come into my shop to buy fruit for his pregnant wife and, of course, cause havoc. Everything was built around what he had to do – I don't think he realised what the rest of us were going through. I remember being surrounded by these apples and oranges, rehearsing my lines to myself while Michael was saying his to himself as well. Suddenly he turned to me and said, 'Well, if I can't hear you, Elisabeth, the audience won't.'

The bloody cheek! It wasn't a tech run or even a proper rehearsal; I was just trying to fix it in my head.

Generally, though, Crawford wasn't exactly unpleasant, just nervous – really, really nervous. He had been in those Hollywood musicals and Michael Winner films and I think his career was in a bit of a slump. He was desperate for this series to work and that was what made him so uptight. There was nothing you could do to help him, either: he had to deal with his demons on his own. I once saw him in makeup trying to open a carton of milk – he got through pints of the stuff, I think, to calm himself down. But on this occasion he couldn't open the blasted thing and he was getting more and more irate. Literally shaking with nerves. I was just about to go over to help when another actor, Norman Mitchell, pulled me aside.

'Don't even think about it,' he warned. 'Don't even offer. He'll explode.'

He was a wound coil ready to spring at any moment.

Norman played Jackson in my episode. Years later, his son gave me a compliment to cherish. He said, 'My dad always told me that you were the only person he saw who could get a laugh when Michael Crawford was on.'

Maybe that's why he was so off with me?

After the *Some Mothers* experience I had another couple of

adverts lined up but then a pretty empty diary. *Something will come up*, I thought. But as each job passed, I began to worry.

The last job on my books before I had to contemplate another stretch of unemployment was an ad for the liqueur Cointreau. Some people outside the business assume there's snobbery where ads are concerned. It's simply not true. The lunch we'd had with Morley and Paul Tomlinson in the spinning Skylon restaurant proved that. You couldn't ask for better-connected thesps than those two but they called it as I do: acting is acting, whether it's Pinter, Beckett or Kellogg's Corn Flakes. You're bloody lucky to get any job doing something you love. (The pay tends to be better with Corn Flakes, however . . .)

Adverts in the early 1970s were very 'honest'. By that I mean that if you were promoting bacon, you ate bacon on the screen. If you were washing with Daz, that's what you poured into your machine. All of which is fine.

Unless you're advertising alcohol . . .

There was no pretending to drink the stuff. It was quite ridiculous. So from eight in the morning, it was sausage rolls for breakfast, a cup of tea then tipping real Cointreau into our glasses. We went through take after take after take and the ad's star, a French actor, was getting more and more sozzled. In the end he had to go and sleep it off. By the time he returned it was six o'clock and then it was all dark coffees and coping with his hangover. He was obviously suffering, so it was impressive he got through it at all. On the plus side, union laws were so tight in those days I got overtime every day, which was always welcome.

Waiting for your lead to sober up is a time-consuming business. I didn't get home until two o'clock in the morning! I'd been up for twenty hours and I never wanted to smell or taste Cointreau again. *But*, I realised with a fairly heavy heart, *if Cointreau ads are the only offers on the table, then that's what I'll be appearing in*. After all, my career wasn't exactly setting the world on fire.

But I wasn't going to dwell on that now. There was only one thought in my head.

Bed.

Brian was already asleep but I spotted a note in his handwriting. I was so shattered I considered leaving it for the morning. At that moment, I was in no state to do anything about anything. But I did pick it up and, through bleary eyes, could just make out that by the time I surfaced in the morning, Brian would be up and gone.

Fine, I thought. *I could sleep for a week*.

But that plan was put on hold the second I noticed the 'P.S.' at the bottom.

'By the way,' he said, 'there's a message from your agent. You've got an interview with Barry Letts at Threshold House tomorrow morning.

'It's for *Doctor Who*.'

Chapter Four

What Would You Like To Drink, Katy?

*D*OCTOR *WHO*, EH?

I was aware of it, of course, although this was not something I would choose to watch. Science fiction, as I've said, just isn't my thing. *Sorry*! If I'm honest, getting the call for *Doomwatch*, *Corrie* and *Z-Cars* meant just as much to me because all three were such popular programmes. So when I saw the note from Brian I reacted the same way I always did.

Oh, excellent – work! That should keep me busy for a few days. And not a Cointreau bottle in sight . . .

Little did I know how much that 'work' would change my life.

I may not have known much about Time Lords and blue police boxes, but I did know something about the man who'd asked to see me. I remember, at seven years old, being taken on a school trip to the Abbey Cinema in Liverpool to celebrate the Queen's Coronation. For some reason we were shown a film called *Scott of the Antarctic* and Barry Letts had been one of the actors in that. Ever the performer and looking for inspiration even at that age, there had been something about him that had captured my interest: the way he moved, the way he delivered his lines, the way he interacted with props and his co-stars . . . everything was so considered. Twenty years on, as I wandered over to Threshold House and through the familiar front door, I was really rather excited.

There's always a certain trepidation when you meet someone you admire, but Barry didn't disappoint. In fact he couldn't have been more charming – 'Come in, come in, so glad you could make it at short notice.' Such a refreshing fillip after my *Some Mothers'* experience; I was amazed that as producer of the show he was so hands-on. To greet and audition all the extras and minor characters struck me as a very nice touch.

Barry handed me a script and I had a quick scan through. The audition scene was a girl called Sarah Jane talking to a normal-looking chap who, when she wasn't looking, had this snake-like forked tongue that would dart out. Typical *Doctor Who* stuff, of course, but I'd never seen anything like it. *Still*, I thought, *at the moment it's just two human beings having a conversation*, so that's how I played it.

We had a couple of goes with Barry playing the snake-tongue fellow before he shook his head.

'This isn't working,' he said.

Well, that's another audition I've blown then. My face must have said everything.

'No, no,' Barry laughed. 'It's not you – I can't do this monster chap justice! Tell you what, let me get another actor in to read with you.' He paused. 'Thinking about it, if we go to North Acton, Jon Pertwee's rehearsing there at the moment. You can meet him and we'll find an actor there.'

I thought, *Bloody hell, they're very thorough*. Normally you arrive, you read, you go away, you wait to hear.

North Acton – or the Acton Hilton as it was known – was another BBC building, but this one was seven floors full of entertainers. Everyone was there. Just walking through the doors that first time I saw Cilla Black, the Two Ronnies and the cast of *The Onedin Line*. By the time we got upstairs my mouth was agape. You soon got used to all the stars of the day coming and going, but I can't deny I wasn't still thrilled to spot Sean Connery there one time and I'll never forget, for some reason, Prunella Scales – Sybil from *Fawlty Towers* – struggling to buy chocolate from the vending machine.

A brilliantly chatty concierge welcomed you in at the door and good old Ruby was in charge of the till and the food in the canteen on the top floor. On every floor there were three rehearsal rooms and a green room for each one. The rehearsal rooms were massive – plenty of space to work through any show and mark it all out on the floor. Each room that we used was square with two walls that were full of windows so the light absolutely poured in. It was a brilliant set-up because you could pop along the corridor or upstairs to peer through and watch other shows when you were on a break. The BBC no longer use the Hilton, which is a shame: everything you needed was there.

On that day I followed Barry into an empty rehearsal room, where a chair and desk had been set up. Barry introduced me to Stephen Thorne, who I would later work with on the *Who* radio plays, and I was given a bit more information on the scene: I had to climb through a window into an office and have a nose around. That's all I was told.

'Just feel your way,' Barry advised.

Auditions can be very intimidating but I really enjoyed this one. It was exactly like the sort of imaginary adventure you might act out as a kid. I think it helped that I just seemed to know instinctively how to play this character. That happens sometimes – there's no real detective work, you get a handle on what she's about as soon as you read the words.

I was so happy when we finished that I said, 'Thank you so much.'

'No – thank *you*,' Barry replied. 'That was lovely, I really enjoyed it.'

Casting can be a bit of a conveyor belt and I assumed they were seeing other people, so I picked up my bag ready to leave. But Barry said, 'Jon's just upstairs. He'd love to come down and say hello.'

Crikey, this is thorough – all this just to meet the extras! I'm surprised they have time for any rehearsals.

Jon Pertwee was a big name then, more as a personality than an actor, although he'd done plenty of good work. Quite a fuss had been made about *Doctor Who* reaching its tenth season so anyone with access to newspapers, TV or radio would have been aware of him at that moment. Even I'd noticed.

And I certainly noticed him in the flesh. Talk about making an entrance.

I was standing with my back to the windows with the sun pouring in from behind me. Suddenly the double doors opened and there was Jon Pertwee, bathed in golden light, flanked by a girl on either side. Honestly, it was like the Second Coming!

I could barely look at him, though. He was wearing a denim jacket covered in badges boasting trendy messages like 'Ban the Bomb' – always ahead of the fashion was Jon – and the sun was pinging off these badges in all directions. He was like a walking glitterball.

It was so OTT I burst out laughing.

Jon came straight over and said, 'Hello, how are you? I'm Jon Pertwee.' As if there was any doubt! We shook hands and chatted about my audition and then Jon said he had to get back to rehearsals. That was it, short and sweet.

Well, whether I get the part or not, I won't forget that meeting in a hurry, I thought. I turned to say goodbye to Barry and that's when he dropped the bombshell.

'The Doctor needs a new assistant. Would you like to be our Sarah Jane?'

'His *assistant*? You mean I'm not just here for one episode?'

Barry shook his head, smiling.

Talk about out of the blue! I'd had no idea that I was auditioning for such an important role. It was all a bit overwhelming: *The badges, Jon's celestial descent – and now this*.

I realised I still hadn't given an answer.

'Yes!' I gasped. 'I'd love to.'

'Excellent!' Barry said. Anything that happened afterwards is a bit of a blur. All my tiredness from the night before seemed to catch up with me in one go. It was so much to take in.

Not everyone was knocked out by the news, though. When I rang my agent later that afternoon he had only one question:

'Did you accept?'

'Yes, of course.'

There was this great long pause then, 'Christ, you could have let me talk money first!'

* * *

You don't think about these things at times like that. There's a lot I didn't think about, actually. Some of it I should have spotted, other bits I never would have guessed. When eventually Barry told me the whole story of my audition I was shocked. I owed it all to . . .

Z-Cars?

It's true. Katy Manning, who played Jo Grant, was leaving and so Barry had been quietly auditioning for a new companion. Eventually they thought they'd found the right girl, so they signed her up and began rehearsals. I can't tell you who she was – I don't think that would be fair. But I can say she didn't get on with Jon. It just didn't work between them, apparently. On-screen chemistry between the leads is so important – audiences have to believe in a relationship. It's all very well saying anyone can play any part but it's simply not true. If I were watching *Romeo and Juliet* on stage and Juliet was Sophie Dahl and Romeo was Jamie Cullum, I would find that unbelievable. Heavenly for them in real life and everything, but as a theatrical couple they'd be a mismatch.

And that was the problem with this girl. Evidently she was quite big – by which I mean very busty. If you're spending half a show running along dark tunnels, that's going to pose one or two problems. More importantly, I don't think it's unfair to say the Third Doctor's character was exactly the sort who thrives on being surrounded by smaller women. Jon loved Katy because she's mad as a hatter, warm and funny – but crucially she's little. And I think Jon was the same as his Doctor in that respect. His personality, his very being, responded differently to having smaller girls around him and so it didn't work out with Katy's replacement. They paid her off, and started again.

Of course, by now they were behind schedule. All the production offices at the BBC are in the same building, most of them along the same corridor, so Barry literally stuck his head outside the *Doctor Who* room and yelled, 'Look, does anyone know a girl who could play this part?'

Ron Craddock emerged from the *Z-Cars* office.

'Have you seen Lis Sladen?'

'No,' said Barry. 'Is she good?'

'I think she'd be perfect. You should meet her.'

So that was it. I have Ron to thank for everything.

Apparently Jon had said, 'Look, Barry, when you cast the next person, can I have a bit of a say?'

'Of course, dear boy.' Anything not to make waves! But, true to his word, once Barry had decided I was right for the part that's when he wheeled me out in front of Jon at the Acton Hilton.

Looking back they must have had a good laugh at my expense. While I was being dazzled by Jon, quite literally, Barry was standing behind me with his thumb up. Meaning: 'I think she's great – what about you?'

They'd worked this code out beforehand.

Then when Jon had said goodbye to me, he'd walked behind me and given the same thumbs-up back.

'Fine with me if she's OK with you.'

The decision was done and dusted, there and then. And I was none the wiser to any of it.

Some things on *Doctor Who* have changed beyond all recognition over the years, while others have stayed the same. Secrecy concerning the series may have gone through the roof since Russell T Davies' reboot, especially with information getting out so quickly on the Internet, but it was ever thus. I was bursting to tell the world about my new job but I was sworn to secrecy.

'There'll be a press call in due course,' Barry said. 'But for now, mum's the word.'

Everything happened in a bit of a whirl after that. My character was to join in Season Eleven, but they wanted to film the first episode at the end of the last Season Ten recording block. That was only a fortnight away. I was sent a production note saying we'd be on location for a couple of days and then my first script arrived.

Normally this would be where you get all the background info on the character. Things like: she's been molested by her father, she's fifteen years old, she's got one leg shorter than the other, some key detail that you can peg your performance on.

I opened it up and just saw the words: 'Enter Sarah Jane.'

My worst nightmare – they want me to play myself!

After a long line of supposedly subservient female companions, Sarah Jane Smith was intended as the show's nod towards the nascent Women's Lib movement. I didn't want to make a big thing of this, though, assuming the Doctor to be a more liberal thinker than 1970s Britons. As the only girl running around UNIT's military set-up, Sarah Jane needed to make herself heard, but I figured this could be achieved simply by making her a strong character. Of course the writers occasionally had other ideas. In *The Monster of Peladon*, for example, the Doctor actually orders Sarah Jane to give the Queen the full 'Women's Lib' lecture, no punches pulled. The irony of male writers getting a male character to 'order' a woman to talk about feminism wasn't lost on me. And when the adorable Ian Marter (Dr Harry Sullivan) joined the show, the gender battle became even more overt, although always playful.

All Barry had said to me, however, was, 'We want Sarah to be very much her own person, someone of today, with her own job, and always questioning everything.' That's what I worked with.

So, Sarah Jane was a journalist, a woman with her own mind and her own private income. She was confident, resourceful and inquisitive – to the point of being nosey. Now the most important question: what would she wear?

I got a call from Jim Acheson, the show's costume designer.

'We need to take you shopping. Sarah Jane needs some clothes.'

That made a change. So often I've appeared on stage or screen wearing my own things. It was refreshing to think they actually wanted to spend a few bob on making my character look a specific way.

Jim Acheson has gone on to greater things, of course, winning Best Costume Oscars for *Restoration*, *Dangerous Liaisons* and *The Last Emperor*. He is such a talent, and always did such stunning work. His are the only aliens you could photograph from the back – the attention to detail was spot-on. I was just getting my head around the character, so it was a relief when he said, 'Come on, we're going to Biba.'

Being dragged round all the trendiest stores by your own personal shopper is such a blast. Jim was my own Gok Wan for the day. He had his own fix on how Sarah Jane should look, so he'd wander around, scanning the racks, then suddenly appear at my side with an armful of potential outfits. Time, ironically considering my new job, was against us and the queues for the changing rooms were horrendous. I remember Jim's face in Biba when I said to him, 'Stand still for a moment', then whipped my clothes off.

'You can't do that!'

By then I was pulling a new dress over my head.

Any modesty I had was long gone. When you've been a dancer or appeared in any sort of theatrical production, you're used to quick changes but Jim had kittens every time. I think he envisaged newspaper headlines about their new star caught in her undies in public. But I didn't give that a thought. *Who'd be interested in little old me?* I was just another girl in a shop.

Like the shopping expedition, everything happened at such a whirlwind pace. I signed my contract on 3 May – for twenty-six episodes – and four days later I was on a train heading towards Manchester.

My life in *Doctor Who* had begun.

* * *

I'm sure the rest of the cast had already done a table read-through, but casting for Sarah Jane was so far behind schedule that I missed out on that. I was starting cold. My introduction to the serial called *The Time Warrior* would take place on location in Cheshire. Fortunately I gleaned a bit of inside info on the way up. Brian had worked with Kevin Lindsay, a typically colourful Australian actor, in Watford and they got on well. When we discovered Kevin was also in *The Time Warrior* – as Linx, the Time Warrior himself, no less – Brian arranged for us to travel together. Typical Aussie, he was so relaxed, which was just what I needed.

'I'm terrified,' I confessed.

'Course you are. But stick with me, girl, we're going to have fun!'

I believed him – Kevin could give a dying man confidence.

We arrived late afternoon and made our way to the hotel, a charming old coaching inn. It was quite a period place, all slanted floors and low beams, but my bed was comfortable and there was hot water for a bath. That was more of a luxury than I realised.

Soon it was time to go downstairs. The crew and cast were assembling in the hotel bar. This was it, my big entrance into the world – the universe – of *Doctor Who*. I'd been in enough shows with enough companies not to be anxious about joining another one, but something about this particular programme made me feel nervous. Like *Coronation Street*, everyone was so established in their roles. Would I fit in?

Only one way to find out . . .

The bar area was already full, although I didn't recognise a soul. Then I spotted Jon Pertwee at the bar. A quick double-take and he recognised me.

'Lissie!'

His booming voice carried across the room and two-dozen heads swivelled my way. Well, if they didn't know me already, they did now. It was embarrassing at the time but actually it got all the introductions out of the way early on. Kevin and Jim Acheson appeared out of the throng and showed me off around the room. It was such a blur but everyone was friendly.

Finally I found my way to the bar where Jon was waiting. He gave me a great big hug, which was his seal of approval to the rest of the cast, I think, like a Roman emperor giving the thumbs-up sign.

Relaxed, he said, 'Now, what would you like to drink, Katy?'

Katy?

I didn't say anything – I didn't need to. A second later Jon realised his error.

And burst into tears.

Oh Christ, I thought, *what on earth have I signed up to here?*

There's not much you can do when the most important – and largest of life – character in the room breaks down in front of you, especially with the whole bar looking on. I didn't know whether to comfort Jon or run. To be honest, I just wanted the ground to open up. I think I stood there awkwardly for a second, but it felt like an age. Then I felt an arm around my shoulder and I was led away. I learned later it was Peter Pegrum, one of the visual effects guys. Right then he was my knight in shining armour.

'Don't worry about Jon,' Peter said. 'He just misses Katy, that's all. It's not personal.'

It was nice to hear. But by the end of the night I was ready to punch the next person who even mentioned that woman's name. (Of course, I didn't mention this when Katy and Matt Smith joined me on the *Sarah Jane Adventure Death of the Doctor.* But then why would I? You only have to spend a second in Katy's company to realise how wonderful and scatty and delightful she is. The idea of anyone holding a grudge with her is inconceivable. In my defence, I didn't know her then . . .)

So it wasn't the most comfortable evening I've ever had. Jon quickly recovered his normal bubbly self and a bit of a party atmosphere picked up again, but the feeling lingered: whatever I did onscreen, I just wasn't Jo Grant.

But sod that, I thought. *This is the age of Sarah Jane.*

I'm sure if you ask anyone else about that night they'll say I was quite drunk. I can reveal now that it was an act. I still wasn't much of a drinker – I might have had one gin, but I pretended to be a lot further gone than I was. It just seemed easier. Almost the diplomatic option, actually, because the next day I could say I didn't remember anything. But I'll never forget that night – as everyone relaxed and got to know each other, good friendships were made. Apart from Jon's episode, there was quite a lot of ribald joking going on, and more than one fellow saying a blue joke then panicking when he saw me. 'Oh, I'm sorry, Lis.' As if I'd never heard swearing before! Jim Acheson's assistant, Robin Stubbs, really took me under his wing. He'd been on my episode of *Some Mothers* . . . and I became strong friends with him and his wife later. That night he was my guardian angel.

At breakfast the next day there were one or two people nursing hangovers. Jon was as lively as usual and afterwards he and I were led into a big room, where Sandra Exelby was waiting to do our makeup. You know I love actors' tales and Jon rattled off a couple of stories that had Sandra and me in stitches. Half an hour later we climbed on the bus with everyone else. I sat next to Kevin and braced myself for the day ahead. The real work was about to begin.

* * *

The reason we were in Cheshire can be answered in two words: Peckforton Castle. Although built as a folly in the 1800s, to the untrained eye Peckforton looks exactly like a mediaeval castle. And that is exactly why we wanted it. Strictly speaking, we needed it to be *two* mediaeval castles.

The Time Warrior, written by future script editor Robert Holmes, was a four-part serial featuring warring neighbours Irongron and Wessex. Irongron, the local aggressor, wants to conquer all before him and unquestioningly accepts the fantastic weaponry offered by the stranded stranger Linx – a Sontaran whose ship has crashed in Earth's Middle Ages.

A Sontaran – an alien! I'd never encountered the like.

In the story, Linx kidnaps scientists from the twentieth century to aid in his repairs, conducted in his laboratory at Irongron's castle. The Doctor sets off in the TARDIS to investigate and Sarah Jane stows aboard. That, in a nutshell, was the start of my adventure.

I've always loved being part of a repertory company, so travelling with everyone on the bus was in my comfort zone. Both regulars and newbies had bonded pretty well the night before so there was a real buzz in the air. The first day's shooting looked like it might actually be fun.

While the supporting cast, including June Brown – later Dot Cotton from *EastEnders* – were getting to grips with their cumbersome mediaeval costumes, I had no such problems. Jim Acheson had found me a smart brown trouser suit, large-collared shirt and jumper. After the state of me in *Z-Cars* and my shopkeeper's overalls from *Some Mothers* it made a change to actually look nice for once.

I think Barry originally hoped to direct *The Time Warrior* himself but had become tied up with Terrance Dicks in preparation work for the BBC's new sci-fi show, *Moonbase 3*. Instead we had a chap called Alan Bromly. When people talk about the 'old school' ways of the Corporation in the 1950s, it's people like Alan they're referring to. The image of pipe and trilby sums him up to a T.

I don't know why Barry hired someone who hadn't worked on a *Who* before – I suppose everyone needs their chance but handing him a new companion to introduce to the series was quite an order. Or maybe it wasn't. Perhaps it only seemed important to me. I found Bromly hard to connect with. Not unpleasant, just distant – we were on different wavelengths. But no matter how hard I tried to retune to his frequency, he wasn't terribly receptive. I thought, *I could really do with a bit of direction here. I'm in this show for 26 episodes. If I don't get the first one right, it's going to be a nightmare.*

But my legacy wasn't at the head of Bromly's agenda: he had a job and a schedule to stick to and no silly little actresses were going to delay him. About the only words I heard from him were, 'Action!' and 'Cut!' Point and shoot, move on quickly. Meanwhile I just had to trust my instincts that I was doing Sarah Jane justice.

I wasn't the only one introducing an important recurring character, though. Kevin Lindsay, as Linx, would do such a sterling job that the Sontarans would return again and again – even popping up in *The Sarah Jane Adventures*. Jim Acheson designed the costume and Sandra Exelby helped the effects people with the head mould. Linx looked like a squashed frog in shining armour with a big bowl-shaped helmet. Of course, the joke was that when the Sontaran took off his helmet his head was the same shape underneath. I love twists like that. About the only bit of Kevin you could make out were his eyes and tongue. It was an incredibly inventive look created on the usual BBC shoestring budget.

For Kevin's first scene he had to step out of his spaceship, which looked like a giant silver golf ball. With one hand on his hip, he announced, 'I am a Sontaran.'

Kevin's lazy Aussie vowels really made the word sing: 'Son-TAR-run.'

Bromly was puffing away on his pipe, not saying much as usual. Then he beetled over, script in hand, and said, 'Kevin, I think it's "Son-terran",' emphasis on the first syllable.'

'Well, I think it's "Son-TAR-run",' Kevin snorted. 'And I come from the fucking place, so I should know!'

And that's how it's been pronounced ever since.

To his credit Alan didn't push it and we all had a laugh.

Coming from a stage background I had been trained to accept the director as king. Tony Colegate or Alan Ayckbourn could squeeze miracles out of anyone's performance. Their attention to detail was phenomenal and every man jack of us responded – or we were out. I soon realised that the *Doctor Who* set-up was different – there was no shortage of advice and leadership but it didn't come from the director.

Take my first scene, for example. All I had to do was emerge from the TARDIS, creep up on Hal, one of Wessex's soldiers, and make him jump. Hal was played by Jeremy Bulloch, who was a lot of fun. He'd been a child star – I remember him from *Billy Bunter* – but sci-fi fans will probably know him as Boba Fett from the *Star Wars* films. He's had an impressive career, really, always busy.

I was nervous as hell, of course, so I'd found a quiet place away from the pack to go over my lines. (We didn't have the luxury of trailers in those days.) When I was given the five-minute notice to take my place I was pretty confident, though. Then I heard a shout from Jon.

'Lissie!' he beckoned me over. 'Come and say hello to our fans.'

Fans? Here?

A truth I soon learned pretty quickly is that wherever you go in the world to film *Doctor Who*, the fans will find you. I don't know how they do it. The BBC has always been pretty hush-hush with its arrangements, for the very practical reason that if you have to worry about an audience then you can lose valuable filming minutes. Timing is so essential when you're involved in an outside broadcast that you can't afford to waste a single unnecessary second. I looked down the hill and there was Jon surrounded by a gaggle of men and women, boys and girls with their autograph books and cameras out. Jon loved his fans and was totally in his element among them. He couldn't do enough for them.

But at that moment I felt like punching the lot of them – and him.

I've just spent half an hour getting ready for this, I thought. *The last thing I need is to be distracted now*.

'Jon,' I called back, 'they don't know who I am.'

'Nonsense,' he bellowed. 'Come along.'

Suddenly everything had changed. This wasn't a request to join him – it was an *order*.

I thought, *OK, I'm getting a handle on this operation now. Somebody is going to need to be pleased quite a lot*.

Of course, no one there was the slightest bit interested in me – I'm not even sure they knew Katy had left by that stage. I did some hellos, then thought I would slip off to do my take.

Jon had other ideas.

'Look, everyone,' he addressed the masses. 'Lissie's about to do her first scene for us.'

For *us*?

Then he unfolded his shooting stick – a walking stick that turns into a seat – and he sat, arms folded, surrounded by his fans, waiting for me to perform. If someone else had done this you might think it was a joke but Jon was serious. I'm sure he thought it would give me confidence but honestly, I could have kicked him in the teeth.

OK, maybe that's a tad harsh, but I just thought, *Let me do this first scene, please. Then I can relax.*

Of course Jon, bless him, had only the best of intentions. All he wanted to do was make me feel special by giving me the honour of him as an audience – it was his show after all. But what a way to do it: parading me to a bunch of fans who didn't know me from Adam, while I was getting ready to shoot my first-ever scene. It felt all wrong. I'm not a method actor by any means, but I prefer to put a bit of distance between the real world and my character before a take: I like to focus, gather my thoughts. I suppose Jon didn't know that.

Kevin Lindsay got along famously with Jon. Being an Australian, he was a natural charmer anyway. Barry Letts was the master, though. The trick with Jon was to keep him in the loop on all decisions. Whether they affected him or not, he liked to be aware. Jon hated thinking anything was going on behind his back. Keep him up to speed, as Barry – and the good directors – always did, and he was a real pussycat. Pull a rabbit out of the hat and you'd have a fight on your hands. You'd see Jon and Barry in confabs and every so often you could make out Barry saying, 'Yes, dear boy, of *course*, dear boy.' He really knew how to play Jon.

It was a skill I needed to master . . .

* * *

One of the questions I'm asked most (after 'What is so-and-so really like?') is 'What is the TARDIS like?' Even I was aware just how iconic this strange blue box was. Seeing it out in the grounds of Peckforton had been quite impressive. When fans spot it for the first time you can almost see the hairs rising on the backs of their necks. The whole mythos surrounding it is so vast and so very well layered in the psyches of entire generations' that you can't help but gasp a little. Even when you see one of the old working police boxes in the street in Edinburgh or somewhere like that, you can't help but wonder.

Unfortunately, actually working with the thing is slightly less romantic.

I know this sounds obvious, but it was literally a box. It's no more than a shell. Floor, roof, four sides, that's it – completely empty inside. No console, no library, no heart. These days it's lit from the inside and there's a painted backing, so the magic sort of spills out when you open the door. We just had a solid back wall, which is why you rarely saw the door open face-out.

Apart from the fact our TARDIS had a special key (compared to the modern Yale lock), there's another advantage the modern model has over ours: it's bigger. These days five or six people will pile out and you think nothing of it. Back then it was a bit cosy with just me and Jon inside. Once you start adding Ian Marter or someone else then you're all a little too close for comfort. You certainly notice if someone's been eating garlic.

But I remember how excited I was stepping in there for the first time. The door closed and the importance of what I was about to do suddenly hit me. It was a massive moment. I was entering that funny blue box as Lis Sladen but I'd be emerging as Sarah Jane Smith.

Thrills aside, there was still work to be done. After all the build-up I couldn't wait to get inside and enjoy a few moments cut off from the outside world – and especially Jon on his bloody shooting stick! There was no light, and it was cold. In fact, it seemed the perfect place to gather one's thoughts. But I could hear the voices outside and the longer I stayed in there, the more nerve-wracking it got. Then I heard someone call for quiet. Even Jon's gaggle of fans hushed. I took a deep breath, focused on what I had to do.

'Ready, Lis,' a voice said.

Here we go.

'And action!'

* * *

Normally, I don't suffer from nerves but the sense of relief when that first scene was in the bag was palpable so I must have been quite tense beforehand. But from that moment on, I knew I would never have a problem: I'd broken my duck and I knew my character. Now I could just enjoy myself.

I must say, I had a ball – I think everyone did. It was a really low-key shoot but there was a lot going on. Bromly certainly didn't hang around with reshoots. And I really loved the physical stuff. *The Time Warrior* was a good old-fashioned adventure and I was thrilled when I saw I'd be doing as much running and jumping and fighting as Jon. It was very feisty for me. Where I get scooped up by Bloodaxe and dragged into the castle like a rag doll I was really fighting him. It was great and I've had lots of letters over the years from fans who've detected the fact I yelled a very Scouse-sounding 'Gerroff!'

I'm actually rather sad that I can't do as much rough stuff these days because you can achieve so much with body language. As a dancer and theatre actor, you're very aware of the unspoken communication possible through the body – a fact I think a lot of purely television actors seem oblivious to. And I'm such a fan of the silent film era, D.W. Griffith and the like, that if you look closely at those moments where I'm being manhandled across the courtyard, I swear I was channelling Lillian Gish in *Broken Blossoms*.

There was actually a fight co-ordinator for that scene, although there wasn't much he could teach me on this particular occasion. Terry Walsh was a stunt man and Jon's double for the more dangerous scenes; he would also do the same job for Tom. On top of that, if there was a part requiring a man in a helmet then Terry usually got those as well. Check the credits of my *Who* serials and count the different characters he plays! You never knew where he was going to pop up next.

I became great pals with Terry over the years. He saved my life at least once – which I'll tell you about soon – and spared me countless broken bones and twisted ankles (although not all of them!). Because any companion of the Doctor spends so much time running, and because I was lucky enough to be comported in heeled boots for most of it, if I ever needed to run down a path Terry would say, 'I'm just going to move Lis's stones!' Then he'd come over and tell me, 'I've cleared a path – keep away from the right-hand side.'

Once I'd seen how physical the part was going to be I made the decision that Sarah would attack each hurdle with gusto. In a way, that part of her character wrote itself. I really tried to put a stamp on it, though, by showing she was as much of a swashbuckler as any man – or Time Lord. I'm not sure I quite nailed other aspects of her character. Considering she's meant to be a journalist, Sarah nearly missed the biggest scoop of her life – the fact she'd gone back in time! Despite sneaking up on bowmen and watching the locals run around wearing Lincoln green, the best she can gush is, 'Oh, it must be some sort of pageant!'

Any more subtle character development, I decided, would have to be attempted back in the studio the following week.

Jon was great fun to act alongside because he adored all the rough-and-tumble as well. He was a big man, very physical, and he brought a lot of his personal get-up-and-go to the role. The Third Doctor's Venusian aikido came in as a direct result of Jon's willingness to get his hands dirty and show off his sporty side. I was acutely aware of him leading me around those opening performances, which was fine. Bromly just went along with it. By now, I understood that that was how the relationship had to work.

We had one terrific scene where we needed to flee the castle. Irongron's men were trying to shoot us with futuristic rifles supplied by Linx. Our effects guys wired up boxes of explosives in the ground to be triggered remotely as we passed nearby.

'*How* nearby?' I asked Peter Pegrum.

He laughed – we had a lot of giggles over the years. 'Don't worry, Jim Ward's in charge and he's the best special effects guy in the business.'

When I was introduced to Jim I couldn't help noticing he had only one eye.

'OK, I admit, he made one mistake,' Peter said. 'But he's never going to make another one!'

A scene like that is hysterical. Those squeals are genuine. You don't need to act at all – it's pure reaction as each bomb goes off, nearer and nearer. I'd never done anything like it – and I loved every second.

We were in Peckforton for a few days and mostly the weather stayed dry. When it did rain, though, without a trailer or any other vehicle, we took to getting changed in the church attached to the folly. It may have been a fake castle but there was nothing false about the vicar. I was getting changed one morning, leaning against the altar and struggling to pour myself into this 'authentic' archer's costume that Jim had created, when I heard this 'Oi!' ring out. I don't know where he appeared from but the vicar was standing there, red in the face, indignant as could be that I was showing my smalls so brazenly in a house of God. That was me banned, rain or not.

Not everyone was so easily offended. The American family who were renting Peckforton at the time – I think they were attached to the US Airforce – invited all of us to a meal on our last night. That was very charming of them, so we all rushed to the hotel for a wash and a change, then jumped in taxis to get back there. Don't ask me how, but I ended up perched on Jon's knee for the duration of the drive.

'What have you got there?' he asked, spying the Tupperware pot on my lap.

'Oh, it's nothing, just a little salad. I was raised never to turn up empty-handed.'

'A *salad*!'

Jon's face lit up with wonderment. For that second he was a child again, full of wonder, bombarding me with questions about my recipe. When he heard I'd added mustard, it was like all his Christmases had come at once.

'You put mustard in your salad as well? So do I!'

Of all the things to bond over! Seriously, I really think we connected on that journey. It was just one example of the incredibly sweet side to Jon that I would see so many times over the years.

Actually, if I took one thing from my first experience on *Who*, it was the genuine camaraderie among the whole team. It was truly the nearest I got to being back in rep in Manchester, where I'd had the happiest time of my life. There were some amazing people on that crew. I'm sure it was just another job to most of them, but it certainly didn't feel like it as they were willing to go that extra mile, put in the extra hours, sweat blood for the show.

Some of them took the teamwork too far, I realised, when I finished a scene and sighed, 'I could murder an orange now.' Half an hour later Robin Stubbs appeared next to me – clutching a bag of Jaffas.

'There you go, Lis.'

I was dumbfounded.

'Where did you get those from?'

'The shop,' Robin replied. 'In town.'

I must have looked pretty vacant.

'You asked for some. It's my job to get them.'

I've never felt so ashamed – I couldn't apologise enough but Robin just kept saying it was his job to look after the stars. Well, that simply made it worse. I didn't feel like a star. In fact I didn't want to be one, I never had: I wanted to be an actress, that's all. And if that meant fetching my own oranges, it was just dandy.

It took me a while to get used to being looked after like that. I remember getting a similar shock when I worked with David Tennant on *School Reunion*. It was another rainy day – that's Cardiff for you – and this kind fellow held out a brolly for me. I thought, *Oh, the perks of being part of a successful series!* As I went to take it, he wouldn't let me.

'No, this is my job, Lis,' he said, and just stood there holding it for me.

I must admit, I find those things a little easier to accept these days, but before any accusations of 'pampered star' rain down – excuse the pun – you can bet no bugger would lift a finger if we weren't so important to a given day's filming. An unscheduled return to hair and makeup after a deluge could be the difference between finishing on time and on budget, or not.

I don't know if it's my old ASM training but as soon as a break was called I found myself naturally gravitating towards the areas staffed by Jim Acheson and the makeup team. I've always been much more comfortable among the crew. It's a calmer place – and, to be honest, I learned over the years that they were often the only ones who had chairs and, occasionally, a roof over their heads!

By the end of the week I'd made so many friends that the idea of a long coach ride home didn't seem so daunting. On the contrary, there was an end-of-term feel in the air and everyone was in a party mood. The plan was to head off as soon as the last scene wrapped (so as not to waste licence payers' money on another night of hotel rooms). I was lugging my bag towards the coach with Robin, Peter and the rest when I heard a car horn toot. When I looked around there was Jon leaning against this beautiful Lancia.

'Lissie, you're coming back with me!'

Am I? Thanks for asking, I thought. But I said, 'How kind, Jon.'

OK, I'm going to sound a bit catty but I really didn't fancy travelling with him at all. I was tired, I was looking forward to curling up on a seat on the coach, maybe having forty winks, then joining in with whatever high jinx were occurring. Besides, I saw it as a valuable bonding session – everyone would be there.

Except me.

Jon, of course, thought he was doing me the greatest favour. Why slug your way back to the Smoke on a clumsy old charabanc when you could travel in style with the star of your show? I'm sure a lot of people would agree with him but, you know, it would have been nice to have been given a choice.

Trust me, though: there was no choice. Resigned to the way of things, I humped my case into the boot and climbed into the passenger seat.

'Here you go,' Jon said, tossing a map onto my lap. 'You can be navigator.'

Oh joy, I thought. *I came up by train for heaven's sake and was picked up by coach. I haven't got a clue where I am now.*

Jon was already manoeuvring the car. 'Is there anything behind us?' he asked, before slipping it into reverse.

I didn't even look up from scrutinising the map.

'No.'

Off we shot, backwards at top speed – and crashed straight into the props van!

I have to say Jon took it incredibly well. He loved his cars and the Lancia was his latest pride and joy. After a quick inspection of the damage he clambered back in and we set off. This time he didn't ask me for any help.

For quite a while we spoke about the show and how proud Jon was to be part of such a TV institution. He was happy I was aboard as well. We were going to have fun, he promised. Then as the miles passed and Manchester became a mere dot on the map, the mood in the car changed. Suddenly I went from navigator to Mother Confessor. He poured out the whole story: how much he'd enjoyed working with Katy Manning and how it had broken his heart when she'd quit the show.

What was I meant to say to that? I just thought, *Oh God, please, I don't want to know.*

Just like on the first night, no sooner had he sunk into a depression than he snapped out of it. Spotting a sign for a service station he suddenly chirruped, 'Lunchtime, Lissie,' and swung in. Of course he was dressed flamboyantly as the Doctor and so heads turned everywhere we went. And to everyone who came up to speak to him, he said the same thing: 'This is my new assistant.'

It was so embarrassing. No one could have cared less about this stranger staring back at them – I could have been the bag lady for all they knew. I just thought, *No, Jon, people don't want to know. Just take your bow and leave me alone!*

The rest of the journey passed in a blur. I'd already heard too much so we chatted about the industry. He'd said it before but he repeated it then: 'If I can do anything for you, Lissie, just ask.'

And he really meant it. Such a kind man, he really just wanted to help.

That was 10 May 1973. My first day in the studio was not until the 28th so I had a fortnight to really get to grips with the scripts and my character. I just prayed I'd be allowed to do so without interference.

* * *

The filming sequence for *Doctor Who* back then was extremely regimented. But what did I expect when the whole place seemed to be filled with ex-military men? Serials in those days ran for four or six episodes, with the odd aberration. Episodes were recorded in pairs and for every pair we had ten days, working ten to five, to do everything: rehearse, technical rehearsal – where lights and camera positions etc. are worked out – costumes, record. It sounds a long time but actual filming hours were in extremely short supply. If we had a four-part serial, we filmed four days. Six days for a six-episode story. No time at all, when you think about it.

Rehearsals took place at the Acton Hilton in one of their vast rooms, working through each show sequentially as that's how they would be filmed. I have to say, it was an exhilarating atmosphere. There was a great energy in the room – in the whole building, in fact – and the sense of creativity was almost tangible. The BBC in the 1970s was a tremendously fertile place to work. The talent on show was immense.

Of course there were the odd teething problems. Having joined the cast late and missed out on the table read-through, I'd gone up to Manchester cold, needing to make friends from scratch. A lot of the cast and crew hadn't been required for the location scenes, of course, so now I had to be introduced as the new girl all over again.

I don't like to bring up gender issues because there were as many women acting as men, and yet, I have the feeling that had I been a chap joining, there'd have been a tad more respect thrown my way. As it was, I was perceived as the latest in a long line of ditzy girls employed to scream 'Doctor!' every five minutes, which, I felt, was all that certain people wanted to see. No one apart from Barry and Jon really knew what I'd done in the past. All that went completely under the radar and assumptions were made about my ability – or lack of it. I remember later saying to one person who'd tried to position me for a scene rather than describing what he wanted, 'Oi, hands off! I'm not a Dalek.' Patronising really isn't the word. (Actually, yes it is – it's the perfect word.) Unfortunately this wasn't something that disappeared with the first episode. A constant turnover of directors, crew and production personnel meant I repeatedly encountered new people who assumed I'd been hired from a modelling agency and not from a background of twenty-odd years, girl and woman, on the stage.

Fitting in back in London was a lot easier with Jon there to show me the ropes, although even that seems, on reflection, to be just another example of the casual sexism on the show at the time. He was almost giving me his blessing, like the thumbs-up he'd originally given Barry, but to some people that blessing counted for a lot.

Replacing an established character like Jo Grant was quite a hard nut to crack. I had to win over not only an audience used to watching Katy, but the actors accustomed to working with her. You get to know how your co-stars act after a while, you can predict their moves or mannerisms, and a certain shorthand creeps in, but all that disappears when a newbie turns up. Then it's back to the drawing board for everyone.

Doctor Who in those days could be a bit of a boys' club, I think it's fair to say. A lot of my predecessors were written to be supplementary to the action. I needed to shoehorn Sarah Jane into the action as quickly and firmly as possible – and that had to start with the boys of UNIT (the United Nations Intelligence Taskforce, you know) who acted as Earth's military response to the threat of extra-terrestrial invasion.

Brigadier Lethbridge-Stewart, Captain Mike Yates and Sergeant Benton were a familiar, well, *unit* by the time I arrived. From what I gathered, Yates had had some romantic interest in Jo Grant.

I didn't want Sarah Jane to go down that route because it would disempower her but boyish flirting would be OK, as I demonstrated when the Doctor was ignoring me in *Invasion of the Dinosaurs*.

The only one of the triumvirate I met at Acton on my first day was the Brig, played so clinically by Nick Courtney. He's a great thinker, is Nick, often off in his own world. Over the course of our time together I didn't think I'd actually got to know him that well at all, so it was such an unexpected bonus when he joined us on *The Sarah Jane Adventures* for *The Last Sontaran* to discover just how much we knew about each other. When you've worked so closely you build up a joint history, shared memories. It was really moving to catch up and realise we both experienced the same things. I can only liken it to a band on tour or an army battalion in the field. When you return to everyday life there are things you can never share with anyone other than those you've served with. And that was what it was like seeing Nick again. Magical.

Jon and Nick were very tight but complete opposites. Where Jon was flamboyant, Nick was so reserved you'd think he really was military top brass. Jon loved trying to prick his veneer. Once we were doing a camera rehearse and he whispered, 'Let's try to make the Brig laugh.'

So just as Nick was running through his lines, we took position next to the camera, both still in our blue makeup capes and Jon with a mop on his head. The crew were falling about. Nick just carried on as normal.

'What's everyone laughing at?'

It wasn't Nick's fault that we weren't close at the time. When I was looking to chat to someone I instinctively gravitated towards wardrobe and makeup. If ever I went missing, that's where you could usually find me, tea in hand, gossiping, and away from the spotlight.

For the last couple of scheduled days at North Acton, we had an audience. All the technicians, the producers, the effects guys and cameramen came in for a technical rehearsal. These were the people who had to transfer what we were doing in the Hilton onto the screen. They needed to see how much we were leaping about, where we were standing, who was doing what in the background, and work out the best angles and whether it fitted in with the space restrictions and the sets that had been built. After a full run-through of Episodes 1 and 2 we were all packed off to the canteen while Barry, Terry Dicks the script editor and co. had a pow-wow with Bromly. Everyone else was completely at ease but I couldn't bear the suspense – it felt like waiting for a jury to return its verdict.

In a sense that's exactly what was going on. By the time we trotted back downstairs decisions would have been made on which scenes worked, which ones didn't, which lines needed to go and, worst of all, who had new dialogue to learn. As we filed back in, everyone was handed notes. 'Emphasise this', 'hold back here', 'scream louder' – all pointers that the consensus felt would improve the show.

Generally I enjoy getting notes on my performances. Producers and directors are the ones you have to please, after all. Unfortunately I was also getting pointers from another quarter.

'Lissie, how about saying that line like this?'

I counted to ten.

'I think it works as it is, Jon.'

I know he was only trying to be helpful but that rubbed me up the wrong way, I'll admit.

My first studio day finally arrived on Monday, 28 May. I was up at six, hair washed and then at BBC Centre in White City by seven. As I was led along the labyrinthine corridors to my dressing room, I wondered whom I'd be sharing with. We stopped outside a door and I noticed the tag on the front: 'Elisabeth Sladen'.

I had my own room!

When I told Jon how surprised I was, he just grinned. 'Number two on the call sheet, Lis,' he said. 'It does have its perks, you know.'

Sandra and her team managed to get on as much makeup as they could, but the priority was putting the rollers in my hair. By the time the camera rehearsal started at ten, I looked a complete state.

Over the course of the day we went through all of that first episode, going over everything again and again so the lighting chaps had us where they wanted us, the sound man had the right places miked up and the cameras were ready to follow the action. Tape went down on the floor to mark out everyone's spots. Stray too far from the spot and you could end up out of shot.

One more thing to remember.

Every time there was a lull in shooting or I wasn't required for a particular scene I'd disappear to the sanctuary of the dressing room. It was such a thrill having my own private bolt-hole – with its own bathroom! But I'd only snatch a couple of minutes before a knock on the door and I'd be summoned to see Sandra again for a bit more makeup. That way, by the time shooting started in the evening, we'd all be ready.

The first casualty on filming days was lunch. Only once rehearsals finished about six o'clock did the food trolleys come out, but I couldn't eat by then. Now the nerves really started. Costumes had to go on, touch-ups to makeup happened, then at half-past seven we did it all again – for real.

BBC studios in those days had extremely hard, flat surfaces to enable the cameras to whizz around. My feet were killing me before the cameras were even turned on. But the biggest difference back then was that the director sat above the action in the producer's gantry with all the other technical staff, whereas these days he's virtually by your side crouched behind a monitor. Instead we had a floor manager with headphones permanently fixed to his ears, whose job it was to relay commands from on high. The thing I liked most about the studio – and which you don't get now – was the camera screens hanging from the gantry. These were monitors showing exactly what the director was seeing. There was no downside to having them, as far as I could tell – I could be just about to start a scene and realise that I was too far over for the scenery. They'd really come into their own, however, in the later story *Invasion of the Dinosaurs* when the monster models were shown on those screens and I could see where I was in relation to them.

As break time came to an end the tension in the room built up. The cameras that had been hovering around all day were about to be switched on. Rehearsal time was over, now we were doing it for real.

I like to get into the zone before going on stage, as I mentioned. Script rolled tightly in my hand, like a relay baton (although more for comfort at that stage), I went through my first scene. *OK*, I thought, *let's go. I'm ready to be Sarah Jane.*

Suddenly there was a holler from the other side of the studio.

'We're over here, Lissie!'

What now, Jon?

I trotted over to where Jon, Nick and the others from the episode were all huddled.

'What's going on?' I asked.

Jon winked, beaming like the Cheshire Cat. 'After three, everyone!'

And then on three, everyone who'd gravitated around a hanging mic bellowed out the name 'Harry Roy!'

'It's just our little tradition,' Jon explained afterwards. Apparently it got the mouth loosened up and was a good team-building exercise.

It might be your tradition, I thought, *but it's not mine.*

A lot of actors have superstitions. Mine on *The Sarah Jane Adventures* is always having to pull my left boot on first – don't ask me why, it's just something I follow. In my defence, it's a minor thing. No one knows (until now!), and no one else is impinged upon.

Bloody 'Harry Roy' was different. I'd just spent ten minutes getting into the mindset of Sarah Jane – I didn't want to be thinking of some old actor. And more importantly, I didn't want to be made to do things just because the last girl did them, but I went along with it.

Anything for a quiet life, Sladen . . .

* * *

Recording on Episode 1 finished at half ten on the nose (the unions were very powerful in those days so the knock-off time was fixed in stone). Then on Tuesday we did it all again for Episode 2. It was hard work, but God I had fun.

I was very happy with the way Sarah Jane was set up. You could see a genuine twinkle in Jon's eye when the Doctor first meets her – especially when he rumbles her lie about being Lavinia Smith, her aunt. There was also the indignant feminist tease, 'If you think I'm going to spend my time making cups of coffee' from me before Jon disappeared inside the TARDIS to boil his own.

What I adored most of all about filming, of course, was the feeling of being part of a company. Yes, the 'Harry Roy' thing annoyed me intensely (we had to do it again on Tuesday and again the following week) but Jon was right: it did make the supporting cast feel part of 'us'. I was hired for twenty-six episodes while some of them were only with us for one or two, but for that night they were made to feel as essential to proceedings as the Doctor himself.

I was still finding my feet, of course. *The Time Warrior* was the first thing I'd worked on where I had to perform in front of a blue screen to film scenes to which special effects would be added later (in those days the effect was known as CSO – colour separation overlay). The camera guys were very patient with me while I got to grips acting against imaginary explosions. Watching the raised monitors I could just about follow proceedings.

I was pretty pleased with my first attempts on the blue screen. On stage you're regularly expected to act with imaginary sets, props or even people. This was no different. Once I'd mastered the mechanics of it, I had a blast. As I came away from the screen I noticed the studio had cleared, though. There was just me and the cameraman – and he was looking a bit awkward.

'Was that all right?' I asked him.

'Really good, Lis,' he said. 'But, um . . .'

'Is there a problem?'

I've never seen a man look so shy.

'Lis, did no one tell you what you're supposed to wear for CSO?'

'No, they didn't. What am I supposed to wear?'

He looked nervously at his shoes again.

'Come on, out with it,' I said.

'I'm sorry, Lis. You should have been told to wear the special CSO underwear. We could see everything you've got, that's why everyone left,' he added. 'We're going to have to go again.'

'Why didn't bloody Jim tell me?'

I flew round to the costume room just off-set and tugged on the handle. It was locked – from the inside.

'Open up, you buggers,' I said, hammering on the door. 'I need the special underwear!'

Eventually the door was unlocked to peals of laughter. Finally the penny dropped.

'You bastards!'

There was no special underwear at all. It had all been an elaborate wind-up. I felt a bit of a fool but I had to admit, they'd got me.

On the Tube home that night I remembered Jim's face, pink from laughing at my initiation test, and I had to smile. *I think I'm going to enjoy my time on Doctor Who.*

Chapter Five

O.O.B., Sladen?

W E FINISHED recording *The Time Warrior* in the second week of June 1973. It wouldn't be broadcast until the December. Working so far ahead to meet TV broadcast schedules throws up its own little quirks in time. I remember gossip in the press (denied, of course) saying Freema Agyeman had been dropped from Series Four of the new *Doctor Who* even before the third season had started! And when Chris Eccleston was doing promotional interviews for his landmark relaunch season, everyone in Cardiff already knew he had quit – but luckily none of the journalists thought to ask.

It was just as confusing back in 1973. Literally as we were recording *Time Warrior*, the final serial of Season Ten – *The Green Death* – was being aired. There I was replacing Jo Grant before anyone had even seen her leave. No wonder those fans at the motorway services had stared at me so blankly.

The Green Death's final episode had further significance for me. That was the day when the BBC publicity department decided I should be unveiled to the press. I can see the logic. Old series ends, viewers disappointed to see Jo Grant swan off into the sunset with Cliff Jones. What better time to introduce her delightful new replacement?

And so it was on a sunny June day that I was persuaded to put on a ridiculous pair of denim shorts and T-shirt in a look that predated Daisy Duke by a few years and pushed out the front door of BBC Television Centre to the main entrance area – where they shoot all the *Strictly Come Dancing* intros – and where the national press's snappers were assembled.

I'll never forget the sight of all those lenses. Thirty-odd photographers all calling my name was something I hadn't expected. 'Lis, do this', 'Lis, over here', 'Give us a smile, Lis'. I was pulled from pillar to post, made to turn this way, perch on this thing, lean against that. And then there were all the questions to answer. Going back to Freema, I know she was given a course at the BBC on how to handle the media. I had no such training – we were thrown to the lions in those days completely unprepared. So I struggled gamely, all the while my rictus grin beaming unlovingly outwards.

Fortunately I wasn't alone out there. Jon was on call as well and as soon as he saw I'd had enough, he very gallantly swept over to join me. That was my cue to hide behind him. I'd never been so glad to see that great flowing cloak of his. This, I felt, was where I belonged all along: by the Doctor's side, not in the limelight.

I was glad to have the ordeal over and quickly forgot all about it. The next day, though, reminders came in their droves. A few lines appeared in one or two of the papers, and at home the phone rang off the hook. My parents were proud as punch, of course, and Dad promised the *Doctor Who* snaps would replace my Anita Reynolds stills in pride of place on the lounge wall. Every other call came from family and friends in Liverpool. Everyone was so pleased for me. It was flattering, if awkward. Brian was just as chuffed for me, of course, but he was the only person who understood. *I'm just doing my job . . .*

The script for my second story, *Invasion of the Dinosaurs*, came through in mid-August. This one was written by seasoned *Who* scribe Malcolm Hulke. A couple of things leapt out. First, not only was the Doctor still Earth-bound but the action took place entirely in London – I wouldn't be getting a jolly away-day with the cast this time. Secondly, the UNIT boys were back in numbers. Nick Courtney's regular assistants Mike Yates and Sergeant Benton were both in this one. Once more, I felt the challenge to impose myself on the set in the face of some very established relationships. *I need to let them all know I deserve to be here.*

It wasn't just a fresh cast I had to master, though. On *The Time Warrior* Jim Acheson, Sandra Exelby and their teams had been my support network, my comfort blanket whenever I needed to get away from the glare. On *Dinosaurs* I'd be working with new costume and makeup people. It really was like starting all over again.

I met Jim and Sandra's replacements soon enough. After a call from Jean McMillan, the new makeup supervisor, I was whisked away to an upmarket hair salon and given a neat, bouncy bob cut. That was a treat. Then our new costume designer Barbara Kidd and I had to pick out Sarah Jane's look for the serial: a smart brown trouser suit and a white, wide-collared shirt. I think it's a look that would still work today. More importantly it reflected the character – the strong feminist journalist. No dolly-bird outfits for Sarah Jane. Not yet, anyway.

I was a bit apprehensive as September arrived but nerves gave way to excitement as I pitched up at North Acton for the table read-through. Obviously I'd missed out on the last one so this was something of an eye-opener to see how things worked. As I made my way in everyone was chatting about what they'd been up to – it was like the first day back at school. New faces mingled with familiar ones – everyone seemed to know someone. I was delighted to see George Gallaccio, whom I'd met on *Z-Cars*. By the time I'd said a few hellos all my nerves had gone. I saw Jon regaling a couple of chaps with some tale – he was a natural raconteur – and went over, determined to get off on a better footing than the first time we'd met on location.

'Lissie!' he boomed, breaking off from his story. That was good of him, rather than leave me hanging. We hugged and then he looked me up and down.

'What have you done to your hair? No, I don't like that!'

Oh, Jon. It's going to be a long series . . .

I always like table read-throughs and they're exactly how they sound. Everyone sits at a table – all the cast, someone from makeup, someone from costume, someone from camera, Barry, Terry, sometimes the writer, and the director – and we literally read through the script. The technical team would make notes about what they could achieve and how we might have to amend things. For *Dinosaurs* I'd prepared inside out. Later I realised this was the time to suggest changes, especially if I felt a writer hadn't quite nailed Sarah Jane as well as they might. (It made sense that the writers wouldn't necessarily be as au fait with my character as I was. Some of the scripts might have been written before I was even cast.) I began to alter the odd word, then sentences, then whole exchanges. I'd never ask, I'd just do it. Afterwards I'd look up at Barry and he would simply nod. You've no idea how satisfying that is, as a newbie, getting the blessing from the highest authority in the room. Well, the highest authority on paper . . .

Mostly we had a very collaborative working arrangement where everyone contributed. Jon probably contributed more than anyone else. Whether he was in a scene or not, he loved to have input. 'Why don't you try this?' 'I don't think that's working.' He had so much experience after all. Unfortunately he didn't always agree with my interpretations and he really didn't like it when I stood my ground.

'Oh, I think the moon's in the wrong position for someone today, isn't it?'

His heart was in the right place but I could have throttled him sometimes. We got on better with every passing day. I just had to remember, now and then, not to stoke the fire.

As with *The Time Warrior*, Barry was still too snowed under with *Moonbase 3* to direct. His replacement, I was pleased to see, was a woman. Paddy Russell had previously held the reins for the First Doctor some seven years earlier, on *The Massacre of St Bartholomew's Eve*.

If anyone is going to go softly on us, it's her, I thought.

Well, I got that one wrong.

I don't know if it was because she was trying to overcompensate for being a woman in a man's world – and we all have those moments – but Paddy was not an easy person to work with. She didn't set out to make friends, not even with Jon, so there was friction right from the off. Her way was to treat everyone like children. It was the job of the assistant director – known as the 'First' – to keep us all in order, like naughty schoolkids. Ridiculous, but that's how Paddy wanted things.

We'd get to a location and normally you'd walk around, mull over the logistics of what we needed to do. Not with Paddy.

'Silence!'

For me, joining the show was all about fitting in, how you could meld and interact and find the best way of being part of something that had been going a long while. Not so Paddy. At one point she completely lost it with Barbara Kidd and bawled her out in front of everyone over some minor costume detail. I'm sorry, but you don't do that. We all lost respect for our director that day but I don't think she cared.

I'm sure Paddy cared deeply about the programme. How else can you explain why she made us go over some scenes a dozen times until we were incapable of bringing any vim or vigour to the lines? There's an optimum time for a scene and she sailed past it so often, always pushing for something better – which, of course, rarely came. I never thought I'd miss Alan Bromly!

Paddy didn't care who or what she trampled on, including film regulations. Completely unscheduled – and without a permit – she took a camera team out early in the morning before official shooting started to get shots of a deserted London (I think they all posed as tourists). The official location shots started a few weeks later, which was fun – lots of running around London streets and reacting to the sight of dinosaurs in the distance. But more on them later!

Speaking of dedication, if you ever needed proof of how much the programme meant to Jon, the evidence was there for everyone to see on 23 September, the first 'official' day of location shooting. Earlier in the year he'd commissioned a car builder, Peter Ferries, to construct a futuristic vehicle suitable for his Doctor. I think he was expecting the BBC to pay for it. When Barry said 'No', Jon went ahead and financed it himself. Typical BBC, of course – once the thing was built, they were happy to include it in the show.

'You wait till you see it, Lissie,' Jon gushed. 'It will blow your mind.'

He was right there. When this thing turned up I was shocked to see it really was part-car, part-hovercraft, part-spaceship. Jon called it the Whomobile – although I think its real name was The Alien – but in the script it just said the 'Doctor's car'. Barry always vetoed any puns on the show's title and certainly wouldn't let anything like that into the script.

Jon loved whizzing around in the Whomobile. Afterwards he took it on *Blue Peter* to show off all the gadgetry. When you think of it, the BBC really wrung every opportunity out of that car – and yet they wouldn't give him a penny for it.

Jon wasn't the most technically minded person but he was a magpie with anything modern and shiny. And if he couldn't use it, he knew someone at home who could. After every show he would go up to the props guy and say, 'You don't need that any more, do you?' Before you knew it, some new toy was in his pocket ready to give to his young son, Sean. I remember one occasion we had to do a reshoot and Jon had already snaffled the prop. Barry said, 'We really need it back, Jon.'

'Leave it to me.'

He was as good as his word.

'Sean gave it back, then?' Barry asked.

'Oh yes,' Jon sighed sheeplishly, 'but I had to bloody pay him for it!'

I enjoyed filming out and about in London, although as well as Westminster and Trafalgar Square there were the less glamorous locations of Southall and Wimbledon Common. Apparently when the TARDIS put down for the first time the 'Police Call Box' sign was missing but I didn't notice – and neither did anyone else at the time. That gives you some idea of the time pressures we worked under. We had enough to do just keeping track of where we were in the script – always a problem when you're shooting out of sequence. I remember waiting with Jon for our first take at a new location.

'Remind me, Lissie,' he said. 'Have we been running?'

I nodded.

'Out of breath, then?'

'Out of breath.'

Those three words became our shorthand before every new scene. Later, Ian Marter abbreviated it further.

'O.O.B., Sladen?'

'O.O.B., Ian.'

I got to know script editor Terry Dicks a bit during this shoot, which was a treat. He's a very approachable man and will still happily talk about *Who* for hours with anyone. He cared, and still does care, so passionately about everything on the show but he could have a laugh all the same. Jon wasn't renowned for having the best memory – it wasn't completely unknown for him to write some of the more complicated lines on the frilly cuffs of some of his shirts. You'd see him just before a take flipping his sleeve up and down, trying to sneak a peep. Terry, of course, just loved trying to get Jon to say more and more complex phrases – and when you're talking about time and space and all manner of far-out technology, that can be exceedingly complex. So it was Terry who came up with the classic 'reverse the polarity of the neutron flow' – as much to vex Jon as anything else. He put it in *The Sea Devils* and thought, *Jon will never go for that.*

'But he loved it!' Terry laughed. 'He kept wanting to say it in every programme.'

And sure enough, there it was in *Dinosaurs* when the Doctor decides to 'reverse the polarity' of the Timescoop. (Fans will be able to recite all the other references over the years, but I do recall David Tennant saying in *The Lazarus Experiment*, 'It really shouldn't take that long to reverse the polarity. I must be getting out of practice.' It's incredible how a little piece of jargon can take on a life of its own.)

* * *

Picking up the character of Sarah Jane after so many months off was almost like starting again. *The Time Warrior* had yet to be broadcast so I was still in the dark as to how I'd come across. Still, I was anxious to capture the same characteristics as far as possible. I tore off a piece of my script, found a quiet corner in the Acton Hilton and jotted down a few things that I decided I must never forget about her. After that, whenever I felt lost in a scene I'd pull that scrap of paper out and remind myself how Sarah Jane should be. I used it for ages. In fact, I've still got it.

One of the things I wrote on it was Sarah's purpose. Sometimes you'd be handed a script and have to really dig for the character's story. Her role in the show – like any companion – is to ask the questions the audience wants to ask. She's the foil for the Doctor, so he can prove how clever he is. There's no shame in being less intelligent than a Time Lord but one or two of the writers tried to get me to say all sorts of rubbish. I'd then have to pull them up. Sarah had to be an intelligent audience, that was very important to me. I remember Tom pulling one director up, saying, 'Lis can't say that because that would make her stupid and I don't take stupid people around with me.'

As far as Sarah Jane's actual character went, though, I had two very different people in mind. The first was a cousin. She was eight when I was in my teens and my overriding memory of her is her sheer indomitable attitude. She was young and naïve enough to really rail against any perceived injustices with the words 'It's not fair!' She said it all the time, with the absolute certainty you have before you realise that life just isn't fair. Taking her attitude on board, Sarah Jane became a fighter: she wouldn't give up, whatever the odds, just because she felt slighted. She could fall down a quarry every week and still come out, fists clenched and ready for revenge.

There was another influence on Sarah Jane and it's one that I didn't even realise myself until years later. I was doing a magazine interview and I said, 'I think I may have based Sarah a little bit on Barry Letts.' And once I'd said it, the more obvious it was that it was true. Interviews can be very therapeutic like that – they force you to think about things in different ways. Imagine how much writing this book has taught me about myself!

Barry had great strength of character. He would never say yes if he meant no and he would never be devious; he wasn't interested in playing games. I don't know anyone who would say a bad word about him. And yet he was very strong-minded. I've seen him really lose his rag big time – really big time – because he's so committed. So that was something I wanted to incorporate: Barry's honesty and his straightforwardness.

After that little epiphany, which happened during the press for the third series of *The Sarah Jane Adventures*, so quite a long while after I'd been playing her, I got a text from Russell T Davies. 'I've never heard you say that before,' he said.

Honestly, that man must read everything!

* * *

Filming for *Dinosaurs* ran as before, with three lots of eight days at Acton culminating in two filming days at Television Centre. Rehearsals were fun, actually. One or two of us struggled not to smile at a couple of the lines, and there's always a bit of a laugh when a bunch of you are acting to a chair and being told to pretend it's a Stegosaurus. But we all took it very seriously – with Paddy around, there was little choice. No one was dismissive; you can't be an actor if you're going to be condescending about your material. Once you stop believing, you're lost. I don't care if I'm doing *Play for Today* or *Jackanory*, acting against an imaginary dinosaur or Banquo's ghost – it makes no odds.

Beginning on 15–16 October, we concentrated on the first two episodes as usual, plus some of the underground stuff from Episode 4. As usual it was all against the clock. Ten p.m. was the cut-off point. A second after that and the plug would be pulled.

As I said, the unions were so strong in the Seventies, there was nothing we could do, so it wasn't out of the ordinary to butcher the odd scene just to get something in the can. You'd get to half past nine, see how much was still left to do and know you were going to have to fly through it. Anything, just to get it done – all that hard work, all that rehearsal, being pushed and pushed by Paddy Russell, just to see a terrible last-minute hatchet job of a rewrite rushed through.

Worshipping Harry bloody Roy before the cameras rolled was still *de rigueur* but something even more disruptive was around the corner. With everyone ready to go at 7.30, a flurry of activity at the back of the studio announced the arrival of the BBC's press team chasing promotional shots for the serial. Jon and the others were happy to oblige but I found it really disruptive. We'd just spent two days in the studio trying to hone the most realistic performance among occasionally wobbly sets and now here were people with no understanding of the script telling me to act in a completely different way. 'Lis, can you come out from behind that desk and look surprised?', 'Stare at Jon and look afraid?' The very antithesis of everything we'd been slaving over and over with Paddy to perfect. I really struggled to shake all that artificiality off. When it came to filming my real scenes in the same space I still had the photographer's barked requests ringing in my ears when it should have been the script.

At the first opportunity I grabbed Barry – 'I can't do all this fake posing – it's ruining my performance. Is there anything you can do?'

And being Barry, of course, there was something.

'Leave it to me.'

For the next photocall Barry made sure he was there. He let me do a couple of poses cowering at Jon's side then said, 'Sorry chaps, I need Lis elsewhere.' And that was it, I was excused. He did that every single time. Jon didn't mind going solo, of course – he'd pose all night if he thought it would help the show. But that's why, if you look, there aren't many publicity stills of me from the serials.

As each day ended and I trudged home at eight, nine, ten o'clock – or later on filming days – it was only the thought of weekends that kept me going. They were the first chance I got to spend with Brian, if he wasn't working.

Prior to our first shoot in Studio 6 there were two model-capture days. Bearing in mind the feats Jim and co. had pulled off with the Sontaran costume, I was expecting great things from the dinosaurs. I think everyone was. Unfortunately, the work had been farmed out to an external company. Whispers around Acton were that Barry et al. weren't happy with the results. By the time Paddy actually had to film the things everyone knew they weren't good enough. You can imagine how much this improved our director's mood!

When I saw one of the models I could have cried. We all could. Awful, just so amateur looking! But what can you do? The serial was called *Invasion of the Dinosaurs* so they had to be included, terrible as they were. I think the scene where I have to photograph a sleeping T-Rex looked OK, but as soon as the creatures needed to move a bit, then any magic was lost. *Jurassic Park* it wasn't.

Most embarrassingly, the monsters weren't even accurate. Shortly after airing I received a letter from a six-year-old boy saying, 'Your Tyrannosaurus has the wrong number of fingers. Five instead of four.' The *shame*.

* * *

Although each serial was one continuous story, working on *Dinosaurs* was as close to being in theatre rep as I could imagine. Each fortnight of rehearsal and recording was just as punishing as my time in Scarborough. No sooner have you cracked one script than you're on to the next. Rehearse, perform, rehearse, perform, rehearse, perform . . . Boy it was tiring. It was like a conveyor belt, really – we were all just hamsters on a wheel.

At least with summer season you could always see the end in sight. No such luck in *Doctor Who*, though. Drawing towards the finale of *Dinosaurs* merely meant it was time to begin shooting the next story. Suddenly I was receiving scripts for the following serial, as well as the final *Dinosaur* updates. In theatrical terms, that eleventh season of *Doctor Who* was like five or six Scarboroughs bundled together.

After *The Time Warrior* I'd had a three-month break to get my breath back. Not this time. In fact, I didn't even get a weekend to recover. Our last studio day on *Dinosaurs* wrapped on 13 November – the very day location shooting started on the next serial. So after a couple of hours in my own bed I found myself hurtling down to Dorset on an early train, desperately trying to shake *Dinosaurs* out of my head and get to grips with the new scripts.

And what scripts they were! Some characters take on a life outside of their programmes, don't they? From the moment the Daleks had first appeared in the 1960s they'd leapt into the wider public's consciousness. Comedians made jokes about them, kids ran around pretending to be them, non-fans would exclaim 'Exterminate!' in imitation. So even as a non *Doctor Who* fan I was aware of the Daleks.

I was even looking forward to working with them. Quite a few of the darker moments on the *Dinosaurs* set had been lifted by Jon saying, 'Don't worry, Lissie, the Daleks are in the next one. You'll enjoy them.' He wasn't the only one excited by them. There was a palpable buzz about North Acton among the regulars once news of the next serial came in. Partly I suppose because it's always nice to work with something so iconic but also you just knew, as Barry said, that thousands more people would tune in to see the Doctor come up against his most famous enemies.

Death to the Daleks, I think, is one of the great underrated serials. It tends to get overlooked when people talk about the classic episodes. To be honest, it's even disregarded when people talk about Dalek episodes. Unfairly, I think.

It was written by Terry Nation, the monsters' creator, although as usual there was a lot of input from Terry Dicks and Barry, as well as Robert Holmes, who was being groomed as Dicks' successor.

As well as the Daleks, it was on this shoot that I was introduced to another mainstay of *Who* folklore – the quarry. If you see another planet being represented on television, especially one with a rocky surface, chances are it's been filmed in a quarry – and I've probably been there. I don't think *Doctor Who* would have lasted so long without them.

ARC Sand Pits at Gallows Hill, Dorset, was our quarry of choice – masquerading as the planet Exxilon – for five November days and, I have to say, despite the cold weather it was a fun time. One of the first people I met when I arrived was Jon. As usual, he couldn't wait to show off the team, even before I'd caught my breath.

'Lis, come and meet our Daleks.'

Bloody hell, Jon, can't I just get my bearings first?

Then he did this weird thing of looking like he was going to put his arm around my shoulders, but actually he just grabbed my neck. It was like he was steering me! There was no hint of menace, and it didn't hurt, but he needed to be in control.

I've met a lot of men like that over the years. They want to impose themselves physically on smaller women. You see them in bars, leading their partners in with firm hands. I'm always amazed at the things I've put up with in the past. If someone touched me like that now I'd break their fingers but when you're young, you don't want to rock the boat, you just go with the flow.

A lot of people think Daleks are controlled by wires. There were actually men working them from the inside. They weren't midgets or anything, just actors who were not particularly big. (Russell's Daleks are bigger and, I believe, Steven Moffat's are larger still, so I imagine the same restrictions don't apply.) Our main Dalek operator was John Scott Martin – he was the one who tended to roll out first. We got on famously, actually. John was another Liverpool lad, so we had that in common, and it was a terrible shame when he died from Parkinson's in 2009.

The other two operators were Murphy Grumbar and Cy Town, who played Baby Dalek. Murphy looks like a munchkin from *The Wizard of Oz*, but larger and grumpy with it, although nice enough when you got to know him. Michael Wisher supplied those terrifying electronic voices, as he had on the last Dalek story. He was a dear man and, like Terry Walsh, a jack of many trades. Later, he would get his moment in the sun as Davros but also cropped up as Morelli in *Planet of Evil*, Magrik in *Revenge of the Cybermen*, as well as making several appearances before my time.

You can make new friends in any walk of life but on *Who* I was spoilt by the number of amazing older actors who crossed my path. I'm such a glutton for tales of yesteryear – I love the old tradition of passing stories from one generation to the next. You can learn so much, although sometimes it's just a pleasure to become immersed in that other world. For me it's as romantic as the tales of knights and maidens.

The thing I always forgot is how delighted they are to be in *Doctor Who*! These great thespians arrive, rubbing their hands with glee, genuinely thrilled to be involved for a couple of months.

On *Death to the Daleks* we had Duncan Lamont, who played Dan Campbell. He was a joy. Duncan was married to Patricia Driscoll, who had played Maid Marian in *Robin Hood*, so there was a connection to my childhood right there. I could have listened to stories about their work all day. Actually, though, Duncan paid me a huge compliment. He was worried about offending me, I think.

'Do you know what you remind me of?'

Oh here we go, I thought.

'The way you do things – it's that old Hollywood style of acting.'

I could have hugged him. All those films I used to love as a child, the silent ones and the early talkies, they're still my favourites. I particularly loved the body language in those pictures, the way the actors could achieve so much without words. Lillian Gish in *Broken Blossoms* is an absolute masterclass – that scene where she goes down rapids on a raft should be in drama textbooks. All actors then were trying to add another dimension to the piece. Maybe that's why I love doing action myself. And the reason they managed it was so simple – a lot of the actors had other lives before they found the movies. So many people, like Joseph Cotton in Orson Welles' company, had backgrounds in vaudeville or radio that they arrived in Hollywood as all-round entertainers with an armoury of tricks they could apply to film. Cary Grant started out being a juggler and an acrobat and it's there onscreen in the way he moves. There's one film where he's sitting by a side table and he knocks the table and his hat goes down. He just reaches out and catches it so effortlessly. It's so clever, so understated and light and funny. I'm not that good with props so I do admire anyone else who is – I'm all right on the rehearsal and then it comes to the take and I become really cack-handed.

There were more new faces behind the scenes as well. L. Rowland Warne was in charge of costumes – and boy did we have fun with this one! – while Magdalen Gaffney was my third makeup supervisor in as many serials. Obviously Magdalen had a lot of other people to tend to and those requiring most makeup, like the alien Exxilons themselves, dominated her time, so an assistant was assigned to do me.

We were chatting away while the slap went on and then proudly she showed me a mirror. God, my face was so shiny it was almost silver!

'What have you done?'

The girl bristled. 'This is a space programme, isn't it?'

'Yes – but *I* come from Earth!'

Magdalen just fell about. 'What's she done to you? You're luminous!'

For the rest of the week she did me herself.

Coincidentally, it was while I was in makeup the next day that I got a shout to nip outside. Obviously Daleks can't easily negotiate sand dunes so a network of train track had been laid for them to roll around some rocks and down a little hill. *Why have I been called out for this?* I wondered.

But I was so glad I went.

The director called 'Action!' and the three Daleks, led as usual by John Scott Martin, started gliding along this track, as smooth as if they were in a studio. They'd only been going a second or two, though, when they began to pick up speed. Suddenly we heard this almighty 'Wheeeeee!' coming from them as they realised they were going too fast – and with the corner approaching. The next thing I knew, there was a pile of Daleks on their sides, rolling around like skittles!

Everyone rushed over to get the poor guys upright again but we couldn't do it for laughing. Forget the joke about the most terrifying force in the universe having a problem with stairs – they can't even handle bends.

Watching the Exxilons navigate the terrain was just as funny. In fact, considering it was their planet, they were hysterical. Exxilons were these sack-like creatures who crept around the hills, taking pot shots at the rest of us. Not being able to see their faces always makes villains seem more sinister – at least that was the theory. But every time these scary savages had to stagger up the hill, one of them would tread on their costume and you'd see a surprised head pop through the hood.

There was a nice feel to the whole shoot, I have to say. A lot of that, I think, came from Jon getting on better with this particular director than he had with Paddy. Jon was a bit like Bagpuss in that respect. If he was having a good day, then everyone would, too.

Michael E. Briant had directed *The Green Death* among others and he knew how to get the best out of Jon. When it came to it, I can't say I felt a similar bond – he really didn't seem interested in much to do with Sarah Jane at all.

Some of Michael's techniques with his star were a little off-the-wall, though. I remember one chilly day us being lined up for a shot when he looked at me and said, 'Lis, give Jon a slap, would you?'

Well, that's not in the script, I thought.

Jon virtually did a double-take. 'Why would Sarah Jane slap me?' he spluttered. 'We're great friends.'

'I know you are, Jon,' the director laughed, 'but your face is turning blue.'

Actually, there was one occasion when we did actually slap each other for real. Jon loved diving and had spent a lot of time in the South Seas. His house was full of bits and pieces plucked from the seabed. When he was drunk he would sometimes tell bawdy stories from his trips over there. I always assumed he was joking but one day I made the mistake of referring to one of his tall tales when we were both sober. That was it – his hand went *smack* across my face!

Well, he got a slap straight back.

Safe to say, although we immediately kissed and made up, that was probably the lowest point in our relationship, but I guess he had been telling the truth.

* * *

God it was cold, but being in a quarry in Dorset in mid-November, what did we expect? There were no Winnebagoes or trailers to hide from the elements in those days. Any spare half hours and I'd smuggle myself onto the bus for a nap or just to warm up.

Just when I thought I couldn't bear the temperature any more, Michael announced the final scene of the shoot. I'd been dreading this. It was bad enough being out there in Sarah Jane's suit but now I'd have to do it in a bikini!

The last *Dinosaurs* episode ended with the Doctor promising to take me to the holiday planet of Florana, so as *Daleks* begins I'm all set to go with swimming togs, lilo and parasol. I know Sarah Jane is meant to be striking a blow for feminists across the universe, but I was actually quite excited by the idea (it's nice to be a bit playful with a character every now and again). It was my idea to have a beach ball, I remember – I thought that could be fun – and I didn't mind being asked to put a swimsuit on. I just thought, *I must remember to shave my legs!*

Most of those scenes were filmed later in the studio but first we had to capture me exiting the TARDIS, dressed – that's right – for 100 degrees, not 30. Anyone who thinks acting is all lipstick and glamour should really think again. As there was no way I was leaving the hotel dressed like that, I had to get changed on the bus. Heating systems on coaches in 1973 left a lot to be desired, let me tell you. Even worse, I had to stand semi-naked for ages while they hosed me with fake tan – a hideous experience to end a pretty good week.

* * *

I always enjoyed the camaraderie of location shoots and everyone being at the same hotels, eating at the same restaurants and sharing the same buses. You don't always get on with everyone but there are enough people around for you all to have your own friends.

After a week away, however, it was still a relief to get back to the home comforts of London where even the relentless slog of the rehearse, record, rehearse, record at North Acton seemed quite welcome. Before we got going at the read-through, however, Barry had some news – and it wasn't good.

'I just wanted to let you all know that this will be my last series as producer,' he announced. 'It's time to move on to other things.'

Oh my God! We all sat there in shock. As far as I was concerned, Barry *was Doctor Who*. Jon might be the star, but Barry was the *programme*. Barry had overseen the show's transfer into colour, he had forced the Corporation to investigate and then adopt the latest Colour Separation Overlay techniques. Thanks to his close relationship with Terry Dicks he had also influenced and written storylines, and had even directed several episodes. His influence was truly extraordinary. And, of course, he had created Sarah Jane Smith and cast me in the role. What a great decision that was!

Barry wasn't the only hole we had to plug. Terry Dicks had announced his departure some months earlier and his successor, Robert Holmes, had been shadowing him for a while now. Rumour has it that it was Robert's idea to call our current serial *Death to the Daleks* out of pure wishful thinking because he hated them so much. Robert, of course, wrote *The Time Warrior*, so I had a lot to thank him for. He could have turned my character any which way (although I'm sure Barry kept a very close eye).

I liked Robert. We both enjoyed all things gothic. Over the

coming months I drew comfort from spying him in the wings, pipe in mouth, very tall, very upright, but always nodding, like a dog rocking in the back of a car. You always felt brainy in his presence, he just oozed quiet confidence. I'd sometimes go and stand by him just to feel his strength.

'Hello, Robert.'

'How are we, girl?'

'Fine, fine.'

'How's the work today?'

'Fine, fine.'

He and Terry were chalk and cheese. Whereas Robert was extremely contained, the thinking man with the pipe like his namesake, Sherlock, Terry was so ebullient, so funny and so very open. When we went to the fortieth anniversary celebration of *Doctor Who* at the Houses of Parliament, he was such a scream. 'When does the bar open? I wouldn't have come if I'd known . . .'

With Terry and Barry, the lynchpins of the show, leaving so soon after Katy Manning and following the tragic death in a car accident of Jon's close pal on the show, Roger Delgado, who played fellow Time Lord the Master with such sinister class, I was apprehensive as to the future of the programme. Audiences don't always embrace change. Mess with the ingredients too much and viewers start disconnecting. *At least we've still got Jon*, I thought.

* * *

North Acton was such a divine environment to work in and by our third serial Jon and I were in a comfortable groove. The regimented rehearsal/recording demarcation was quite liberating, actually. On day one Jon and I would arrive and we'd go through our scenes, script in hand, working things out. Gradually over the course of the session the lines just seep into your memory. It's a lovely way to work, actually, very organic. You block sections out, work on them, have fun experimenting and don't even realise sometimes that you're memorising quite large chunks of text. And as changes get made as you go, you're not lumbered with having to re-learn something in a different form. I wish we still had that system now. On *The Sarah Jane Adventures* we're expected to have the whole episode in our heads from day one. You've got to be good to go on the first day – it's more like cramming for an exam.

Rehearsals at the Acton Hilton began in the last week of November after a hurried trip back to Dorset for some extra scenes. Script under my arm, I met Jon in the canteen and we had a guess at what the day would hold. It turned out we were wrong. Michael E. Briant declared right at the start that we would not be working on Episodes 1 and 2, as expected. Instead, we would work through the script on a strict set-by-set basis. In other words, all tunnel shots from all episodes were done at once, TARDIS shots bundled together, Dalek ship scenes paired up, etc., regardless of where they fell in the serial. My initial reaction was, *OK, whatever. Let's go*. Jon, on the other hand, wasn't happy at all. And when Bagpuss wasn't happy . . .

But it was no good arguing. Briant had decided to try and avoid wear and tear on the sets by not using them, storing them, then digging them out again. Get a set in place, film everything, put it away – it made sense but only if you treated the actors as chess pieces.

It was the filming equivalent of completing a jigsaw puzzle before you've got the edges in place. After one day my script was littered with notes. 'O.O.B.' didn't begin to cover it. Running, walking, happy, sad, chatty, quiet, close to Jon, coat on or off, hair neat or messy . . . And, of course, it wasn't just me I was trying to keep track of: Jon was completely at sea filming in this way. In five seasons I think this was the first time he'd been asked to do anything like it.

I didn't envy the person in charge of continuity on *Death to the Daleks*, although I didn't exactly make that particular job any easier. There is a scene where I've been captured by the Exxilons and am being prepared for sacrifice. In the script I think I should have been hung from the ceiling. In reality I was told to stand, arms above my head, with my hands tied to a pole – which was actually a broom handle. That's how thought out this particular scene was. I can't remember if it was the floor manager or the assistant studio manager, but he was the one who held the sweeping head out of shot while I was dangling away. What I do remember, however, is that this scene went on for bloody ages while the Exxilons danced around their fire.

As soon as they stopped pointing the camera at me I unhooked myself from the broom handle and tried to shake some life into my arms. 'I need to have a sit down,' I told Chris D'Oyly-John.

As floor manager Chris was the director's voice on the studio floor, so he said, 'Fine. Just don't wander off.'

So off I went to find a piece of scenery to rest on while they got on with preparing for another angle shoot of the sacrifice set-up. I was so busy trying to massage some feeling back into my wrists where they'd been tied that I didn't notice another camera angle change. The new angle focused on the Exxilons – but the camera was pointing exactly where I should be dangling in the background.

Oh Christ, I thought, pulling myself up, *I'm in this scene!*

'Chris,' I said, but he just waved a hand dismissively and called, 'OK, everyone, action!'

'But, Chris . . .' I persevered.

'Not now, Lis,' he hissed.

Well, sod it then, I thought. *You're not having me.*

So I sat back down.

To this day I don't know if anyone has ever noticed but look carefully and there you see me – and there you don't.

* * *

As I mentioned, I really think *Death to the Daleks* is one of the forgotten classics. It had everything – impotent, double-crossing Daleks, a mysterious alien planet, a pretty tense chase scene – even a bit of Venusian hop-scotch. Acting with the Daleks in the studio was a lot more satisfying than out in a glorified sand pit. For a start they were designed to roll around on a flat studio surface, so their mobility wasn't an issue but up close, in the right setting, they really did look intimidating. I'm no sci-fi fan, as I've said, but within context they are damn scary, I can assure you.

At least they are in the studio. In the rehearsal room it's quite a different story.

Obviously John, Cy and Murphy didn't want to be lumbered with the whole Dalek paraphernalia at North Acton but neither was it any use if they simply wandered around normally. So they would learn all their lines, bless them – because obviously they were dubbed by Michael for broadcast – then hop into just the bottom half of the Dalek suit. Watching these three wheel around the room, using their hands as the sink plunger and whisk, took a bit of getting used to before the laughs stopped but it was the perfect compromise, really.

I don't know if Terry Nation ever saw one of these rehearsals. Maybe that's where he got the inspiration for the look of Davros.

When it came to the studio days, Michael sat there at the side with headphones and a mic so we could hear the words in real time.

I say 'studio days' – that was another thing Briant meddled with. Rather than shoot on both Mondays and Tuesdays as was tradition, he decided to dedicate Monday to rehearsals and Tuesdays to all-day filming. What an ordeal! It wasn't just that we were used to the old way, although that certainly contributed to our annoyance, but such a gap between rehearsal and 'action!' was way too long. Worse, having to cram the equivalent of two episodes into a single day piled on too much pressure. By the end of each Tuesday I was ready to kill; we all were.

If I hate something, I have a moan but then I get on with it. Jon couldn't do that – this new way of working knocked him for six. As much as anything, he hadn't been consulted and I could see his temper getting worse as the weeks went by. Learning lines was more of an effort for him, focusing on rehearsals seemed arduous and keeping a civil tongue in his head with Briant around was sometimes a chore too much. I really felt for him. It was Jon's show, he was the name above the title yet he was being forced to work in a way that really didn't get the best out of him.

The second Jon realised he wasn't enjoying it any more his mind went into overdrive. 'I'm not being paid enough to work like this,' he announced during a break. 'It's time to have a word with the powers that be.'

At the time I didn't think much of it. *He's probably just letting off steam, like the rest of us*, I told myself.

* * *

Shooting on *Death to the Daleks* finished for me on 18 December. How on earth it was nearly Christmas already I had no idea, but as we wrapped late at night there was a spring in everyone's step – even Jon's – and it wasn't just the prospect of a few days off. Three days earlier, on Saturday, 15 December, the first episode of *The Time Warrior* had finally gone out on BBC1. I don't know how they work these things out, but viewing figures were good – nearly nine million people!

Of course, when I sat down with Brian at 5.10 that Saturday afternoon I had no idea whether it would be a success or not. I know it's only television and I'd recorded the show back in May, but I had a real case of first night jitters. As the continuity announcer introduced the programme it felt exactly like that moment when the curtain is about to go up – and you're not sure you remember all the lines.

I don't know what I was so nervous about. You never know what's going to be added afterwards but I was pleased with how it turned out. The special effects were unlike anything I'd ever seen before and seeing how they worked the TARDIS was mind-blowing, really. I thought I did all right, too, but I still had that nagging doubt: what if the viewers don't take to me after Katy?

'Stop fussing,' Brian said. 'They'll love you.'

I wasn't convinced.

Half an hour later, the end credits barely faded from the screen and our phone rang. It was Mum. The whole family had gathered round the telly at home, she reported, and they were all so proud of me.

'You were the star, Lissie!'

Dad was a bit overwhelmed, I think. He and Mum had seen all my plays and everything I'd been in on television but I suppose I did have a lot of screen time in this one. And I would for another twenty-five episodes. Perhaps that was the difference. Either way, that became our Saturday night ritual. As soon as an episode finished, Mum or Dad would jump on the phone to tell me what they thought about it. Who knew my parents would become such fans of science fiction?

Brian had to slip off for a play but it didn't matter. The phone rang off the hook all night with friends and family congratulating me. It was nice. I hoped I'd done Sarah Jane justice – I thought she deserved it.

Unfortunately, even as I watched that episode, I knew things in Sarah's world were about to change. Viewers didn't know it yet but Terry Dicks was off and Barry wouldn't be far behind. But the most devastating news had just reached me: Jon had quit.

We would be looking for a new Doctor.

Chapter Six

There's Nothing 'Only' About Being A Girl

I STILL REMEMBER Jon regaling me with the story. He'd never been more upbeat.

'So, Lissie, I bowled in to see Shaun Sutton and said, "Hello, old boy, the programme's doing well – better than ever, I hear. How about a rise?"'

Shaun was head of drama.

'How did that go?' I asked.

'Shaun looked up. Didn't smile, just said, "I'm sorry, Jon. The answer's no."

'That was it, Lissie. Can you believe it? No discussion, no "we'll consider it" or "maybe next year". Just a big flat "no".'

I felt for Jon, I really did.

'So, what did you do?'

'Well, it left me in a very awkward position. So I said, "Then, I have no alternative but to inform you that I'm leaving the show."'

'You didn't!' I gasped.

'I certainly did.' Jon puffed himself up as he spoke. 'I walked out, closed the door and that was that.'

'And how do you feel about it now, Jon?'

'Best thing I ever did,' he assured me. And I believed him.

Wow! The Doctor was leaving. I hadn't seen that coming and Jon hadn't either, I think. To be fair, he seemed content with his decision, which was great. Where it left the programme, however, I had no clue. Would they replace him? Could they replace him? And if they did, would the new Doctor want me?

Ah well, I thought. *I only signed for a year. I may as well enjoy it.*

* * *

Speaking of enjoying it, strange things had begun to happen to me since *The Time Warrior*'s transmission. As a young girl in London it's not out of the norm to attract the odd stare or comment from men of a certain disposition but after Christmas it seemed to become more frequent, and not just from men. I felt women studying me as well. When the first young boy rushed up to me near my house the penny dropped: they were *Who* fans.

I'd seen the effect Jon could have on complete strangers when we were out and about but, naïvely I suppose, I never for one moment expected the same treatment. He was the Doctor. Who was I?

It turned out that for a surprising number of people I was apparently quite important.

Signing my first autograph was an amazing feeling. It's one of those skills you practise as a child but you never expect to use on anything other than cheques. I had no idea signing sessions would become such a large part of my life later on.

Jon was amazing with fans – he never felt more comfortable. I don't know how he did it. I love meeting new people and having conversations but, to this day, there's something unnerving about having a conversation with someone who knows so much about you when you don't even know their name – especially when you've just popped out to buy a pint of milk.

My postman noticed another change. Aside from bills, circulars and the odd bit of family correspondence, I was now receiving bundles of letters every week, forwarded from my agent. It became a point of principle to reply to each and every one. But they don't tell you about that when you sign up.

* * *

Jon's news was still top secret when we began work on the next serial. I thought it would be tricky to keep schtum but once you're in the flow again the real world flits out of your head.

If *Death to the Daleks* had brought back familiar villains, *The Monster of Peladon* reintroduced an entire planet. Brian Hayles' *The Curse of Peladon* had done well when it was broadcast in 1972 and so Terry and Barry asked him to conjure a sequel. The finished result, set fifty years after the original, was also intended to convey comment on the bubbling mining dispute in the UK and the growing enthusiasm for feminism.

For the sake of cost-cutting and also continuity, many of the original *Peladon* sets and costumes were to be used again. Not only that, Barry attempted to regroup as many of the team from the earlier production as well. I was so glad he did. After three serials where I'd felt all at sea with the director I was delighted to meet the next one. Australian Lennie Mayne had also directed the tenth-anniversary special, *The Three Doctors*, so he had his *Who* credentials. More importantly he was just so easy to get on with.

He was a small man, about my size, but he had none of the chip on the shoulder that shorter men sometimes have. Maybe that's the Australian confidence – or perhaps he was just a nice bloke. He was such a bundle of energy, quite manic actually, and because he used to be a dancer he was always pirouetting around the studio and talking away. He had such a florid vocabulary and he was so irreverent. For one of the royal palace scenes he waited for Nina Thomas, as Queen Thalira, to get into place and then said, 'Right, now Mum's in the bog house sitting on the throne!' No airs and graces with Lennie.

He loved calling ladies 'Mum'. Don't know why. You could always try things out with Lennie, though. He was never rushed.

'Lennie, what about if I do this instead?'

'Good idea, Mother, good idea!'

Plenty of others would have said 'no' or worse but Lennie was a real people person. You could see that in the way he looked out for his wife, the actress Frances Pidgeon. He liked to have her around and so he found her a small role as a handmaiden. He was always fussing – 'Hello, Pidge', 'Come in, Pidge', 'Join the group, Pidge – you're one of us, Pidge.' He just wanted everyone to be happy.

Working with Lennie also coincided with me finally relaxing into the show. Looking back, it definitely took me the first two serials to get my bearings. I was still finding my feet, getting to know the team and doing my best to get a bead on Jon. It was in everyone's interests if we got along off-screen as well as on and that was my mission. By the time we did *Daleks* I think we were close. *Peladon*, though, was the first time I thought, *Yes, I'm part of this show. Jon and I are a team.*

These relationships can take time. *School Reunion* was David Tennant's third *Doctor Who* episode – after the Christmas Special and *New Earth* – and I know he was still feeling his way with the crew, the character, Billie Piper and everything else. He's said in interviews that he didn't really feel he owned the part until *Tooth and Claw* – his fourth episode (although broadcast before *School Reunion*).

So with *Peladon* everything just clicked. Obviously I got notes from Jon about my costume, but that was just him. I turned up in a jumper one day and he said, 'Oh no! You should wear a blouse, Lissie.' Now, I hate wearing blouses, anything with collars, really. 'It's quite dark in the tunnels,' he added. 'If you had a nice white blouse . . .'

'I'd be easier to shoot!'

We had a laugh about that, which shows how our relationship had matured.

I knew Jon's comments about my jumper weren't personal – it was just his obsession with all things fashion. (According to Jon, he and Gerald Campion, who played Billy Bunter, had been the first Teddy Boys in London. These things were important to him.) But Jon wasn't the only one, unfortunately. After a morning of crawling along tunnels I received another piece of advice. 'Lis, perhaps you might wear a bra for the actual shoot?'

For God's sake, I thought. *You can't see anything!* But, 'OK, fine,' I said, all teeth and smiles, and duly traipsed off to wardrobe. I counted to ten before returning, still completely bra-less. 'Is that better?'

'Oh much! Thanks, Lis. We don't want to frighten the children.'
Ridiculous.

Even the soundman threw his two penn'orth in on my costume
on that one, I seem to remember. I felt like saying, 'If you think
you can do better,' but you just grin and get on with it.

As far as working and rehearsing and workshopping the script,
Jon and I had never been better. For the first time it felt like we
were totally in tune with each other, bouncing things back and forth
so naturally. After a bit of a slow start it was really an honour to
work with him so closely.

One of the things *Who* has always been famous for is its running
– exactly the same under Russell T Davies and Steven Moffat as it
ever was. As Peladon was a mining planet, a lot of our scenes
seemed to involve haring up and down narrow corridors at full pelt.
I remember one early scene, setting off after Jon, and he looked
round at me. It was a really patrician, caring look and I'm sure
anyone watching would have thought he was checking to see if
Sarah Jane was OK, that she hadn't fallen over. What they didn't
notice was him hissing, 'For God's sake, Lissie, slow down!'

That was hysterical. Of course, I know exactly how he feels now,
having to keep up with the kids on *The Sarah Jane Adventures*.

Jon wasn't the only person who struggled to keep pace with
me on *Peladon*. It was getting near curfew time and we weren't
anywhere near ready to wrap so the pressure was on. I had to be
chased down a mine by an Ice Warrior. I won't mention his name
but the actor inside was a great guy. He enjoyed being on *Who* and
was always happy to go the extra mile. This time he nearly went
too far.

Lennie gave the word – 'Time's short, people, let's get this right
first time' – and off we charged, me in my heeled boots and him in
a heavy monster suit with an oxygen unit on the back, like a scuba
tank. We hadn't gone far when I realised I could hear loud wheezing.
He sounds like he's in trouble. Why doesn't he stop? I wondered.

Then I realised: he didn't want to be the one to push us over time.
The show must go on, and all that.

Right, I thought, and threw myself to the ground.

'Sorry, everyone!' I called, 'I just tripped. Sorry, my fault.'

I looked behind me and the Ice Warrior was slumped over, struggling to get his helmet off. When they checked, we'd been in such a rush to get going that they'd forgotten to plumb his breathing apparatus in. He was gasping in that airtight helmet and he hadn't said a word. That's what *Who* means to people.

Although there were no outside scenes for *The Monster of Peladon* we still had a week's location shoot. The only difference was that the shoot took place in another studio. And I couldn't have been happier.

As a film buff I can tell you there are a few studios in the world that really have a history. Ealing Studios is one of those few. *The Cruel Sea*, *The Lavender Hill Mob*, so many classics were filmed there. They've got the big sea tank used on all those war films. The magic that has been created there! It's one of those places where you can feel the past as you walk around. It also made a change not to be in a chalk pit or a quarry or even a dust bowl in freezing January. And, of course, it was so close to my home!

I really think Lennie achieved wonders with the mood on set. Everyone was willing to go that extra mile for him – just look at that Ice Warrior. The new rapport between Jon and me probably helped as well. We certainly tried to lead from the front. Jon was suffering quite bad back pain at the time and had to wear a corset to keep everything in place. Although Terry Walsh was always on hand to step in (although you probably shouldn't see as much of his face and Pertwee perm-wig as you do during one fight scene), Jon still insisted on doing as many of his own stunts as possible – afterwards he'd literally have to be stretched on a human rack. A couple of chaps would grab Jon under the arms, hoist him up and wait for his spine to click back into place.

I had my moments of sacrifice, too. There was a scene where Jon and I had to leap into the pit with Aggedor, the so-called 'monster' of Peladon. I agreed to do the stunt myself and Terry talked me through it.

'Now, Lis, we've got cushions at the bottom, perfectly safe. We can get someone else to do it, if you like, but I think you can do it easily.'

I looked down at the hole. It was only about six feet but in the darkness it seemed to go on for miles.

'I'm not sure about this, Terry.'

'You'll kick yourself if you don't.'

So like an idiot I agreed. Lennie gave the cue and off I jumped. Terry came rushing up to me afterwards.

'Well, did you enjoy that?'

'No, I bloody didn't!'

But he was right – I was glad I'd done it. Unfortunately, I'd forgotten that I'd have to do it again – and again – until Lennie was happy.

By coincidence Todd Joseph was on set that day. Agents never miss a trick, do they, and I saw him talking to Barry.

'Half past nine and look at the energy she's got!' Always trying to squeeze some negotiating power out of a situation.

Afterwards I knew how Jon felt with his back because my ankles were killing me and I'm sure my hip was out of joint. Max Faulkner, who played one of the miners, said, 'You're walking oddly. Lie down on that table.'

I was desperate for a rest so I climbed on while he had a look.

'Thought so,' he said. 'One leg is longer than the other. You'd better go and see someone.'

I didn't do any jumps after that and I've had weak ankles to this day, but at the time I was just pleased to have managed the stunt. *At least we got our shot. It should look pretty spectacular on-screen.*

Anyone who has seen the episode knows it didn't. It looked about as dangerous as hopping into a bath. What a waste of time – all that pain for nothing. *Wait till I see that bloody Terry . . .*

* * *

As usual there was a lot going on in the *Peladon* story. Some of it, perhaps, passed over one or two viewers' heads. If I'm honest, even I might not have noticed the allusion to the then current miners' strike if it hadn't been pointed out to me. I mean, yes, workers on Peladon are abused and so, according to them, were the miners in the UK, and they had no choice but to strike and fight for their rights. But, you know, I had enough to do: remember your lines and don't bump into the furniture and all that. At the end of the day, it's a kids' programme and it's an adventure and that's what I preferred to focus on. If Barry and Terry wanted to put anything else in, then that was fine.

It wasn't just the miners' dispute that Barry asked the writers to focus on, though. After a couple of serials building Sarah Jane up as this thoroughly modern Millie, there's a cracking scene where the Doctor gets so frustrated by Queen Thalira's backwards thinking that he unleashes Sarah Jane to give one of her 'feminism' talks. He doesn't stay around to hear it, of course, but I get to say that unforgettable line: 'There's nothing "only" about being a girl, Your Majesty.'

Once again there were some marvellous older actors in the show who I adored chatting to. Rex Robinson, who played Gebek, was great. And Donald Gee (Eckersley) was another fun one to have around, always a twinkle in Donald's eye. He got to swan about in marvellous black leather. I think he'd been in *Coronation Street* by then and he was doing something for kids with Bob Hoskins, because he was talking a lot about that.

Stuart Fell had me in stitches, of course, playing Alpha Centauri, the alien with a giant eye for a head and myriad arms beneath his green cape. It's hard to keep a straight face when you're talking to what looks like a bobbing head in a curtain. In rehearsal Stuart would just stand there, saying his lines and hopping up and down like he needed a wee. Hysterical. Originally he didn't have a cape but someone said he looked like a 'giant dick'. So they draped this shawl around him, then Lennie, I think, said, 'Now it looks like a giant dick in a cape.' Not my finest, hour, I think, acting with Alpha Centauri. It was like doing *Romeo and Juliet* with a Teletubby.

While we were having a blast, I guess Jon was going through his own turmoil. On 8 February, a Thursday, Barry authorised the press announcement that he was leaving. I remember when David Tennant made his big goodbye speech live at the TV Awards – that made headlines around the world. I don't think it was quite such a big deal in 1974, although it didn't stop the press door-stepping us for a couple of days on our way into White City and Acton. The question on everyone's lips was: 'Do you know who the next Doctor will be?' And of course I didn't have a clue. Jon swam through it without a care in the world. Or so it seemed.

We didn't have to wait that long to see the true impact of Jon's resignation on him. If *Peladon* had seen him attack the part with renewed vigour, his swansong, *Planet of the Spiders*, saw a very morose Doctor trundle into work each day. I couldn't blame him. By then, of course, the whole world knew he was leaving. Even worse, they knew his successor – that announcement had been made a week after Jon's farewell. And as we trudged into rehearsals at the start of March, we only had a month before the Third Doctor regenerated into the Fourth.

You can't say the Beeb didn't pull out all the stops for Jon's finale, though I think Barry should take most of the credit. As producer he may have kept a tight grip on the purse strings, but as a man he was determined that his friend Jon should go out in a blaze of glory. Clearing his schedule, Barry announced that he would take the helm for *Planet of the Spiders* himself. And, he promised, he'd make it one for Jon to remember.

And I really think he did. Jon loved his gadgets and all the physical stuff so this story was loaded with them. I just wished I didn't have to 'enjoy' them as well! But when Bagpuss jumps into a helicopter, all his friends jump in too . . .

Live and Let Die had been the big Bond movie of the previous year, full of speedboat, car and all other sorts of chases. That was definitely an influence on Terry and Barry when they came to shaping Robert Sloman's script. In one episode there's hardly any dialogue at all. Jon is either on the water, in the air or pounding the tarmac in an incredible pursuit sequence.

Part of the chase had Jon haring across a lake in a speedboat. By the time he got out, he looked like the proverbial drowned rat. He was happy to go on but Barry said his hair needed attention. It had been completely matted by a combination of wind and water. So, there he sat, rollers in his hair, when a PR person appeared and said a local journalist had arrived early for her interview.

'Fine,' said Jon. 'Bring her over.'

People who say Jon was vain really didn't get it, did they? And trust me, since his death I've heard quite a few whispers to that effect. The truth is, the vanity was all for the programme: he wanted his Doctor to look a certain way and he was very protective of that. But personal vanity? Yes, he liked to look good, but only if he was on show. Behind the scenes, or off duty, he was as laid-back as anyone. It was all about the show. Why else would he give an interview in full rollers and back corset?

And remember, Jon was always the first one to make a joke about his nose – or his lisp. He had us all in stitches trying to get through the line, 'Don't struggle with the spiders, Sarah!' In fact, I remember him moaning back on my very first day, 'Christ, with my S's, why did they give me someone called Sarah Jane Smith?' So, there was no ego in that respect.

Even so, Jon could be proprietorial at times. On one occasion Nick Courtney, on location with us, offered to drive me in Bessie back along this muddy track to the catering truck.

Jon literally put his arm across me and said, 'Darling, I wouldn't advise going with the Brig.'

So I didn't. A minute later, Nick jumped behind the wheel and, honest to God, within moments he was nearly in the ditch. Thank you, Jon!

Bessie wasn't the only old favourite recalled for Jon's farewell. Barry also found a way to include the Whomobile in the chase sequence – in its new, improved flying mode. I had to jump in as well, which was fine. Not so fine, however, was driving around in it beforehand. We were being made up outside the BBC, somewhere near Kingston. Then Jon said, 'Come on, I'll drive us to location.'

So he did – right through Kingston High Street!

In rush hour!

If you've seen the car, you'll know from the outside it looks like a silver manta ray. On the inside, however, it feels like being in a goldfish bowl on wheels. Everywhere we went people were staring and Jon was waving back. Then we hit the high street and all hell broke loose. Cars were weaving all over the place, so Jon had to take evasive action a couple of times. We couldn't have had more close calls if he'd fitted a giant magnet on the front. It was as if every road user was doing a double-take at the same time. My heart was in my mouth because the Whomobile didn't seem to be made of the sturdiest stuff.

And then, inevitably, there were sirens.

'I think they're for us, Jon.'

'I think you're right.'

A policeman came over, so Jon wound down the window.

'Hello, officer, how can I be of assistance?'

'Hello, Doctor,' the policeman said, as if it was the most normal thing in the world to be talking to a Time Lord. 'I'm afraid you can't drive this through Kingston High Street.'

'But it's got a registration plate.'

'That may be so, but in my view it's a hazard.'

In my view it was as well, but I never mentioned it.

Boats and cars were only half the story. The Whomobile took to the skies at some point to chase the villain's gyro copter so there was a BBC chopper on standby to do the filming. During one lunch hour at Membury Airfield Jon couldn't resist suggesting, 'Come on Lissie, let's go for a ride.' I didn't have time to say no; he just pulled me over to where the pilot was polishing it. Bearing in mind my Toronto flight, you'll understand I really wasn't happy, but Jon was so excited and I climbed in.

Whoooosh! It was like going up in a rocket. Suddenly the ground had vanished – and so had my stomach for flying.

'Isn't this wonderful!' Jon beamed.

He was lucky I didn't throw up on him there and then.

'That's the last time I go up in one of these things!' Famous last words . . .

Climbing out, the pilot warned us to mind the rotors which were still spinning. He didn't have to tell me twice – I was almost doubled up clutching my stomach anyway so I was safe. But accidents do happen.

The pilot of the gyro copter wasn't so lucky. His blades were much lower than the bigger chopper's and he got caught. He was lucky not to lose his head. As it was, the blood poured out like water from a geyser. He screamed the place down and everyone ran out to him, of course. By the time I got there I noticed our makeup girl, Deanne Turner, crouching next to him.

'Oh, Deanne, aren't you lovely, looking after him,' I said.

She stood up and leant into my ear.

'I'm actually matching his blood against all my fake colours,' she confessed.

God, I thought, *that's TV for you.*

I remembered that event years later. We were filming a scene in *The Sarah Jane Adventures* in a wood and I'd decided not to risk running down this narrow pathway in the dark. With branches everywhere it seemed foolish to take the risk. So Katherine, my amazing stand-in, was all kitted out in my coat, boots and wig – which is a thoroughly disconcerting image to look at, I must tell you – and ready to go.

On cue she shot off into the wood, twice as fast as I could have gone. A yard from the end, she stumbled and fell arse over head. Watching from the sidelines were me, Stuart our costume designer, and Emma on makeup. As soon as Katherine went down we all leapt up together, hands in mouths like the three brass monkeys.

'Katie!' I screamed.

'Jacket!' cried Stuart.

'Wig!' went Emma.

It just shows you . . .

* * *

We packed a lot into that week. Tidmarsh Manor served as a monastery, Mortimer railway station was where I joined the action answering Mike Yates' call, while Le Marchant barracks in Devizes and the River Severn also provided various location opportunities. Before we headed back to the Acton Hilton as normal, Jon announced a little surprise. By way of a thank you to everyone on the team and to give his further career a leg-up, he was throwing a drinks party at his house in Castelnau, near Barnes. I'd never been before and I was expecting it to be grand but this place was something else, absolutely stunning. I don't know how much of it was down to Jon or whether his wife, Ingeborg, was responsible, but it really was beautiful. I know who the cook in the family was, though, and Ingeborg put on an impressive spread. Jon was on drinks duty that night and he could have done with one or two himself because he seemed on edge. As soon as I stepped in, he fell on me like a long-lost brother and pressed a glass into my hand. 'There you go, Lissie, enjoy that.' God, it was the strongest vodka and tonic I have ever tasted in my life. The next day at North Acton he said, 'Lissie, were you all right last night? You were awfully relaxed.'

'Bloody hell, Jon, after that drink I wasn't relaxed – I was comatose!'

It really was a nice touch to have Barry directing Jon's final episode. They had a natural understanding and this time, more than ever, Barry was inclined to humour more of his star's script suggestions. To be honest, though, there wasn't much Jon could add to a story heavily weighted in his favour. Venusian aikido, plenty of running, lots of saving-the-day action; they'd even brought back the Brig and his UNIT team for a final hurrah. Barry wanted all Jon's friends to be around him when the moment to say goodbye came.

In the circumstances I was really pleased that Sarah Jane had such a dominant role, especially in the earlier episodes. Called by Yates to investigate the mysterious Buddhist retreat – a personal interest of Barry's – she stumbles upon the heart of the Doctor's last adventure. As another fillip for Jon, Barry cast an old friend in the role of Cho-je – Kevin Lindsay, the first-ever Sontaran. Looking back, I'm not sure quite how we got away with converting Kevin into an oriental by sticking a few bits of Sellotape on his eyebrows, but standards were different in those days. It was nice to see him, though. Even better, from a personal point of view, I was so happy that my old Clapham landlord Terry Lodge got to play Moss. I had nothing to do with the casting but if I could have put in a word, I would. It was so nice to chat about our old Manchester days in the breaks and reminisce about how he used to go over Pinter text with me. So much had happened since then, it seemed like a lifetime ago.

* * *

Since the start of the year all the buzz around the BBC had been 'Who will be the next Doctor Who?' When the announcement of Jon's retirement went public that speculation burst into overdrive. At one point every Tom, Dick and Harry seemed to be in the running. I tried to keep on top of developments because obviously it affected me more than most, but work on *Peladon* meant my information was occasionally behind the times. And obviously the lid was being kept very tight on this particular secret.

As I recall, Tommy Steele was seriously mentioned at one point. And *Carry On*'s Jim Dale – it would have been nice to make him apologise for nearly running me over all those years ago! Richard Hearne was another one. He was famous at the time for comedy character Mr Pastry but, so the story goes, he wanted to play the Doctor in the same style. Can you imagine? Fortunately, Barry couldn't and they continued the search. Years later I met Ron Moody, the original Fagin, in Los Angeles. Ron had worked with Brian in a TV play called *Village Hall* so he came straight out with it. 'They offered me the part,' he said. 'They offered me it after Troughton and after Pertwee and each time I said no.' He looked me straight in the eye.

'Biggest mistake of my life.'

Then one day Barry bounded over, full of energy. I remember exactly the spot where I was standing.

'We have got the most perfect Doctor for you, Lis. Have you heard of Tom Baker?'

The name rang a bell but I couldn't place it.

'No,' I said, 'I don't think so.'

Barry wasn't fazed in the slightest.

'Well, you might have seen him in—'

And then it came to me.

'*Rasputin*! Yes, I do know him. Wonderful. Wonderful!'

Barry vanished as suddenly as he'd arrived – off to spread the news further, probably. And I was left to ponder my future with this strange wide-eyed actor with the slightly beak-faced stare. *Interesting*, I thought, *very, very interesting*.

I don't know how Jon took the news – I presume he was told at some point before the press announcement but I never felt comfortable discussing it with him. What I can say is that I wasn't looking forward to our first days of studio shooting. I don't know if it was intentional, to get it out of the way, or whether the schedule just worked out that way, but out of a six-episode show, Jon's regeneration scene with his successor was to be filmed in the first batch.

The day arrived and we all pitched up as usual. Hair, costume, bit of slap every now and then as you went along – the same old pattern. Everyone tried to pretend nothing out of the ordinary was going on, which was so hard because we all knew things would never be the same again. This was the day I had to say goodbye to my Doctor. I was trembling at the prospect; I can't imagine how he must have been feeling.

Those moments of Jon lying there in the lab will stay with me. It was so poignant. In a way I'd sort of delivered my elegy during *Peladon* when I thought he'd died then: 'I still can't believe it – I can't believe that he's dead. You see, he was the most alive person I ever met!' This time, of course, it was Jon who uttered the immortal lines: 'A tear, Sarah Jane?' If I had a pound for every time those words are quoted back to me. (Although it's not the most common quote. I'll let you guess what that is.)

There were no real tears, certainly not from Jon. In fact, there was no emotion at all. One minute I was hunched over his body, sobbing at the Doctor's death, then as soon as we heard 'Cut!' he leapt to his feet, nearly knocking me over. And he did so completely wordlessly, just pulled himself up, dusted his clothes down, then strolled off. It was quite eerie. A minute later another figure was lying down to take his place: Tom Baker had arrived.

The whole regeneration was such a cold affair. Tom simply dashed in and back out again because he was already rehearsing for his debut story. And Jon – well, I don't know what was going through his mind, exactly, except that he refused to be in the same room with his successor. In fact they didn't exchange a single, solitary word. *A pity*, I thought, *a very great pity*.

After that the mood back at Acton was very different. The penny had finally dropped, I think. Jon was leaving – and the show was carrying on. I know later on David found handing over to Matt Smith harder than he'd possibly imagined. From star to history in a matter of seconds; it's a phenomenal fall. No other show does this to an actor.

And Jon, of course, with every day that passed, was wishing he could jump into the TARDIS for real and turn back the clocks. Yes, he was getting tired of the physical stresses on his body; yes, he could do without the fights with directors and yes, he honestly believed he deserved more money, but were those things worth giving up his beloved *Who* for? The answer, he had realised with a sickening thump, was no. By the time he admitted it to himself, though, it was too late.

'Are you all right, Jon?' I asked as he arrived at Acton the morning after regenerating.

'Don't you worry about me. I'm fine.'

But he didn't look fine. In fact, the first chance he got, he dragged a table and chair over to the far end of our massive rehearsal room, then methodically began going through his fan mail. Hundreds of letters and cards, and one by one he replied to them all. He still joined us for tea breaks and lunch, he wasn't avoiding anyone, but whenever the Doctor wasn't required for a scene, he threw himself back into his paperwork. I don't know if he wanted to remind himself how popular he was, or whether he just needed to get all *Who* correspondence out of the way by the time he left – he probably wanted a clean break.

It was so sad to watch and it must have been killing him not to be involved in what we were all doing as well. We were so used to Jon buzzing around, encouraging or giving notes or saying, 'Maybe try it like this . . .' even when he wasn't in a scene. He could be so annoying, I admit, but Jon was also our chief cheerleader. Without him it all felt a bit empty.

* * *

It's strange how things work out. A couple of days after the crushing low of recording his own death scene while still having to concentrate on the rest of the serial, Jon was thrown a nice little fillip. The BBC had licensed a *Doctor Who* exhibition at Blackpool and they wanted Jon and his trusty companion to open it.

It really couldn't have come at a better time.

I can't say I was terribly thrilled at the prospect because it promised to be such a whistle-stop visit. There wouldn't even be a chance to call in on Mum and Dad, even though they were so close. Jon promised it would all be worthwhile. 'It will blow your mind, Lissie, trust me.'

Whether he genuinely expected the event to be that exciting or he was relieved to be out of the same building where Tom was rehearsing, I couldn't say – I was just happy to see him smiling again.

We had a meal in a seafront hotel with some of the BBC suits, then turned in. The next morning at breakfast Jon was all aflush. Apparently he'd been getting ready for bed, stripping in the moonlight, when all of a sudden there was this tremendous roar.

A lamp at the back of the room had illuminated his little striptease routine for all and sundry below.

'I looked out the window and there's a hundred people cheering!'

I thought he must have been exaggerating but my mind was changed the second we stepped out of the hotel. I've never seen so many people in my life – and they were all screaming for Jon. I was literally speechless, so stunned I couldn't move. If Jon hadn't put an arm around me to guide me towards the waiting Bessie I think I'd still be standing there now.

As we scrambled into the old yellow car it dawned on me that Jon had been expecting this. After so many years as the Doctor he must have been used to it but I'd never seen anything like it. I just began to get my bearings and then I heard someone shout, 'I love you, Sarah Jane!' and I crumbled again.

They love me? I certainly hadn't expected that.

The next half an hour was the most surreal of my life. Somehow Jon negotiated Bessie out of the car park without running anyone over and we drove at a snail's pace along the promenade. You couldn't see an inch of pavement anywhere. People were lined five deep along the route, all waving and cheering, calling out their appreciation – and, yes, love! – for *us*. It was like the Queen's Coronation – and we were only off the telly!

I was so glad for Jon; this is how I wanted him to remember *Who*. And this is how I wanted to remember him. Adored by thousands, playing to the gallery, living and breathing *Doctor Who*. Not squirrelled away in a rehearsal room with just his post for company.

I was genuinely amazed to be treated so warmly by the fans. When I joined the show I'd felt so conscious of replacing Katy. In a way I half expected them to be calling her name, not mine. But *Who* fans are the best in the world: if you're good to them, they're magnificent to you. *Peladon* had just started airing by then and I suppose they'd had fourteen or fifteen episodes to get used to me.

I must be doing something right.

A lot of the exhibition itself didn't mean much to me. The Daleks I recognised, of course, and Exxilons, but I think there were plenty of exhibits from before my time. If Jon didn't recognise all of them you would never have guessed – 'Look at this, Lissie', 'See what this gadget does'. He was so masterful at interaction, all the while oblivious to the barrage of camera flashes in our faces. I'd never seen a person command so many people with such ease. Never seen him happier, in fact.

And, I suddenly realised, *I'll never see him this happy again.*

* * *

It would have been the humane thing to have ended Jon's involvement in Blackpool, let him go out on a high, but we had work to do. Even with Barry in charge, those final days on *Spiders* seemed to drag on forever.

And then suddenly, on 1 May in Studio 6, we were done. There was a party, of course, and I seem to remember a cake with Jon's face on it. But I couldn't enjoy it (the party, not the cake!) – I had to get in a car for Hereford where the next serial had already begun shooting. I felt such a fraud bolting out like that but it couldn't be helped. Jon's association with the show may have ended but mine was continuing as normal.

It was just continuing with a different Doctor.

Chapter Seven

What If A Snake Slides Up My Skirt?

TOM BAKER was once asked: 'Why did you get on so well with Elisabeth Sladen?' He gave the interviewer one of his transfixing stares and then said, 'That's easy – she laughed at my jokes.'

Who wouldn't laugh at Tom's jokes? He's one of the funniest people I've ever met. Anyone who has seen him regale a convention with tales of OAP shopping adventures and the like knows he can spin comedy gold out of any subject. Tom has such an energy, a genuine impish delight in the absurd; always playful, always alert to the possibility of a punchline – a treasure. I'm so glad he's known to a whole new generation now, thanks to *Little Britain*. As he says, 'I'm in that lucky position of the people who liked me as a child now offering me work.' And, as he also says, 'No one does Tom Baker quite as well as me.'

But I didn't know any of this as my car hurtled down the roads towards Worcester that night in May 1974. I'd met Tom briefly at Acton, just hellos and handshakes at that stage, because he was hard at work on his Doctor's character upstairs with new producer Philip Hinchcliffe and I was flat out on *Spiders*, but I remember he was big, very big, and had piercing eyes that seemed to be constantly scanning for something in your face when you spoke to him, and there was that mellifluous, rich voice. But, honestly, our time together had been so brief. Anyone can turn on the charm for a meet-and-greet – many an unpleasant actor has mastered that little trick. The proof of the pudding, I decided between snatches of sleep in the car, would be in the meeting.

I've always had a fairly *laissez-faire* attitude to employment. Or maybe that should be *que sera, sera*. I've never worried terribly about the next job and I've always been all right. So as the end of my contract with the Beeb approached, I took it in my stride. Change was in the air, you could almost taste it. Jon was leaving, UNIT was being downplayed to give the new Doctor breathing space, Terry Dicks was off and, of course, Barry Letts was about to produce his last serial. Philip Hinchcliffe, who had been shadowing Barry for quite a while, would obviously want to put his own stamp on the series when he officially took over in the autumn. If he decided the incoming Doctor deserved a fresh companion, then so be it. I wouldn't take it personally. I'd had a good year. A tiring one, definitely. And I'd learned a lot about people in that time. But it had been fun and I was confident I'd done some good work. Damn it, I was *proud* of Sarah Jane Smith.

Fortunately for me, so was everyone else. Even though Barry was handing over the reins, I think he had a lot of influence with the new production team. His opinion – very sensibly, I think – was that audiences are comfortable with continuity. It was one thing giving them a new Doctor; replacing his companion as well might be a step too far.

Actually I think audiences are far more forgiving than that (look at Matt Smith and Karen Gillan as the Eleventh Doctor and Amy Pond). The truth was Barry was as proud as I was of Sarah Jane. Most importantly, from the compliments and comments I'd been fed throughout the year, I know he was very content with the direction I'd been taking her. So, when a new contract for another twenty-six shows was presented on 16 April 1974, I duly signed.

Bearing in mind my value to the show as the cement binding the Third and Fourth Doctors – on more than one occasion I heard Barry say, not for my benefit at all, 'We can't do without Lis' – Todd Joseph went into negotiations on my behalf in bullish mood. 'Without my client your show will struggle this season', 'Lis is already such a popular character – did you see the turnout at

Blackpool?' – he said all the right things, I'm sure. But he was up against the people who had let their star leave rather than even *consider* a nominal raise. In the end, I think Todd did well to scrape a £5 a week increase, but it scarred him.

'Seriously, Lis, it's like getting blood out of a stone.'

Yet when I saw Barry later that day he looked as if he was still in shock.

'Your agent drives a hard bargain, Lis.' He was being deadly serious!

While I hadn't been replaced, I had been added to. In Barry's initial casting meetings with Robert Holmes and Terry, they had pretty much settled on going for another older actor as the Doctor – no names at that stage, but that was the feeling. The dilemma facing them, however, was that Jon's gung-ho energy and hands-on style was very popular with viewers. An older actor might not necessarily want to – or indeed be able to – pull that off. The solution was to introduce a younger male sidekick who could take care of the fisticuffs. In the end, of course, they went with Tom who was more than capable of handling himself. By then, though, they'd already met and liked Ian Marter. So, for the forthcoming series, the TARDIS would have one extra passenger.

I didn't appreciate it at the time, but this was actually a throwback to the Sixties. William Hartnell's Doctor had surrounded himself with friends and family in Susan, Barbara and Ian (Carole Ann Ford, Jacqueline Hill and William Russell), and so it continued throughout the decade. As far as long-standing *Who* fans were concerned, Ian and I were merely our (re)generation's Maureen O'Brien and Peter Purves.

I suppose I should have worried my screen time might be cut with someone else there to ask questions for the audience, but it didn't actually occur to me. I was pretty sure they wouldn't be asking Ian to scream 'Doctor!' every five minutes.

It was such a rush down to Worcester that I was still in my costume when I was bundled into the car. We arrived at 2 a.m. Call time was four hours later and I didn't have time to worry about my co-stars.

The new serial, *Robot*, was written by Terry Dicks as his parting gift to the show – or vice versa. It took the serial number 4A, which I assumed denoted the Fourth Doctor. Rather fittingly, I felt, *Planet of the Spiders'* production code had been 'ZZZ' – the end of the alphabet and the end of the line for Jon and so many others. The director this time was Chris Barry, who had worked with Jon on *The Mutants*. They used to call Chris the 'Mad Monk' – I've no idea why. But later he was so kind to Sadie when we were all in Chicago in 1993, and I still get Christmas cards from him and his wife Venice.

That friendship had yet to bloom, however, when I strolled on to set on 2 May. In my first scene Sarah Jane had to climb over a wall. I was so tired after the big finish on *Spiders* and then the journey. We did the scene and I was running, not looking, and somehow found the energy to scramble over the wall. Panting on the other side, I was actually pretty pleased with it. So was Chris – at first.

'That's awfully good, Lis,' he called over. 'But next time could I have your face in camera and not your bum!'

By the time I'd finished I noticed my co-stars had arrived on set. I had no expectations really – to be honest, I was too shattered to think much at all. When I caught a glimpse of Ian and Tom, leaning against a building and just chatting, my mood lifted. They barely knew each other and yet there they were just getting on. No airs, no graces, no coterie milling around them – just two actors, two men, chewing the fat. In that one snapshot I knew I was going to enjoy working with them.

Whereas Jon had always craved company, Tom was content to do his own thing. His Doctor didn't require a companion to fawn on his every utterance and Tom didn't expect that from me either, and even though he was the star, it was his name in the opening credits. Watching him so at ease with Ian I realised, *I don't have to walk over and doff my cap with this one. I don't have to pay my respects.*

Don't get me wrong, all actors are vain in a way – Tom's vanity was just different to Jon's. Tom loves taking the floor, holding court on his own: the more people watching, the better. Jon preferred his audiences closer to him, that was all – just as I'd known from his first spectacular entrance at North Acton during my audition. It made you feel like you were at his beck and call, whereas Tom gave everyone that little bit of space.

Another positive was that the problem I'd faced joining *The Time Warrior*, of being an ingénue in an established set-up, had disappeared. Now I was the old hand while Tom and Ian were the new boys feeling their way around. You'd never guess to look at him but Tom suffered terribly from nerves – he got these really gripey stomach aches, coincidentally just before filming each scene. So he had that to contend with every day, and no time left to be concerned with what I was doing. I responded to that. It was like turning up for the first day at a new school – you can reinvent yourself; be whoever you like.

In a way, of course, that's exactly what each new actor gets to do with the Doctor. I know Tom had worked very closely with Jim Acheson on getting the right look. They were going for something a bit more eccentric, closer to Pat Troughton than Jon's interpretation. More alien, if you like. (This was going on while we were working on *Spiders*, so of course Jim passed down all these nuggets of gossip as they went along!) Eventually they settled on the coat, the hat and, of course, the oversized scarf. That came about when Jim sent a bag of wool to a knitter called Begonia Pope – and she used the entire amount! It was Tom who said, 'No, let's keep it. I can have fun with that.' Typical Tom. And the rest is history.

I remember shooting that scene in TV Centre when Tom nips into the TARDIS a few times to trial various looks. He had everyone in hysterics, especially with the Viking outfit. You knew what he was wearing before the cameras started rolling, yet the second he stepped out of those blue doors, sparks flew. It was so damn good I thought, *Bloody hell, we've got a hell of an actor on our hands here*! I was going to have to seriously up my game or get left behind.

So, in a way, the arrival of a new Doctor actually gave me the freedom to regenerate Sarah Jane as well. If someone comes in who's the same person but is actually totally different, they do things differently and that in turn makes you react differently. So I discovered all sorts of new things I could do; it gave me a new lease of life and allowed me to expand. I loved that. I don't know why, but as welcome as they made me during my first year, I always felt on trial, but no longer. Isn't that funny?

Even the introduction of a new companion couldn't dampen my renewed confidence. I thought Ian was tremendous. He often gets overlooked, but stuffy naval doctor Harry Sullivan is a very difficult part to play. Modern audiences probably can't relate to him. He's like a character from *The Cruel Sea*. Men like that talk in a certain way, act in a certain way, wear the uniform with such pride. I think Ian was spot-on for that – he never overdid it.

Harry also took the brunt of the Doctor's venom on occasions. In *Revenge of the Cybermen* Tom delights in yelling, 'Harry Sullivan is an imbecile!' And in *The Ark in Space* he has another little dig when he says, 'My doctorate is purely honorary and Harry here is only qualified to work on sailors.' So from that point of view he got to do a lot of the things that Sarah Jane would otherwise have been lumbered with.

In the car down to Worcester I'd been looking forward to our summer break. Eight months of solid shooting without pause can really take its toll – I wished I could have knocked it on the head after *Spiders* then started again, fresh, with Tom in the autumn. I didn't want to be the tired one while everyone else looked so perky and up for anything.

As soon as I arrived all those cobwebs were pretty much blown away, though. There was such a buzz on set from working with the show's first new Doctor in five years that any end-of-term malaise was simply swept away. By just being there Tom had given us all a shot in the arm.

There is always such a lot riding on the new Doctor's first appearance, of course. Will he be liked? Will he live up to billing? David Tennant had to follow Chris Eccleston, which must have been terrifying. Then, of course, Matt Smith has had to follow David, arguably the most successful Doctor in history. As good as Tom was going to be, nobody really knew how he would be received. Wisely, Barry and Robert Holmes decided to pack his debut with some *Who* staples. Apart from me on the acting side there was a return for the Brig and Sergeant Benton; they also brought back Bessie. I thought the car would always be associated with Jon but Tom immediately made it his own. The way he clambered all over it like a Whipsnade monkey was uniquely him, right from the start. And the message to viewers was clear: same, but very, very different.

Location shoots can seem a little detached from reality. There's a real Dunkirk spirit in the air: you're all away from home, you're stuck together for a few days so you might as well get on with each other as best you can. Any negative opinions or arguments could wait until we got back to London and the comfort zone of the rehearsal rooms. That's how Jon used to be. Perfectly charming when you're halfway across the country, but a royal pain in the backside, on occasion, when you're locked in Acton for a week. So, as lovely as it had been so far, the real nature of Tom was yet to be seen.

Or so I thought. In the event he was exactly the same playful, powerful, kindly presence. And, most importantly, he was happy working together as an ensemble. Even though he was the star, he never needed to establish himself as the leader.

The only hitches, in fact, came at Television Centre. The 1970s were littered with industrial action from one quarter or another. TV certainly wasn't immune. Our recording slots on *Robot* were really hit when the scene-shifters laid down tools. It sounds incredible, but these were the only guys who were permitted to move things on set. If they didn't do it, no one else was allowed to either. One whole day was scrapped, I recall, and on the other we had to shoot around a step ladder that had been left out.

Honestly, I'm an Equity stalwart, but this was a joke. We were all aware of ten o'clock getting ever closer and one scene just could not be finished without moving a chair – which, of course, we were not allowed to do or the rest of the crew would down tools in sympathy.

Chris was pulling his hair out at this stage and I could see Barry was ready to throttle someone. Anyone would be with that deadline hanging over you and both hands tied behind your back. So I wandered over to the chair I was supposed to sit on. It was about a foot out of place. Not much on paper but with the camera angles and lights, it may as well have been a mile. *This is ridiculous*, I thought. After checking all the other crew members were otherwise engaged, I suffered a sudden fit of coughing and fell theatrically back into the chair.

When I stood up it was miraculously on its mark and ready to shoot.

'I think we're set to go over here, Chris.'

You don't often see someone do a double-take in real life, but he did then.

'So we are. Positions, everyone!'

The games we had to play . . .

* * *

No sooner had we wound down for summer than new scripts arrived, it seemed. The next serial scheduled for broadcast was *The Ark in Space*, but the first production of Season Twelve would be *The Sontaran Experiment*. For Robert Holmes' first full season as script editor it made sense for him to revisit the race he had invented – especially if, as instructed, writers Bob Baker and Dave Martin adhered to the 'one Sontaran only' edict, which meant they could economise by using the same suit made for *The Time Warrior*. Money was very much an issue. Rather than have another six-parter, which Robert disliked as a format, he had decided to investigate having two serials of two and four parts. The latter would be shot entirely in the studio. Every shot of the former, however, would be filmed outdoors.

After a scout for a suitable West Country location failed, recharged after the break, we all jumped on the bus and headed down to Dartmoor. It was super to see everyone again. Tom was raring to go. I imagine *Robot* had felt like a false start – just as *The Time Warrior* had for me after the gap before *Dinosaurs*. Now he was fully fired up and bursting with fresh ideas for his character – never a dull moment with Tom, even then.

As well as Tom and Ian, it was also nice to see Kevin Lindsay back. Even though he was playing a different Sontaran this time – Styre, not Linx – he'd done such a sterling job on *The Time Warrior* that he was the only actor considered. Unfortunately he wasn't in the best of health and requested a lighter suit, which was duly created. So much for Robert's money-saving idea . . .

I don't know what weather we were expecting on 26 September, but I do know that no one was dressed for it. Just staying warm and dry between takes was impossible so Philip Hinchcliffe sent us all down to the local chandlers to choose waterproofs and Wellingtons. The only things in my size were completely bright yellow: a hood, yellow bottoms, yellow top and yellow wellies. I looked like a giant canary – but at least I was dry.

For shooting, though, I was expected to wear a skirt and jumper and just hope for the best. *Fine*, I thought, *it's only for a few days*. Then I noticed a line in the script: 'Sarah Jane falls in the foliage'. I looked at the long grass all around and thought, *No bloody way! What if a snake slides up my skirt?*

I was head-to-toe in my Big Bird gear at the time, so I said, 'Wouldn't it make a spectacular shot if I was rolling around the grass in this yellow outfit?'

And do you know what? They went for it! So I got to spend the rest of the shoot in my sou'wester and Wellies.

Snakes were a genuine fear. The terrain was bushy and hilly – perfect to represent future earth – and the perfect habitat for all sorts of wildlife, including adders. One lunchtime Terry Walsh and I were walking to the nearest pub to try and warm up when something came slithering out from under a boulder. For the first time in my life I genuinely screamed in fright. And what did our brave stuntman do?

He leapt about four foot off the ground!

It was like watching Nureyev at Covent Garden. One moment Terry was walking beside me, the next he was yelling, 'What was that?' and doing this sort of entrechat up in the air.

The pub was the highlight of the day – the weather on the moors at the start of the week was so bitingly cold you couldn't stay out during breaks. We were filming at the top of the hill and lunch was right at the bottom. By the time we'd fought our way down in the howling winds there wasn't actually time to eat and get back up, so on the really cold days we'd traipse over to one of the two pubs. The important thing was to grab something to warm you up. We used to come back full of rum and shrub, or brandy and lovage. Boy are they strong! We would literally weave back. Amazing how the freezing conditions sober you up.

We were staying in a place called Chagford in a charming old hotel, the emphasis being on 'old'. The main problem with the place was the hot water. I don't think the hotel was geared up for an army from White City descending upon it out of season. Basically, the first person to run a bath in the evening had the lion's share of the hot water. I came home shivering and almost cried when I ran an ice-cold bath the first night. The second night I was cleverer. As soon as the closing scenes for the day were set up, my dresser offered to scoot back to Chagford and hit the hot tap. What a treasure! She dived in it first, which was fair, then I leapt in as soon as I made it back. Tom, Kevin and the rest had to make do with boiled kettle water or the icicle option.

Filming had some odd highlights. Back on *The Time Warrior* I discovered the amazing ability of *Who* fans to come out of the woodwork, no matter how remote the location. Sure enough, halfway up a rocky crevasse in Dartmoor, Ian and I were leaning against a rock with a flask of tea when a burst of giggles erupted behind us. Suddenly we were surrounded by a dozen schoolkids with autograph books. The difference this time, of course, was that I was the only one they recognised!

Towards the end of the week the weather improved enough for us to hang around the location for our snacks. Base camp was at the foot of the steepest hill so we all huddled for shelter in the makeup tent or behind the largest rocks. It was all a bit much for Kevin, though, whose scenes were shot at the top of the hill. His new suit was still pretty cumbersome to walk in and the head took ages to get on and off. So he said, 'Look, I'm just going to stay up here during lunch.'

I said, 'I'd love to stay and join you but I need to go down for a wee.'

'No problem,' he said. 'I've found this cosy little nest in the rock. I'm all covered.'

So that day someone took his lunch up for him on a tray, with a little salt and pepper pot and a drink, and he sat there on his own, bless him! As soon as I'd finished, I started the long crawl back up. As I came round the last corner I saw the empty tray on a rock and Kevin relaxing in full Sontaran head and suit.

'How are you?' I asked.

'Well,' he said, 'I am fine, but a woman and her dog who came by will never be the same again!'

Jeez we had fun with Kevin! It was so sad, about six months later, when we heard he'd died of heart trouble – a great loss of a great character and a great friend.

* * *

That woman and her hound weren't the only ones to get a rude awakening, though. At the end of September we shifted base to Hound Tor, near Manaton, to capture the scenes with Styre's spaceship. In typically gung-ho fashion, Tom threw himself into recording. While he wasn't as keen for his Doctor to be the Ultimate Fighting Champion that Jon had enjoyed playing, he didn't want him to be a pushover either. When the script called for a duel between himself and Styre, Terry Walsh offered to take over but Tom insisted on handling his end personally.

Meanwhile I'd been caught with manacles on my wrists that turned into snakes. With so many adders in the undergrowth anyway, it wasn't hard to fake a reaction. The hardest part was keeping still enough for the overlaying images. As the fight went on, I was sitting on the ground on some sort of plastic sheet. Everything felt so damp it was like sitting in a wet nappy. I had my eyes closed when I heard this 'crack!' and a shout.

God, that sounded realistic, that's good! I thought.

Then I heard fussing and Tom squealing in agony. The whole area was full of rocks, and so slippery and wet and muddy. But he hadn't fallen – I think he was so cold that a sudden jerking movement had been enough to do some sort of damage. He was carried down the hill and then driven to the nearest hospital. Word soon reached us he'd broken his collarbone. I thought, *Well, that's the end of this serial. We can't do it without the Doctor.* With his new TB wig and coat, Terry stepped in to complete the fight (as I think you can see from the final version!) and took over lots of the other, more physical tasks, but the following day Tom was back, bandaged and sore, to take his place again in front of the cameras. We were grateful for that scarf and oversized coat because they hid his neck brace so well.

A lot of actors would have been quickly irritated by something so impossible as a long multi-coloured scarf but Tom revelled in it. Just having it there, potentially underfoot or wrapped around the wrong prop, gave every scene that sense of danger. He thrived on that, though. I did, too. Playing with uncertainty is one of the strongest things an actor can do – a quality we each admired in the other.

Speaking of costumes, I enjoyed a spot of fun with mine at Tom's expense. I was trying – and failing – to get the Doctor's attention while he was inspecting the transmat system. Tom naturally turned into an irascible grump for the scene – as you would in a relationship when one of you is concentrating and the other is messing around. I responded by taking Sarah Jane to an even more childish level. One minute I'm trying to talk to him, the next I've pulled my hat down over my eyes. Pure, ridiculous attention-seeking – boy, it felt good!

In that little scene I think we cracked the relationship between the two. It was so much more than master and pupil. Tom's Doctor allowed me to have fun but there were plausible parameters, just as there would be in real life between two companions. He could be playful or stern and I would respond accordingly. It was so warm, not artificial in the least; instinctive as well. We found a way to read every script that just made perfect sense.

I was watching a scene in preparation for a DVD commentary a year or two ago when Sadie said, 'Tom handles you so gently, Mum. It's beautiful to watch.' And it is. He was just so caring and utterly rounded as an actor and a character. There are no shortcuts with him, everything counts.

Tom hit his stride far quicker than I did. He walked into the Doctor's role and I think even he was surprised at how well it fitted him. He never had to reach for it, it's the part he was born to play.

I wasn't the only one impressed with our star turn. *The Sontaran Experiment*'s director was Rodney Bennett, a graduate of *Z-Cars* and *Thirty-Minute Theatre*. After a run of happy experiences I was back at square one with this guy: it wasn't that he didn't like me, he just didn't seem to notice me. He only had eyes for Tom. It was like working on *Some Mothers* again – the star was all, the rest could work it out for themselves. I had no empathy with him at all and I'm sure it was mutual.

The Sontaran Experiment was the first serial in five years which didn't have Barry Letts as producer. His protégé, Philip, was a visible presence in Dartmoor. Without a studio shoot for this one there was little choice. I got on very well with Philip, as did most people, I think. But one comment – a compliment, actually – made me reconsider my entire future.

I was at the top of the hill shooting the scene where I'm captured with ropes. There was one camera and a microphone with me. The director and the rest of the team were at the foot of the hill as usual watching on monitors. We captured the scene in the first or second take, then as I was getting ready for my next scene I noticed Philip puffing his way over. He'd climbed all the way up the hill just to have a word.

'Lis,' he said, 'that stuff you did with the ropes really was top drawer. We were all watching below and a shiver went through us. How did you do it?'

I've thought about this moment many times over the years, wondering if I overreacted. Whichever way you look at it, Philip was simply paying me a compliment. Not only that, he'd put his body through the agony of hiking up a steep hill to deliver it. Yet, my instinctive response was: I've been training for this all my life. I've dedicated my career to getting the most out of every line, every look and every physical action. I can struggle with ropes all day, it's what I do.

It's called acting.

At the time, of course, I took the compliment in the spirit it was intended and thanked Philip for his kind words. Later that night I pondered further. *Do you know what, you're my new producer and you don't really know anything about me, do you? It's one thing having Barry choose your Doctor for you, but soon enough you're going to want your own girl to accompany him, aren't you?*

In that moment my whole future crystallised. As much fun as I was having with Tom, I began to think about life after *Who*.

When I go, it's going to be my decision. It's going to be when Sarah Jane Smith is still popular – I'm not going to be pushed.

And from that moment on I knew I had to leave.

Chapter Eight

Tom, I Don't Need A Coat!

MORE THAN thirty years later, I can't believe how long it took me from deciding to leave to actually going through with it. The important thing, I guess, is having that epiphany; realising you don't need to do a job for the rest of your life. Once you appreciate that – and it's the same whether you're an actress, a bank teller or a waitress – *you* have the upper hand. You're free. I always like to know there's a door to walk through when I'm ready. I'm not saying break a contract, just don't be afraid to walk away. Too many people stay in jobs because they're scared to leave. Embrace the freedom – I did.

But not yet . . .

The Sontaran Experiment was the first two-parter for ten years. I think it worked. Some of the six-episode serials could drag on; you wondered whether the end result justified the airtime. But it was the last one I would do. A week after nearly freezing to death in Devon, we were back at the Acton Hilton working our way through *The Ark in Space*. The good news: this one was entirely studio-bound. And the bad news: Rodney Bennett sat once again in the director's chair.

The Ark in Space enjoyed quite a tortuous conception. Eventually Robert Holmes took the writer's credit, with input from others, including John Lucarotti. As it was part of his master plan to split a single recording period into two separate stories, Robert had a lot riding on it.

The end result is one of Russell T Davies's favourites. In fact, the

Top left: Proving that the 'S' in my name was for 'star' from an early age!
Author's collection

Above: With my parents, Gladys and Tom Sladen.
Author's collection

Left: Sailing at Salcombe. To his dying day, Jon Pertwee refused to believe my family's history in the area. *Author's collection*

As Alice with the rest of the cast of *Through the Looking-Glass*. Sitting next to me, oblivious to the indignity she would suffer on Saturday night, is Edwina Currie (or Cohen as was). *Author's collection*

The programme to the National Youth Theatre production of *A Midsummer Night's Dream*, signed by the cast. In a toss-up between me and Helen Mirren, I was voted 'most likely to succeed'. How she must rue that day! *Author's collection*

Queen's Theatre
one shilling

The National Youth Theatre

A MIDSUMMER NIGHT'S DREAM

By arrangement with H. M. Tennent Ltd.
The National Youth Theatre presents

A MIDSUMMER NIGHT'S DREAM

by William Shakespeare

Theseus, Duke of Athens	...	Michael Newby
Hippolyta, Queen of the Amazons, betrothed to Theseus	...	Mary Payne
Egeus, father to Hermia	...	Peter Scott
Lysander } young gentlemen	...	Andrew Murray
Demetrius } in love with Hermia	...	David Taylor
Philostrate, master of the revels	...	Haydn Biddle
Hermia, daughter to Egeus, in love with Lysander	...	Diana Quick
Helena, in love with Demetrius	...	Helen Mirren
Peter Quince, a carpenter	...	Clive Wilmer
Nick Bottom, a weaver	...	Ken Cranham
Francis Flute, a bellows-mender	...	Trevor Adams
Tom Snout, a tinker	...	Dallas Adams
Robin Starveling, a tailor	...	Edwin Simpson
Snug, a joiner	...	Duncan Woodcock
Oberon, King of the Fairies	...	Jeremy Anthony
Titania, Queen of the Fairies	...	Carol Griese
Puck	...	Tim Haunton

First fairy	...	Katherine Dyson
Peaseblossom	...	Nancy Sykes
Cobweb	...	Myrtle Neel
Moth	...	Elizabeth Sladen
Mustardseed	...	Juliet Green
Other fairies	...	Sophy Cadman
		Prudence Heptinstall

The action takes place in Athens and in a wood nearby.

Settings by Christopher Lawrence

The play is directed by Paul Hill

Assistant to the Director:

Michael Croft

There will be one interval of ten minutes

The running time of the play, including intervals, is just over two hours.

Smoking is not permitted in the auditorium.

PRODUCTION SPONSORED BY THE DAILY MAIL

'Respiration 0 - Aston Villa 2' – Brian's ad lib during Dürrenmatt's *The Physicists*, which caused this corpse to corpse. *Author's collection*

Above: Kissing my future husband, Brian, in *Mirandolina* at the Liverpool Playhouse, 1966. *Author's collection*

Left: Arguing with the lovely Warren Clarke in *The Poker Session*, April 1967. *Author's collection*

Above: Starring as Desdemona alongside Paul Webster's Othello at the Manchester Library Theatre, October 1967. *Author's collection*

Left: Rehearsing *Othello*. Having Brian as Iago only added to the fun. *Author's collection*

MANCHESTER

THE LIBRARY'S resident company opened their new season with a two-weeks' run of "A Taste of Honey".

Thus, ten years after this play by a Manchester playwright received its first production in London it has found its way to its native heath. Much has happened in the theatrical world in the meantime, and Miss Delaney's play about life in the raw in her native Salford has lost some of its impact. But there is still something interesting and appealing about the schoolgirl seeking love and finding the real thing only in the homosexual Geoffrey. The dialogue, too, when it is a piece of reportage is fresh and vigorous, but less satisfactory when the author attempts verbal fireworks which seem out of context.

Director Tony Colegate treats it rather as an interlude between two music-hall turns, perhaps taking his cue from the many asides indulged in by Helen, but the play's natural warmth and life come through, thanks largely to a charmingly natural performance by Elizabeth Sladen as Jo. Linda Polan plays Helen with lots of colour and there is a clever picture of her hard-drinking lover-boy by Peter Childs. Johnny Worthy as Jimmy and Warren Clarke as Geoffrey represent, effectively, two different types of love. Richard Marks' set admirably presents the dingy locale.

Last performance September 7.

Reviewers were very kind. This one mentions 'a charmingly natural performance by Elisabeth Sladen as Jo'. It seems funny hanging onto it all these years but you always need good crits.
Author's collection

Manchester Library Theatre

A TASTE OF HONEY
by SHELAGH DELANEY

Cover star of the programme for *A Taste of Honey*, Manchester Library Theatre, August 1968. *Author's collection*

I played Josephine in *A Taste of Honey* opposite Johnny Worthy as Jimmy. Like *Othello*, the play explored mixed-race relationships.
Author's collection

My wedding to Brian on 8 June 1968. My mother never forgave him for wearing that suit!
Author's collection

Playing Fiona opposite Jeremy Franklin in Alan Ayckbourn's *How the Other Half Loves* during the Theatre in the Round's summer season, Library Theatre, Scarborough 1969.
Author's collection

The 1970 summer season at Scarborough, playing Jenny in Ayckbourn's *The Story So Far...*
Author's collection

With the wonderful, incorrigible Robert Morley at Niagara Falls during *How the Other Half Loves'* Toronto run. He was so generous to Brian and me.
Author's collection

Below: As new *Corrie* barmaid Anita Reynolds alongside my onscreen boyfriend, Len Fairclough, played by Peter Adamson. *Author's collection*

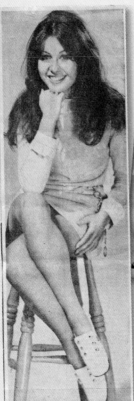

Why all eyes are on Elisabeth now

By SHELLEY ROHDE

THREE weeks ago, Elisabeth Sladen was a relatively unknown actress. Today she is recognised in shops, gets fan mail, and turns heads in the street.

And all because, for just six episodes of Coronation Street, she became Len Fairclough's girl friend, Anita Reynolds.

For Elisabeth, it was not so much a rise to instant stardom as an initiation into the mass appeal of television's longest-running soap opera.

"I certainly never expected such a short stay to produce such a reaction," she said. "I just thought of it as a job, but the pleasure it has given my relatives is quite astonishing.

"It was my first TV part and, although it was fairly small—and very short—it was large enough to get me recognised in shops."

Above: I was only in *Coronation Street* for six weeks but I earned more publicity than in years of theatre work. I never got over the cast calling each other by their character names! *Author's collection*

I absolutely hated my first photocall for *Doctor Who.* Fortunately Jon was more than happy to come to my aid. *Courtesy of Hulton Archive/Getty Images*

My first outing as Sarah Jane Smith in *The Time Warrior*. On location at Peckforton Castle, Cheshire, with Jon and lovely Kevin Lindsay, as Linx. © *BBC*

I could have shot whomever it was who suggested I perch on that bollard outside BBC TV Centre. But when the picture appeared in national newspapers the next day I got my first real clue about how 'big' the show was. *Author's collection*

Elisabeth ..new Dr Who girl

ACTRESS Elisabeth Sladen, above, is to play Dr. Who's new assistant when the BBC-TV series returns in December.

Elisabeth, 25, from Liverpool, will appear as a journalist who stows away in the doctor's time ship—and eventually meets the dreaded Daleks. She has been told not to scream because that frightens the children.

Elisabeth, chosen for the new part after producer Barry Letts had seen thirty actresses, is married to actor Brian Miller.

Her TV roles have included six weeks in "Coronation Street" a couple of years ago as Len Fairclough's girlfriend.

Katy Manning, who ceased to be Dr. Who's assistant last weekend, was heading in the general direction of marriage to the young professor, played by S'wart Betan—her real-life boyfriend.

She has just finished making a film with Brian Rix called "Don't Just Lie There, Say Something."

Invasion of the Dinosaurs was such a wonderful story to work on. But when we saw the dinosaurs themselves, how our hearts sank! © *BBC*

Opening the *Doctor Who* Exhibition at Blackpool, 1 April 1974. 'It will blow your mind, Lissie,' Jon had promised – and he was right. It was an amazing day. So many fans, so many wonderful memories.
Courtesy of Mirrorpix

Jon and I really hit our stride in *The Monster of Peladon*. Donald Gee looked cool in leather as Eckersley but I felt for poor Stuart Fell bobbing up and down inside that ridiculous Alpha Centauri costume. © *BBC*

Riding in the 'Whomobile'. Barry Letts really pulled out all the stops for Jon's swansong in *Planet of the Spiders* and Jon adored playing around with the cars, boats and planes.
© *BBC*

The King is dead, long live the King! With new Doctor Tom Baker and a Wirrn in *The Ark in Space*. The serial's second episode still holds the record for the show's biggest audience, with 13.6 million viewers. It's also one of Russell T Davies's favourites. © *BBC*

Rehearsals with Tom at the 'Acton Hilton'. I loved working there because you could really develop a character or a script. It was as close to theatre as you can get in television. Sadly they don't work like that anymore. *Author's collection*

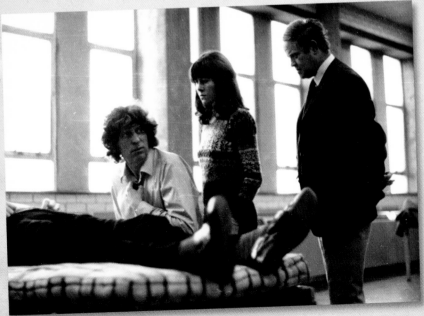

Back in Blackpool again, this time with Tom for the annual illuminations that we had been asked to switch on.

Author's collection

A whole generation of children looked forward to hiding behind the sofa during *Doctor Who* but dear old Mary Whitehouse thought we took it too far. 'Tea-time brutality for tots' she said. Watching *The Brain of Morbius*, she may have had a point!

Author's collection

Holding the actual 'hand of fear' from the title of my last ever serial. I don't think it was the best one to go out on but fans still quote the line 'Eldrad must live!' and ask about Sarah's 'Andy Pandy' costume, so it must have made some impression. © *BBC*

After the whirlwind pace of television it was a relief to get back into theatre. When the chance came to star with Brian in the two-hander *Mooney and His Caravan* at the Liverpool Playhouse, I couldn't turn it down. *Author's collection*

Below: My next TV work after *Doctor Who* was *Merry-Go-Round*, an educational programme for children. The only thing I learned was that I really, really do not like helicopters! *Author's collection*

With Keith Barron on the children's show *Stepping Stones*. It was such fun to do but in hindsight can you imagine Billie Piper or Karen Gillan going from *Who* to this? *Author's collection*

I avoided the convention circuit for years but when the invite arrived to go to LA in 1980 for the first American event I couldn't resist. It was lovely seeing Ian Marter again. I didn't even mind when our old friend from Skaro put in an appearance.
Author's collection

Below: How on earth the photographer talked me into this I do not know. Ian told me afterwards, 'I would never have done that.' But I suppose I trusted both of them. More fool me!
Author's collection

With Jon and his wife Ingeborg in North Carolina, 1983, as part of the Whovian tour.
Author's collection

Below: My name in lights as the tour reaches New York's Beacon Theatre on Broadway – Woody Allen's local!
Author's collection

Fooling around with Brian, Jon and the tour's organizer, Ron Katz.
Author's collection

I'm sure I must have told the same stories a thousand times over the years but fans are always so polite and kind.
Author's collection

Above: The promotional photocall for *The Five Doctors* on 17 November 1983. Spot which Doctor is played by a waxwork figure! *Courtesy of John Curtis/ Rex Features*

DR WHO GIRL PRAISES REAL DOCTORS

Time to be a star just like mother

THE first baby of former Doctor Who actress Elisabeth Sladen is a born star.

Bouncing Sadie, who loves being the centre of attraction, already has her first role—in a video about babies being filmed by staff at Queen Charlotte's maternity hospital, Hammersmith, West London, where she was born last week weighing eight pounds.

Her involvement is 35-year-old Elisabeth's way of saying thank you to doctors and nurses who helped her through her pregnancy and Caesarian operation.

'They were all wonderful,' said the actress who was Dr Who's sidekick, journalist Sarah-Jane Smith, in the mid-Seventies. She is due back at work in July as the dormouse in the BBC's Alice in Wonderland, with her actor husband Brian Miller. 'Fortunately we don't appear together, so we can look after Sadie OK.'

Above: Presenting Sadie Isabelle Amy Miller. No mother could be prouder. *Author's collection*

There was a period when Sadie was the only one in the Miller family working! She made her first appearance on film – and in the papers – when she was just a few days old. *Author's collection*

Above: If I was amazed at the reception we received in America, the welcome from Australia a decade later really bowled me over. *Author's collection*

Left: Sadie getting to grips with a Dalek built by an Australian fan. *Author's collection*

Sydney Harbour, 1996. I still have to pinch myself that a part I first played in 1973 has taken me – and my family! – all over the world. *Author's collection*

How every bride wants to look on her wedding day! In between takes filming *The Wedding of Sarah Jane Smith*.
Author's collection

Below: With the wonderful David Tennant and Anj, Tommy and Danny, my adorable co-stars from *The Sarah Jane Adventures*.
Author's collection

second episode would go on to win 13.6 million viewers in February 1975 – a record audience for the programme. I can see why you'd enjoy it. The sets by Roger Murray-Leach were out of this world – literally. Holmes' script was almost hypnotic in its rhythms, as expected. The costumes for the Wirrn were terrifically convincing as well. In fact, the whole thing was beautifully done.

But I felt invisible.

I blame Rodney for that. He got such a kick out of working with Tom that the rest of us struggled for any recognition whatsoever. I don't think anyone else was in the frame. Subsequently, I found myself in a really uncomfortable costume on a set where there were so many possibilities to run and crawl and bend and really express myself physically. If Philip had been impressed by my bondage scene he would really like what I could do on this vast spaceship. As a result of feeling hampered by the costume and overlooked by the director, I just found myself standing around a lot. I wasn't happy with myself in that one at all, so much potential untapped.

There were highlights. I enjoyed the verbal jousting with Harry. All his 'independent sort of bird, isn't she?' talk focused attention on Sarah Jane's more modern outlook, which was very welcome. Robert and Philip were keen to keep the feminist edge going, so it was important that my character had a life – and sub-plots – of her own and wasn't just arm candy. It was imperative not to agree with the male characters out of habit. Decisions had to be questioned – even the Doctor's.

Ian was the opposite of Harry in real life but equally chivalrous. When I had to lie down in a dress in one scene I was suddenly aware of the camera's position.

'Ian, can you see my knickers?'

''Fraid so, old girl! But don't worry. When we do it for real, I'll pull your dress down.'

And, bless him, he did.

Tom showed himself in an equally gallant light in *Ark* when we had to crawl through a ventilation shaft. I don't know what exactly went wrong but we were going through this pipe and I got stuck.

The script goes out the window for a few moments as Tom attempts to cajole me out, all in character, and I'm desperately trying not to fall flat on my face. Somehow he gave me the shove I needed without breaking stride – and without me landing in a heap. That, for me, was another epiphany moment. It was a genuine, overwhelming emotion of: 'Oh God, I love you for that.' That was the point when I thought, *Oh, I adore working with you.*

It really was an epoch-defining moment. So much so, that nearly forty years later it would come back to haunt me when Matt Smith, the Eleventh Doctor, referred to it when he joined me in *The Sarah Jane Adventures*.

Tom really was on fire on *Ark*. I wasn't the finest authority on all things Whovian, but the word on set was that he was the first Doctor who really 'got' the fact that he was an alien. I would read the script and try to predict how Tom would attack certain lines. Nine times out of ten I was wrong. Whatever I predicted, he would find another way. And it would be perfect.

For a Time Lord.

Sometimes, however, I just needed Tom to be Tom. I remember working on the third and fourth episodes at North Acton. We were meant to be looking at a screen and, being a rehearsal, it was just a prop with the name of a character written on it for a guide. I turned to Tom and said, 'This should be interesting – he died in Episode 2.'

Then Tom turned round and said, 'Rodney – Lis has raised a very good point, I think.'

I'd like to think the director would have listened to me, but I wouldn't have bet on it. That became our pattern for future episodes. I'd bring something to Tom's attention and he'd puff up, summon all his immense gravitas and say, 'Leave it to me, Elisabeth.' Then off he'd go to sort it out.

* * *

Robert's money-saving drive in his first season hit upon the idea of having the same set used twice. I can see why this would be attractive. Somehow, though, he needed to conjure a plot that could make sense of revisiting the same place. By contracting Gerry Davis to reinvigorate his old creations, the Cybermen, he found his answer. More importantly, after a bit of a rummage down the back of the BBC sofa, Philip also found enough money for a location shoot. That's how, on 18 November, just six days after *Ark*'s final studio date, I found myself on the bus down to Somerset.

Wookey Hole, in Somerset, is a series of caves supposedly inhabited by primitive man 50,000 years ago. It's a major tourist attraction now and when you step inside you can certainly picture primaeval Britons scrabbling around. For the purposes of *Who*, however, the caves were designed to serve as the catacombs of the golden planet Voga in *Revenge of the Cybermen*.

Whereas Jon used to give me the heads-up on recurring monsters, there was no one around to plug the return of the Cybermen. When I first saw them, I confess, I wasn't impressed. It was the only serial where I couldn't pretend. Daleks, Exxilons, Zygons, yes, yes, yes. All plausible when you're sharing the same stage – but Cybermen? You'd see them lurching around, huffing and puffing in their silver Wellington boots, and just think, *Not very robotic, are they?* I couldn't see past the costume.

It's possible I'm not the target audience, of course. Years later, when Sadie was about eight, I took her to my first Blue Box convention. As soon as she saw someone marching around in a proper Cyberman costume she just fell in love. She literally hung on to this poor guy for the whole day. I've got pictures of her going up steps clinging to his arm – they're probably still her favourite.

Worse than the villains – and worse than Rodney Bennett – the director this time was Michael Briant. We hadn't enjoyed the best relationship on *Death to the Daleks*, but I tried to be professional and give it a fresh go this time. You never know: maybe it was Jon's presence that got us off on the wrong foot, as much as they liked each other. It turned out not to be so. Michael just isn't what I'd call an actor's director: his focus is on the story, the special effects and the scenery. He's utterly professional, but those are his priorities. Get those right, he seems to believe, and the cast just slot into place. I don't think it was that straightforward, but there you go.

Working in Wookey Hole should have been a fun experience. After all, it's one of the UK's premier tourist attractions. But no sooner had we arrived than things began to go wrong. It didn't take long for us to believe the caves themselves had their own agenda.

The guy chaperoning us around the caves confirmed as much. Pointing to a stalagmite resembling a witch's face, he said, 'The Witch doesn't like you – she doesn't want you here.' *Thanks, mate, a charming welcome!* The next thing we knew, on a closed set, Michael saw a guy in full potholing regalia wandering around. Turned out this man had gone missing some years earlier. *OK, I thought, this is weird*. But we pressed on – we always just pressed on.

Later, Ian and I were sitting under the 'Witch' going through our scripts.

'There's a scene here, Ian, which I just don't understand,' I said.

Ian nodded. 'I know which one you mean.'

We both turned to this funny little half page. It was just dialogue between him and me but, stare as hard as I might, I couldn't make head nor tail of it. Without doubt it was the most unfathomable text I'd ever been asked to learn. It wasn't the first time I couldn't follow some scriptwriter's logic, but even so . . .

I always flag anything in the script I don't understand, so I put an asterisk next to the preceding passage to jog my memory. Slowly but surely we worked through the day's pages. Then Michael announced, 'It's a wrap' and people started packing up. It was then I remembered the confusing lines.

Ian was looking puzzled as well. 'We'd better check with the boss,' I said, and so we went up to Michael.

'What about the scene between Ian and me?' I asked. 'Aren't we going to do that one today?'

Michael stared. 'What scene? There is no other scene – we're finished.'

'Look here,' said Ian and rifled through his script. I watched him flick forwards then back; he couldn't find the scene. Impatiently I pulled my own copy out and thumbed through until I found the margin marks. There they were: an arrow and star reminding me to check with Michael. But where was the text?

The bottom of the page was blank. I swear to you, it had been covered in text. Now, though, it was completely white.

Ian was shaking his script upside down, as if he was trying to tip the missing words out. We both stood there, dumbstruck. Where was that passage? We'd both seen it. Hell, we'd both learned it!

If there really was a curse, we still had more to witness.

Rosemary Hestler, our assistant floor manager, suffered an unexpected bout of claustrophobia so she had to be escorted out. Jack Wells, our munitions expert, also took a turn for the worse and had no choice but to abandon ship. Tony Harding, our visual effects assistant, really struggled to get even basic pyrotechnics to work as they should and an electrician broke a leg after a ladder inexplicably collapsed under him. All in all, it was a jinxed set.

But the worst was yet to come. On 20 November I nearly died.

The Vogans used these little skimming boards to zoom across the rivers that run through the caves. It looks quite impressive – but only if you know what you're doing. At one point I escape from the troglodytes and try to get back to the Doctor. In doing so it was decided I should commandeer one of these boards and jet across to the other side.

'Do you think you can do that?' Michael asked.

'I don't see why not.'

And so it was agreed. I was taken across to the far bank in a little rowing boat. There I was introduced to this motorised surfboard contraption. The guy who made it talked me through the controls. Basically they wanted me to jump on, lie flat on my stomach and pilot it across to the other side where the cameras were waiting to capture everything.

It's only when I was standing at the side that I noticed just how rapidly the water was running by. It wasn't a lake, it was a river –

gushing down through the earth towards a waterfall leading God knows where.

'It's OK, you can do this,' the guy said. 'Remember, just jump on, drive straight across and up on to the muddy bank, leap off and run.'

But I didn't move – I just stared, listening to the whooshing water disappearing into infinity. Terry Walsh came over and put an arm around me for moral support. At that point even Michael sensed all was not well.

'Would you like Terry to do this for you, Lis?' he called over.

At this I scoffed. I was wearing a tight jumper and combat boots – not exactly Terry's sizes . . .

So I said, 'No, no it's fine, it's fine.'

Anyway I did it. I don't know how, I barely remember, it happened so fast. I clambered on, knocked the single control from 'off' to 'on' and it whizzed straight across. I got to the other side, turned it off as instructed and scrambled away. Perfect, no messing about – all captured in one take.

That was at the start of the day. Despite the various inexplicable mishaps that befell the crew, and the tour guide wandering around saying, 'The Witch doesn't like you, the Witch doesn't like you,' somehow we finished the day ahead of schedule.

It's fatal to give a director extra time because they always want to use it. In this case 'fatal' was the key word.

Michael sauntered over.

'Do you know what, Lis – we could really do with a shot of you running towards the board. We've got a bit of time to play with so we'd love to see you getting on it.'

I wasn't happy and obviously it showed in my face. The board owner said, 'Don't worry, you won't have to bother with the controls, I'll leave it pointing in the right direction. You just jump on and push yourself out – you'll soon reach the other side.'

'I've been told the current on that river is about 30 miles an hour. Are you sure I don't need the engine?' I asked.

'No, no. The boat will only go the way it's pointing.'

Now, as I sit here recalling that day, it's apparent that statement was purely nonsensical, but not as nonsensical as believing it. It was a light piece of wood. Of course it would bloody turn with the drift!

But you're on a TV shoot, it's such a world of make believe and you're just programmed to do what other people say. Everyone is an expert on something: makeup, lights, stunts . . . I handle acting. And this guy handled the boat. That's my defence. *They must know what they're talking about,* I thought.

For some reason the Aggedor jump had clean left my mind.

We went for the take and I realised the bank had become really slippery since the morning's scene. You can see in the final version how I struggle to get on the damn thing; I could see the cameras and everyone on the other bank, so far away they looked tiny. I do remember noticing Terry had taken off his Vogan costume (because of course he had a part in this serial, as usual). I thought he must have a stunt coming up – I didn't even question why he seemed to be strapping underwater breathing apparatus to his back.

So I managed to scramble onto this board and gave it a shove off. And what happened? It turned, just like it was always going to do.

Suddenly I wasn't going forwards anymore. I was veering to the left, carried along by the fierce current. Ahead all I could see was darkness. The sound, booming around that black cavern, was louder than in the cable car over Niagara Falls.

Your responses are unpredictable when you're scared. Obviously I should have turned the engine on and powered my way out of it, but I was clinging onto this board for dear life and staring paralysed into the abyss. Everything happened in slow motion. I could see the crew on the other bank, frozen like a tableau, but then I saw movement. Terry was sprinting, faster and faster. By now he was wearing full frogman's rubber – and now I knew why. But I was convinced it would be too late: the end of the line was approaching. I'm no swimmer – I can't stand water on my face, I don't even like a shower. Being underwater is my biggest fear in life, bigger than snakes. If I jumped off I'd be dragged under before I could paddle to safety. I truly thought, *This is it. It's over.*

Then I spotted a rock between the waterfall and me. There was a chance, if I angled my body, of throwing myself onto it. I had no idea if this would work, or whether I would be able to grip onto it, but it was either that or plunging over the edge.

I had to go for it. The boat rammed against the rock and I leapt for it. Stupid things go through your head at times like this. I remember thinking, *I must keep my head up – I need these false eyelashes for the close-ups!* Self-preservation kicked in. I found myself treading water, something I'd never been able to do before. A second later I felt Terry's arms again. Before I knew it he'd pulled me to safety. The boat, on the other hand, was never seen again.

We were both whisked to hospital for jabs. I was OK, a bit shaken. Terry, I think, was quite ill later. Back at the hotel I had a bath, still pretty comatose, then made my way down to the bar. After an experience like that I just wanted company, to feel alive. I was sitting at a table, chatting, when I saw Michael enter. He was standing at the bar and I heard him say, 'Oh, Lis is back. I should really go over and apologise.'

Yes, you bloody should! I thought.

By the time he did mosey over, after everyone else, I could barely speak to him. I was so angry. By contrast, Terry hunted me out as soon as he arrived.

'Hello, Sladen. That was bloody stupid!'

He was right – I only had myself to blame. Always trust your instincts . . .

* * *

Although Tom never billed himself as the show's number one, that's obviously what he was. Ian and I were definitely in the silver and bronze positions as far as the production team was concerned. If Tom had an idea on set, of course he would be listened to more than we would. It might be the craziest, most useless brainwave ever, but because it was him, the director and team would consider it. Obviously Tom did have good ideas and they were always fun, but he wasn't always right. Ian and I knew the score and, because we lived near each other in Ealing, we used to laugh about it on the Tube home.

Really, Tom was such a blast to work with. So many of the stresses of toeing the line of the old regime just peeled away. I may have been the Doctor's 'assistant', as he describes me to the Duke in *Terror of the Zygons*, but in Tom's eyes we were equal. There was no proprietorial hand around the neck, no subtext to any of his suggestions, no accusations of 'women's problems' if we disagreed, just good, honest collaboration – we were in this together.

That's not to say we were the best of friends. I never saw Tom outside work. We don't actually have that much in common. When we were rehearsing, Tom would quite often go to the pub at lunchtime. He wasn't the only one. You'd go in there and bump into all sorts of faces, people from *The Onedin Line*, whatever the BBC had in production at the time. There are only so many days in a row you can bear going to the canteen, so people would nip out for a cheese sandwich and a pint. That wasn't me, though – I never got that claustrophobic sense of being cooped up all day in Acton. I liked having a decent lunch, whether it was on my own or not.

After filming was another matter. Then you'd have a struggle to keep me away from the bar. It was such a release after a day's stresses and I think the camaraderie was helped with everyone piling into the pub together. And it was exactly the same as up at Tommy Duck's in Manchester – you'd shoot the breeze, unwind, relive the highlights and get things off your chest. I think if you didn't take part you'd feel like you were missing out.

We were so unused to seeing each other outside of the BBC's walls that on the rare occasions when we did bump into each other it got quite awkward. I remember running into Tom and his partner Marianne on Regent Street once.

'Ah, Lis,' he gushed, unusually flustered. 'Would you care for a Guinness?'

Before I could answer he'd changed his mind.

'No, no – a coat! Let's go to Harrod's, I must buy you a fur coat!'

'It's OK, Tom, I don't need a coat.'

'But he really wants to buy you one,' Marianne insisted. 'You must let him.'

What a hysterical pair! They were obviously well suited. But I didn't get that coat – or a Guinness.

Tom could drink, no question about that, and over the years he won a well-earned reputation as an old-fashioned carouser. He showed glimpses of this after a serial wrapped, when he always insisted on sharing a pint or two with the director and his team. But was work ever affected? Not one per cent; he never brought it onto the set. The only thing he did bring was the occasional bottle of lemonade on the bus in the morning; that was the only clue he'd had a good night. But I've never met anyone who was better at holding his drink – Tom never let you down.

Ian was a terrific friend to me but there was an innate connection between him and Tom. You just get this between some people. They hadn't known each other too long when they concocted the idea of writing a film – *Doctor Who Meets Scratchman*. And they had it all worked out. Vincent Price would play the villain and it would concern scarecrows that came to life. David Maloney, one of Tom's favourite directors, was slated to direct.

I don't know how far down the line they actually got because I wasn't that involved in it. They'd grab spare moments in rehearsal, put their heads together walking back to set, or, occasionally, go for dinner. You'd hear these animated discussions: 'Yes, that's good.' I'd toddle over to them, uninvited, and witter a few things. Then, bored, I'd wander off to talk to someone else. I wasn't terribly interested in being involved, nor was I asked, although Tom said I definitely would be when it was filmed.

'What about this? He'll be a scarecrow and he'll have a basket, and I could ride in it and you could pedal me down the hill.'

'No, *I'll* ride down the hill with Elisabeth in the basket!'

'What about if . . .'

And so it went on.

At some point they even went away for a week abroad where Maloney had a place. I wasn't there but I did hear that things didn't go quite to plan. For a start, Tom nearly drowned in the pool. Ian and Maloney saw him splashing around and just laughed. 'There's Tom clowning around as usual.'

Eventually Maloney's small daughter dragged him out!

'Without her, Lis, I'd be a goner,' Tom confessed.

* * *

David Maloney may not have been hired for *Scratchman* in the end – sadly the whole project never got off the ground – but he was the director of our next serial. *Genesis of the Daleks* was again written by Terry Nation and this time dealt with the origins of the Doctor's deadliest foes. It was actually drawn out into a six-parter, which could be a little wearing on momentum. How many cliffhangers can you squeeze out of one story? But I think this one was a classic – some really great writing expertly dealt with.

Maloney has to take a large slice of the credit. I would have been happy to work with him every time because he made it such fun. It wasn't just another commission for him: he had such a handle on how things should be, on the camaraderie at the heart of a programme like this. I just remember him and Tom, Ian and me having a laugh and really going for it.

The talent on *Genesis* was extraordinary. David Spode's sets were incredible, Sylvia and Barbara achieved wonders with makeup and costume – and then there were the actors. We had Peter Miles as Nyder, Richard Reeves and Dennis Chinnery – all excellent. But the star of the show, I have to say, was Michael Wisher. It was the third time I'd worked with him – and the third time he'd performed in almost total disguise. On *Death to the Daleks* he'd just supplied the voices. As a Vogan in *Revenge of the Cybermen* he'd been covered in prosthetics. Now, as Davros, the creator of the Daleks, he was stuck under a mask made by John Friedlander, who had also worked on *Death to the Daleks*.

But what a performance . . .

Oh, it's just someone in a horror mask sitting down pressing buttons, you think. Then you watch the hand, study the finger. Michael's timing is impeccable: with the slightest of gestures, he managed to be threatening. It could have been grotesque, over-the-top, cartoon-like. On the contrary, this was a masterclass in restrained, less-is-more, physical acting.

Michael deserved to be a success – he really put the hours in. He used to wear a kilt and kneepads because the Dalek shell was threading his trousers bare. To achieve the feel of Davros being a loner, excluded from his own society, he got a paper bag and pulled it over his head. It wasn't quite the BBC's finest makeup but it did the trick. When you're rehearsing with someone who looks so different, you act differently – we fed off each other.

I didn't see his actual mask until we were about to shoot (I think, as usual, they'd been adding bits and bobs over the day). I suppose, too, I was wrapped up in my own thoughts – going over line changes, rehearsing my own performance, cocooned in my private little world. Either way, it completely passed me by in run-throughs. Then it came to the actual take and I can still feel the shiver up my back. I looked through this wall, in full character now, and there was Davros in all his deformed glory. That's genuine shock you see onscreen. Such a powerful, hideous image!

Those moments are exquisite for an actor, and quite rare, especially when you're on a show as complicated as *Who*. There's smoke all around, I'm concentrating on putting the props in the right place, a hundred things to remember. It's all very mechanical, extremely calculated. And then you get a thunderbolt like that where your whole body just responds to what's in front of you. Seeing Davros that first time genuinely terrified me as much as if I were an eight-year-old watching at home. All my senses responded. The smell of the smoke and the machines was so evocative. He sounded horrible, too. And that mask!

* * *

When I read in the script for *Genesis* that Sarah was to be chased up a large wall as she tries to escape from a missile silo I didn't bat an eyelid. The ceilings at BBC Television Centre are so low that you can't go too high without lights or microphones or even the director's gallery creeping into shot. To get any real height at all, the climb would have to be faked – I wouldn't be called upon to risk life or limb in any death-defying stunt.

There was just one problem with that logic: the scene wasn't going to be filmed at Television Centre at all.

So, on 13–14 January, while everyone else enjoyed a few days' rehearsal at Acton, I found myself at Ealing Studios. Any love I had for the place and its history was temporarily suspended as I looked up at this seemingly never-ending scaffolded wall. I wasn't mad on heights, but back then I had the arrogance of youth – you think you're untouchable at that age. And maybe there was a hint of being a woman and trying just that bit harder not to let the side down. You don't want to give anyone any excuses to have a go.

There's something in an actor's psyche that says, 'If they want you to do this, it must be safe.' That's a hell of an assumption, especially after Wookey Hole, but you plod through life trusting you won't be asked to do things that aren't safe. Oh God, when I look back at some of the places I ended up! My friend in California, Amy Krell, has a photograph of me where I'm leaning over the edge of a skyscraper with Ian hanging onto me. No hidden ropes, no safety net, just us two clowning a mile above the traffic. Afterwards Ian confessed, 'Lis, I could never have done that.'

Oh, it never occurred to me to say no. I assumed the photographer knew what he was doing, I thought.

I've noticed, though, I'm much more careful about these things since I became a mother – I'm far more suspicious.

At Ealing, it transpired, I wasn't the one with the biggest problem. We had a hilarious actor on *Genesis*, Stephen Yardley, who was playing a deformed mutant called Sevrin. His character had this funny arm and he used to come to lunch, dragging his limp limbs around in full costume, and howl, 'I'm not very well!'

An incredibly funny man – and also, it turned out, quite a timid one when it came to heights.

We were saddled with guns and of course he had his dodgy arm, and somehow we'd scrambled halfway up the wall. Then Stephen looked down.

'I don't like this – it's a bit high.'

If we could have faked it on the blue screen, I think he would have been delighted.

I put a lot of trust in our film cameraman, Elmer Cossey, who was the one calling the shots that day. I remember talking to him at Ealing that morning. Just general chit-chat, and then he said, 'So, Lis, do you want to see your wall?' I think he'd been looking forward to seeing my face, the little so-and-so.

The problem with having a technical bod in charge, of course, is they're never satisfied. The first time Stephen and I managed to fight our way up I thought, *That wasn't so hard, we'll be finished early today*.

Not a chance.

We spent the entire day going up and down, up and down this bloody wall. The distance between bars was just too great to be comfortable for me. Another six inches closer together and I could have managed them. As it was, I'd just get a foothold then really have to overstretch to reach the next rung. The following day I could barely lift my hands to head height.

The only plus side of the whole experience is the end result. There was a chance it could have been another stunt that looked rubbish on telly, like my big leap in *Peladon*, but I think Elmer captured the scale of the place pretty well.

* * *

Back in the safe arena of the Acton Hilton we rehearsed as normal for six studio days, filming, largely, in episode order, plus the odd out-of-sequence bit if it saved on scenery. Maloney's inspired idea of only having the Daleks indoors paid off. They're pretty menacing in the right environment, aren't they? As usual we had John and Cy but this time round, Murphy was replaced by Keith Ashley. It's funny to think you can conquer whole galaxies with just three Dalek operators . . .

As before, the Dalek boys all learned their lines for rehearsal. In the studio, however, as Michael was playing Davros now, it was Roy Skelton who took over. Roy is the master of Dalek voices, he really is. Brilliant to watch as well. He'd be in the studio, headphones on, studying the screen and acting out all the parts. When the Daleks argue among themselves, he's just hysterical.

One of the more threatening aspects of *Genesis* is the whole 'master race' undercurrent. I think Terry Nation originally worked a lot of Nazi allusions into the show with Robert and Philip's blessing, although these were watered down in later episodes. (Lovely Guy Siner, who plays Ravon, would of course go on to play a rather camp Nazi in *'Allo 'Allo!*) Spotting the similarities does add that layer of menace, I think. If you're too young or naïve to spot the allegorical references, that's fine too.

There's a hint of a 'final solution' in *Genesis*, of course, which threw up all sorts of issues. The Doctor realises he has the opportunity to connect two leads and prevent the Dalek race from ever existing. Harry and Sarah urge him to act for the sake of the future universe but he can't.

And Tom couldn't either.

It was a big moment at Television Centre when, as we were actually preparing to shoot these lines, Tom just said, 'No, I can't do this.'

He just stopped the whole thing. Refused to go on as it was written.

'Maloney, this isn't right,' he called up to the gallery. 'We need to think this through seriously.'

To put this into some sort of context, Tom's suggestions were often along the lines of: 'What if there was a Mer-man sitting at my feet? Wouldn't that be astounding?'

'Er, I don't think we have the budget, Tom,' would be the normal excuse. 'But thanks . . .'

This time he was being deadly serious.

'Think about it, Maloney. I'm the Doctor – I can't go around wiping out entire civilisations. Do I have the right?'

They struggled with it for ages. Tom was very uncomfortable. Rewrites were drawn up and a lot of his questions made it into the script. It was powerful stuff. Not exactly the sort of debate you find on your average kids' programme.

So we went from an exciting scene in a fast-flowing episode to a major philosophical discussion point, thanks to Tom.

Over the years, of course, the Doctor has theoretically wiped out the Daleks several times (I even helped him in *Journey's End*). If Philip and Robert had their way, they would have been killed off for good in 1975: neither man could stand the Daleks and I think it must have been pretty galling for them to have to work on *Genesis* which, like the rest of Season Twelve, had been commissioned by Barry and Terry as part of their outgoing duties.

* * *

Part one of *Genesis of the Daleks* went out in March 1975 – impressive considering we only finished shooting Episode 6 on 25 February. When you're airing shows so rapidly after wrapping there's a risk the end result will suffer. This one certainly didn't. The whole serial attained, I think, a punchy realism that was hard to beat at the time. Some would argue it was too realistic. In fact, Mary Whitehouse did argue that very fact – and quite a lot more. Younger readers won't remember Mary, but she was a campaigner for standards on television and radio. She was quite a celebrity in the 1970s and 80s, always on the warpath about the levels of sex or violence in this programme or that. Her name has become synonymous with censorship, and not always for good reasons, I think.

In a way it was a compliment if Mary Whitehouse noticed you. Once she started her sabre-rattling about *Who* I thought, *We've really arrived now*. But she really went ballistic at *Genesis of the*

Daleks. 'Tea-time brutality for tots,' she called it. Apparently Davros was too scary, which he was meant to be – Christ, he terrified *me* – and there was too much violence. I heard Terry Nation thought it might be a bit much for kids. Philip Hinchcliffe disagreed and so do I. I mean, the message of *Who* is very clear: it's good versus evil and there's a hero and good always triumphs. And if you take away anything from the programme it's that you should never give up. Time Lords, journalists, navy doctors – we can all make a difference. Barry came to me once and said, 'Do you think it's too much for children?'

'In my opinion the only children who would be bothered by it are the sort of children who would be bothered by a cabbage rolling down the stairs. They're just a bothered child – you can't legislate for them. And you certainly cannot allow programmes to be made for such a very specific minority,' I said.

Of course, we hadn't seen *The Brain of Morbius* yet . . .

* * *

What with the weather and the workload, I was looking forward to the final serial of Season Twelve. I think the plan was to end on *Terror of the Zygons*, then break for summer, rather than record the first serial for the next block. Brian and I had been talking about getting away for a while. Tangiers kept cropping up as a destination, so we began to look at brochures and flights. That put a spring in my step as we finished *Genesis*. When you know you've got a break coming up, it's hard not to count the days.

It was some time in January when all our plans went out the window. ITV, the only competitor to the BBC in those days, announced plans for a new sci-fi series called *Space: 1999*. It was the brainchild of Gerry Anderson, creator of *Thunderbirds* and *Stingray*, so we could expect it to be of quality, although live action and not puppet-based this time. As a non-fan this didn't particularly bother me. What did, however, was the fact it was scheduled to launch in late summer. There were all sorts of confabs at the Beeb and they all agreed: if this programme starts before the new series of *Who* and sinks its claws into our viewers, we might not win them back.

It's a pretty negative view, I believe, and in hindsight probably the wrong one. But we didn't know that then. So, the decision was made to bring forward Season Thirteen. Rather than start in winter, it would now begin in August. The good news was Season Twelve production would now conclude with *Genesis* – which meant we'd finished that block.

The bad news was the new season would commence recording straight after, with no break. I had the offer of a new contract on the table for another series (Todd was in negotiation with Philip), but what about summer? What about Tangiers?

I honestly didn't think I could do it.

Chapter Nine

I Thought You Were Doing A Doctor

I T WAS with a certain reluctance that I started recording *Terror of the Zygons*. Not that I had anything against the script – from what I could tell it looked very strong. Nor the director – from the initial meetings with Douglas Camfield, I thought we were in safe hands here. But knowing it wasn't the end of term, being told this was just the halfway point in a pretty arduous schedule, that was almost too much to bear. And there was no discussion. We were either doing it or we weren't – those were the options.

But that wasn't all. On top of everything else I knew that *Zygons* would also see me saying goodbye to a very dear friend.

Being positive for a moment, 1975 was a good time to be involved with *Who*. Possibly the best time – I'll let others decide. I don't think our stock had ever been higher. Tom was really winning plaudits with every episode and there was a genuine groundswell of love for his Doctor. Viewing figures were largely supporting the new fella as well. I remember being called into Philip's office in February. For some reason he was delirious. He was this close to dancing on the table – and if you know Philip, you will understand how unlikely that image is!

'The figures are amazing!' he said. 'You two should be very pleased with yourselves.'

I guessed he was talking about the second episode of *The Ark in Space*, which had aired the previous Saturday.

'You're absolutely right. Do you know how many people tuned in? 13.6 million people – 13.6!'

Whatever Philip was on was very contagious. It was the first time I genuinely felt, *We're flying, they like us – they really like us!*

The atmosphere in the whole building was electric. It meant so much to everyone. You could taste the enthusiasm in the air. Strangers, people from other programmes, support staff – they all seemed to know our star was in the ascendant. And, do you know what? It felt bloody good! Our hard work was paying off.

We never hit the same heights again, although there was a definite spike in viewers once Tom was established. People loved him. No wonder he stayed for seven years.

A few weeks later there was a lot to love, too, about *Terror of the Zygons*. The plot was intricate, clever and fun and I loved how it tapped into the national psyche, exploiting all those myths and rumours about the Loch Ness Monster. Some of the acting was tremendous as well, the action sequences breathtaking and our director was one of the best.

But the monster . . .

My God, it was *Invasion of the Dinosaurs* all over again. I bumped into Philip one day and he was nearly in tears. Something had gone seriously wrong. The Skarasen was meant to be a sort of cyborg Nessie but it looked like a sock puppet with eczema. So disappointing. Tom and I fell about when we saw it. The plans had, apparently, promised so much. Dougie Camfield did his best but in the end I know he was resigned to using as few clips of the monster as possible, which was a shame.

On the plus side, though, I thought the shape-shifting Zygons themselves were pretty chilling. You can tell when James Acheson is back in the costume department because things get ratcheted up a notch. Need half a dozen giant orange-hooded suits with tentacles and octopus suckers? Jim's your man. It was good to see Keith Ashley again, too, working a Zygon instead of a Dalek this time.

And we did have fun. At one point Harry is cloned by a Zygon and I have to chase him all over the Scottish (hah!) countryside. He's hiding in a barn and I stumble in. It's so redolent of a dozen

1970s thrillers. Really well shot by Dougie, I think. Then Harry has to leap out and try to skewer me on a pitchfork.

OK, so we rehearsed this, but as soon as the cameras were rolling it was like Ian – not Harry – was a man possessed. He came at me with this bloody pitchfork so fast I thought I'd be kebabed for dinner! Boy, I was glad when that scene was over. I remember falling over just to escape those deadly tines. It was a really tricky moment. You learn it, you practise it – then suddenly you see two sharp blades driving towards your face and have to dive for cover. Not a nice feeling at all.

Murder attempts aside, *Zygons* was good for Sarah, as well. I like the fact you actually see me at a typewriter being a journalist – it's a small reminder that she's still an independent career woman, despite the aliens and everything. I think the headline on my piece was 'Another Bermuda Triangle?' – that was clever of Robert, rooting the story in popular myth once again. There are also some good scenes where Sarah is left to strike out on her own – without the Doctor, for example, when she gets to investigate the Duke's library and then saves Harry. In fact, I think I got as much if not more solo screen time in Episode 1 as Tom. That's a real compliment to the character. Whatever my paranoia about Philip's opinion, he obviously felt Sarah Jane was popular enough with audiences to warrant it.

Zygons picked up where *Cybermen* left off and the distress call from UNIT at the end of Season Thirteen. By the time we land in Season Fourteen, there have been a number of costume changes. I'm wearing a sort of pale green safari suit with long boots. Harry is all blazered up as usual, but wearing a familiar inordinately long scarf. And the Doctor is decked out in tartan neckwear plus full Scottish hat and coat combo. The theme continues throughout the start of Episode 1. There's an off-screen bagpipe player puffing his guts out, which is really played for laughs, while the Brig's first appearance is wearing a kilt. It turns out he's related to the clan Stewart, as per his name. And not because, as Sarah mocks him: 'You were just doing a Doctor.'

With budgets not stretching to Loch Ness, Philip and Dougie sourced the ideal alternative locations – in Sussex. In mid-March we recorded all the beach scenes on Climping Beach, plus the TARDIS's arrival on Ambersham Common. The next day we filmed Tom's big chase scene on Tullock Moor. That was action-packed and a half, really redolent of Cary Grant in *North by Northwest*. When it came to the Zygon spaceship landing, however, I think someone somewhere was enjoying an in-joke.

According to the script, the aliens landed their craft in a disused quarry outside Brentford. A quarry actually in the script! When the Brig and co. screech up in their Jeeps, for once there was no need to block out the cranes and diggers. I wonder how many people at home had a giggle at that.

Early April we finally shot the first studio episode in White City; the second followed the day after. I had a good feeling about this one. As usual there were some great auxiliary players, notably John Woodnutt as the Duke of Forgill. It never ceased to amaze me how *Who* could be like this kind of glee club for actors. Some quality talent appeared on our doorstep – and they were so happy to be part of it. John had a couple of parts. When he wasn't being the Duke, or a Zygon pretending to be the Duke, he actually lived inside one of the Zygon costumes. They were very difficult to move inside – I can still picture Jim Acheson guiding John across the room. John didn't let it get him down; he used to tap dance on his mark. Once I went too close and this crazy orange lizard creature said, 'Feel my suckers, Sladen. My suckers are so exquisite, feel them!'

Working with Dougie Camfield was a hoot. Like Maloney, he made you feel part of something special. He wasn't some coach with a megaphone ordering his minions around – we were crucial to the programme.

'Morning, people,' he would holler when he arrived. 'Where's my A-team?'

He was such a flatterer. And because he got on so well with everyone, we'd do anything for him. One day he announced,

'Look guys, we're behind, we're running out of days, and I really need this to be good. Who's going to come in at the weekend?'

Of course, we all told him to clear off, or words to that effect – he would have expected nothing less, I'm sure – especially when he admitted we wouldn't be paid. But we were only kidding: anything for Dougie.

Tom said, 'Yes, I'll bring the soup, Lissie can bring the pork pies.' Everyone was given a task because of course the canteen wouldn't be running on the Sabbath. Then on the Sunday, in we duly marched. Dougie couldn't have looked prouder.

'My beautiful A-team!'

I'd have done anything for Dougie – well, *almost* anything. He had a background in gritty dramas like *The Sweeney*, real urban telly, and so when it came to us he had particular tastes. For example, if the script said, 'Sarah's leg bleeds', he would not have been disappointed to see real blood. It's true. I'm not saying he would ask me to hurt myself – but if it happened I don't think he'd be too put out! Imagine being poor Lillias Walker. For one scene on the moor, her character Sister Lamont has to wield a sickening arm gash. She must have been so nervous around Dougie and sharp objects . . .

Dougie was a mass of contradictions. He was very hippy-looking, with his beard, hat and thin, pale physique, but he was also a military man through and through. More than that, he had an air-raid shelter at the bottom of his garden stocked with bully beef. Everything was set for the bomb to go off. He used to say, 'The invasion is coming – and I'm ready!'

A complete one-off.

There were some nice action pieces, especially Harry's shooting and my game of hide-and-seek with him in the countryside; plenty of comedy too. I get to poke my tongue out at one man, which I think children always like seeing adults do. Tom mimics the Duke's accent at one point, and there's the series of jokes about the incessant bagpipes at the start. Angus Lennie, as the hotelier Angus, had some light moments, too, especially when he's outstaring a mounted moose.

Sadly the fun was about to end for one of us. Early in 1975 Philip Hinchcliffe had mentioned to Bobby Holmes that he'd like Harry Sullivan to be written out. Robert disagreed. Harry, he said, was the perfect foil for the Doctor – and a great companion for Sarah. I think ultimately Philip admitted this was true, but by then it was too late. The decision was made – Harry Sullivan was off.

Filming the studio scenes, especially the ones where Harry is unconscious in hospital, and knowing he was on his way out, were difficult. I still remember getting the news.

'I'm not going to be in it any more, Lissie,' he told me one day.

'Well, I'm sure you'll come back.'

I truly believed he would return. After all, Nick and UNIT came and went. Why wouldn't Harry?

In fact, and I didn't know this at the time, it would be eight years before Nick's services were required again. Ian, however, would be back far sooner.

* * *

I remember when Jon Pertwee went. He himself had set the wheels in motion but by the time the moment came he was devastated to leave. It was when he was going through his lowest ebb that I was offered a new contract. A year later, when my good friend Ian had just been told his contract wouldn't be renewed, I was offered a deal for a further twenty-two episodes. The question was: did I want to sign?

It wasn't just Ian's situation that muddied the waters: my epiphany from that conversation with Philip during *The Sontaran Experiment* still lingered. I was in no doubt – I didn't need this work, it was just another job. The world wouldn't end if I walked away. I stared at myself in the mirror.

Come on now, honestly, Sladen, what's your instinct? What do you want to do?

I considered it for ages. On the one hand this was my livelihood and I owed it to my husband not to throw away good money because as actors it's rare that you're both working at the same time. On the other, it was the perfect springboard to other work. It was make your mind up time. And then the answer came to me.

I want to carry on.

* * *

I signed on 25 March. Tom had added his signature to a contract a few days earlier. That was it; we both were tied in. But what a slog it promised to be. Philip was serious about us working straight through, from Twelve to Thirteen. There would be no break: no summer, no Tangiers.

So why carry on?

The feeling I had with Jon when we were doing *Peladon* – that the stars were suddenly in alignment – was there again. It was a joy to go in to work every day. We didn't have to work at it any more; any teething troubles in the relationship had vanished. My Sarah and Tom's Doctor fitted together so naturally, hand in glove. I hope this came across onscreen, although sometimes I wonder if we went too far. When, decades later, I joined Tom to record the DVD commentary for our next serial, *Pyramids of Mars*, I wondered if we might have been a bit too relaxed! There's something so comfortable about us together. That story's definitely one of our better ones and, you know what, when we started filming I was so glad I'd decided to stay.

Here's a typical example of our partnership. Tom knows I love films. He was always throwing little lines at me and we'd discuss the old black-and-whites. Scenes from the classics became a kind of shorthand between us. 'You remember such and such . . .', 'Let's play it like . . .' Once we were waiting to shoot a scene on *Pyramids* where we had to walk up to a door and enter. Nothing terribly exciting, just one of those bread-and-butter scenes that are so easy to ignore. In the end, I think being in a long-running television show is less about how good you are in the big, confrontational scenes and more about how many different ways you can find to hide behind a rock or fall down a quarry; you have to keep experimenting. That's where we earn our money, I think. And that was what Tom and I were so good at.

I saw the twinkle in his eye. *Tom's up to mischief* . . .

'Lissie, you remember the Marx Brothers in *Monkey Business*?'

'Of course!' I said.

'Remember the three of them walk silently up to a door, change their minds, and turn in unison and walk away?'

'Yes – they see someone they don't want to bump into.'

'Why don't we do that?'

'We'll never get away with it!'

'Let's try.'

He called up to Paddy Russell, back as director, in the gantry. 'Ma'am . . .' – he always called directors 'sir' or 'ma'am' – they seemed to like that – 'Lis and I have had an idea.'

They listened, as they always did.

'It's a great idea,' Paddy said. 'But we only have time for one take. That would be too risky.'

'Right you are,' said Tom.

But to me he whispered, 'Shall we do it anyway?'

'Yes!'

So we did. We had one shot at it, and woe betide us if we messed it up! But it worked perfectly. Nobody said anything afterwards, but they must have been pleased because we didn't have to reshoot and that's the version you see on the screen.

Pulling one over on Paddy was quite rare.

As much as I loved Jon Pertwee, I think it's pretty clear his working methods didn't always suit me – that need of his for control could get a bit out of hand. So when he locked horns with Paddy during *Dinosaurs*, you felt the blame was probably 50:50 on each side. But then I saw how she got on with Tom.

As far as I'm concerned, if you're a director on *Doctor Who* and you can't get along with Tom Baker – you can't get along with anyone.

Paddy had apparently learned nothing about people skills in the two years since we'd last met. Christ, she could wear you down! You can only go over a scene so many times before you start thinking, *I hate this scene, it's like a piece of meat – if you hit it too much it becomes tasteless*. Tom hated that attitude. If you crack something first time, why go on? Paddy seemed to think she wasn't being thorough enough unless we'd explored every potential direction, every blind alley.

'We'll just try it one more time . . .'

Paddy never admitted defeat, never brooked insubordination. Bernard Archard, who I knew from my old Granada days, was playing Marcus Scarman. I remember bumping into him at lunch one day. He was very dry, very measured.

'I'm being kept in after school today. Are you?' he asked me.

I never really got a handle on whether Paddy was like she was because she was aware of being a woman in a man's world or if she happened to be just like that. One episode during *Pyramids* made me think there was a bit of a chip at work, though. The script said Sarah fires a rifle and I thought, *Fine*. When the day came Terry said he'd do it, or a stand-in could. But the director was straight over.

'Lis wants to do it, don't you, Lis?'

'Er, yeah, Paddy, whatever.'

From my point of view, the future of the Women's Liberation Movement would not hinge on whether or not I fired this shot but the gun expert admitted, 'Paddy really wants you to fire this gun because they think a girl can't do it.' How it looked to the outside world was obviously important to her. I really couldn't care either way. All I wanted to know was whether she needed it played straight or for laughs. The answer was straight – although the end result was debatable.

I was put in this recess in the wall and handed the weapon. I'd never fired a gun before, never even held one. And this was a bloody big thing. I was shown how to hold it, how to look like I'm taking aim, and how to fire – all in the space of ten minutes. That was the extent of my training. Where were those interminable rehearsals when you needed them?

Then Paddy called, 'Action!' and I fired.

God – the noise! I swear I was deaf for three hours. Why the hell didn't anyone warn me? Where were my earplugs? The gun let off this awesome explosion and of course it just reverberated off the tiny stone enclave. It was awful. As I put the gun down and walked off, I could see people talking to me but they looked like they were miming. I just went away and hid.

But it's easy to forget Paddy did some impressive things as well. I was working out my response to seeing Sutekh (an evil Ostirian who planned to destroy all life in the Universe) when she just stopped me. 'I'd like to show you something at Ealing,' she said.

Oh God, I thought. *What do I need to go over there for?* But off we went.

When we got to the studios Paddy sat me down in front of a screen and played a series of pre-records she'd already filmed with Gabriel Woolf as Sutekh. At one point I totally leapt out of my seat – much to Paddy's delight.

'Right,' she barked. 'That's the one we'll use.'

For once I appreciated that attention to detail and I was grateful to her for seeking my input.

* * *

People often cite *Pyramids* as one of their favourites and I've lost count of the thirty- and forty-somethings that tell me they genuinely hid behind the sofa in 1975 when the Mummies came out. If they only knew what we'd gone through to get there! Not only did we all struggle to get on with Paddy, I know Robert had an ordeal pulling the scripts together in time. In the end I think he wrote so much new material to add to Lewis Greifer's draft that they shared the pseudonymous credit 'Stephen Harris'. The pressure really was on with this one.

Location work commenced at the end of April – a week after *Revenge of the Cybermen* debuted on BBC1 and with the Mary Whitehouse furore still raging. The location in question was Stargrove Manor in East End, Hampshire – one of several properties owned by Mick Jagger at the time. It sounds glam, but I can promise you that when you've stalked every inch of a building's perimeter for take after take, it loses much of its celebrity allure.

At least I could wear normal clothes. I felt really sorry for the guys in the Mummy costumes. Something about the design wasn't right – no one was comfortable inside them. I think it must have been torture stomping around the woods as they had to. At one point Tom had to put one on and that didn't go well at all. I wasn't there but I could hear his voice being raised because something wasn't right. It wasn't a happy day by any means.

* * *

There are a couple of continuity notes from *Pyramids* which I wonder if people have spotted. One minor detail still makes me smile. Sarah had a nice collection of jewellery but for once I'd decided to wear a piece of my own, this beautiful jade ring.

There's a scene where I'm knocking like mad on the door. With Paddy in charge, I couldn't just do it once, could I? My hand was soon killing me from the various retakes, so I found myself shifting my weight. By the time Paddy said I could stop I thought my hand was going to fall off. Honestly, it was throbbing in agony. As I rubbed some life back into my fingers, though, I noticed my ring was missing its jade stone. I scrabbled around on the floor for a few minutes but no joy. But I didn't dare say anything to Paddy, of course. *If they know it's gone, I'll be doing reshoots all day*, I thought.

So if you watch *Pyramids* I think you can see my ring is there one minute and gone the next – then back again. It's not a major catastrophe, but I know it would crucify Paddy to realise she'd missed this.

For us time was always such a rare commodity that you really had to let a lot of things go, even if they weren't 100 per cent perfect. There's a scene in *Pyramids* where an extra almost stumbles over – and we still kept it in. Generally we'd try to get away with the odd pickup shot if something wasn't quite right. So, for example, in *Pyramids*, you might be walking down a corridor, knocking. Then you get the call: 'Hang on, hang on, nobody move, hold it there!' Depending on where they think it went awry, you can either go back and do the walk again, or do the knock again with that hand. Mostly we just tried to get through the whole scene with as few backward steps as possible.

Sometimes we'd have stop takes: 'OK, we're going to stop that scene halfway through so when you get to that point, just stop. We'll alter some of the props then you carry on.' Generally, though, we filmed entire scenes in one go.

In *Pyramids*, Sarah ends up trapped in a bell jar but they couldn't put a bell jar over me. It would have been such a waste of manpower to lift it. The way around it was to put it on afterwards with CSO. So we began the scene, I reached my mark then the shout came: 'Freeze!' I couldn't move or I'd have arms outside the jar. I don't know how long I was playing statues but it seemed like forever. Then the First's voice rang out, narrating the final version's action: 'Bell jar going on, bell jar over, not long now, bell jar in place – and you can move!'

When I finally broke my pose there was a cheer from the gantry because I hadn't moved. That was nice.

It's so different – so much better – these days. Time is still the one commodity you never have enough of, but so little is left to chance. On *The Sarah Jane Adventures* we film multiple angles of every scene as standard. For example, we'll start with a wide scene that captures everybody, possibly repeating this a couple of times. Then you'll do the exact same scene from every character's point of view. So instead of making do with a couple of pickups we actually have the whole scene played out with, let's say, me in shot for the duration, then Clyde, then Luke, then Rani. Then the editors splice it all together afterwards. I'm sure it's a lot more work for the technical bods and it's definitely a lot more work for us because you have to say and do the precise same things over and over but the end results speak for themselves.

* * *

When the decision was taken to hold *Zygons* back as the new season's opener, Philip was faced with a new quandary: with *Pyramids* following immediately afterwards he'd be left with two Earthbound adventures in a row. After the Third Doctor's economical but seemingly endless Earth exile, it was a pattern he was keen not to repeat. So the call was made to switch *Pyramids* and the next production: *Planet of Evil*. No one could complain about that story being Earthbound. The whole thing was set on Zeta Minor – a planet at the very end of the universe. And for the first time since *Ark in Space*, it was shot entirely indoors. It could literally have been anywhere.

I've always enjoyed the buzz of location shoots. That said, if you're going to shoot indoors for six weeks, you can't go wrong if some of that time is spent at Ealing Studios. The reason for being at Ealing, as it was with *Genesis*, was one of scale. Philip elected to pour the whole of a week's location budget into recreating Zeta Minor in a single expansive studio set. Designer Roger Murray-Leach – the *incomparable* Roger Murray-Leach – was in on meetings from the beginning. His concept of a colourful, malevolent jungle was a triumph, I think.

Tom and I loved having a coffee and a laugh with Roger. We formed a great friendship, actually – just one of many on that set. If I'd been a happy bunny on *Pyramids*, this shoot was off the scale. Looking back, I'd say it was the zenith of my time on *Who*. I don't think Tom and I ever got it more perfect than in *Planet of Evil*. It didn't matter what was going on in the outside world or even in my own head – those doubts vanished when we were together. The magic of television never seemed more powerful to me.

I always say *Planet of Evil* is my favourite serial, but I do wonder if that's because I had such a blast making it. When I sat down to do the commentary for the DVD the happy memories came flooding back. The performances are so chatty, so natural, as though they're not scripted at all, and that typifies how we felt at the time. But I do wonder, with hindsight, if we were having too much fun, if there wasn't the odd moment of, 'Oh, you're dying? Right,

I'd better do something about that then.' I'll let other people decide for themselves.

Once again we had Maloney in the director's chair, which just made the event so enjoyable. Bless him – he's another one no longer with us. I loved him dearly, truly I did, and always had a fantastic time in his company. Like Tom, he had a sense of humour, very left of centre. He would always come out with the most unexpected line. Other times he could be very direct. I remember overhearing him talking to Andrew Rose, my costume designer on *Evil*.

'Look, can we make Sarah look a bit more like a girl?'

Hysterical!

He was right, though. The whole 'journalist' persona had been well enough established by then – I didn't need to keep the suits on anymore to be seen as a 'serious' woman. In fact, I was already beginning to have a bit more fun with her, to play around a lot more. Sarah had been so strait-laced with Jon and now it was time to let her hair down. We began to find a lot more frilly things for her to wear, the more outlandish the better. After all, I thought, *She's travelling in space now. Who's to say what's smart on other planets?*

She's whizzing around the universe in the TARDIS, meeting aliens with eight legs, one eye, fur, clothes, gaudy robes – you name it. Why couldn't she become a bit more off the wall? So in *Planet of Evil* I wore a bodice, nothing like I'd ever worn in the show before. And espadrilles – they were all the rage then – cut-off jeans, a short-sleeve puffed jacket. It wasn't quite so outlandish as *Hand of Fear*, but we were heading in that direction.

The thing about clothes, of course, is that they can alter your behaviour. It wasn't planned when I first picked up the script, but I'm sure Sarah is a bit more girly when she's in more of a fun costume. It seems so natural, why fight it?

I've been thinking about the quality of the scripts on *Planet of Evil* because, as I sit here now, the serial's writer Louis Marks has just died. It's very sad seeing those faces from my past fade away. At least with DVDs and videos a bit of them lives on.

I don't know if Robert asked Louis for a '*Jekyll and Hyde* meets *Forbidden Planet*' storyline – but that's what he got. I love it when there are other references in the programme.

Of course the villain of *Evil* was the actual planet itself. It was quite a clever plot, I think. Extremely forward thinking and ecological – man can't just ride into town, plunder natural resources and suffer no consequences. The anti-matter creature was very futuristic as well. But I don't think Philip was terribly impressed with it, actually. Maybe he had imagined something else. I remember watching it on television at the same time as everyone else – I thought it was fine.

One of the bonuses of filming at Ealing is the fact it's a bona fide film studio. Everything is set up for the director to be at the heart of the action at floor level, not cooped up on an observation deck. I really enjoyed having Maloney up close and personal. It's one thing having a First translate the director's ideas, another seeing on his face exactly what he wants before he says it. In that respect Ealing really was just like being on location.

We also had to do some interesting recovery work at the studio. Roger's vast jungle set was so lifelike and sprawling that Maloney struggled to get the mics anywhere near enough. In the end a lot of our lines on the planet's surface had to be dubbed later. These days we do this all the time but it was a novelty then. If you don't time it right, the result looks like a bad foreign film, with lips and words not synching.

Roger's set might have caused Maloney problems but Terry Walsh couldn't believe his luck. As soon as we'd finished at Ealing Terry ran round and gathered as many of the exotic plants and fauna as he could carry. That night he crept out into his garden and planted them all within view of the house. The following morning his wife pulled the curtains open – and screamed, 'Terry, Terry, you'll never believe what's growing in the garden!'

Poor Terry lost his wife quite young. That's when you find out who your friends are. I got a call one day from Jon Pertwee. 'We must look after him. We'll have to take him round the conventions with us,' he said. It was a sweet thing to do. Jon could be very considerate like that.

* * *

As much as I enjoyed *Planet of Evil*, by the time we wrapped mid-July I was ready for a break. Seven serials in a row – that's thirty-two episodes, one after the other – was a punishing schedule. Worse still, we had fourteen more episodes to film before the block was over. I pored over the calendar with Brian. If we were cute we could actually finagle a few days away. Of course the problem is, as soon as you start imagining these things they just snowball in your mind. I couldn't wait.

First, I had another treat to look forward to. Tom and I were invited to lunch at the Garrick Club by the bosses of BBC Enterprises – the commercial arm of the Beeb. Lovely Terry Sampson was there, Lorne Martin and the head honcho himself, Peter Dimmock. Obviously it's a pleasure to be taken to lunch anyway, but beforehand Tom and I gossiped about why we were being summoned.

'Maybe they just want to thank us for being amazing,' he suggested.

'Do you think so?'

'Don't be ridiculous!'

There always has to be a catch with the BBC – you just need to find out what it is.

We had a drink and a chit-chat before Terry broke the news.

'We'd love you both to turn on this year's Blackpool Illuminations.'

Crikey, I thought only famous people were invited to do that. 'But you *are* famous,' they insisted. 'And you'll be even more famous once you've done this.'

Over the next few years we were followed by such luminaries as Terry Wogan, Kermit the Frog and Red Rum – which gives you an idea of how the Doctor and Sarah were viewed by the world at large.

Back at the Garrick, they really gave us the hard sell and I admit it was tempting (I'd already had a taste of what the Blackpool crowds could be like with Jon). Then I remembered Tangiers.

'Look, I'm sorry, I've got to have a break. Tom doesn't need me there – people only want to see the Doctor anyway.'

At this Peter Dimmock leapt straight in there. 'Lis, we need you! Tom hasn't really been established yet, you're the one people know. You *have* to do it.'

Tom looked at me and said, 'Well yes, I suppose that's true. I've only been around five minutes. They love you, Elisabeth.'

I was flattered, certainly but was my ego more important than a few rare days away with my husband? Not even close.

'Look, I'm sorry, I really am. But if I go to Blackpool I can't take my break, and I really need it – I'm exhausted.'

Terry gave me his most diplomatic look. 'Lis, I understand. Don't make a decision now, talk it over with Brian – we'll pay for him to go as well, obviously. Let us know tomorrow.'

'Fine,' I said. But my mind was already made up – I'd leave it twenty-four hours before giving them the bad news.

When I got home I was even more adamant that I'd soon be in Tangiers. Then the phone rang: it was Mum. She sounded like she'd won the pools.

'Oh, Elisabeth,' she gushed. 'I've just had the most charming call from Terry Sampson. He has asked your dad and me to come down to Blackpool to watch you turn on the lights!'

'*Really*?'

'Oh yes, we can't wait!'

I hung up, feeling thoroughly outmanoeuvred. Mum had never sounded happier. All I could think was, *Sampson, you swine!*

Chapter Ten

Over Here, Cloth-Eyes!

O F ALL the manipulative stunts! I could barely look at Terry Sampson after that. But he was as good as his word: Mum and Dad were picked up by limo and booked into one of Blackpool's finest hotels. It was heart-warming to see them so thoroughly spoiled. I thought they were going to explode with pride when they saw the crowds calling out for me, too. Compared to this, my visit to the Exhibition's opening with Jon had been a washout.

Being flat out in the middle of a consecutive second season, it was a real scramble to get ready. I didn't have a minute to buy a new outfit. Fortunately I had the might of the BBC to help me out. Rowland Warne, the costume guy from *Planet of the Spiders*, really stepped up. He lent me this ornate antique shawl and a beautiful white lace dress that I absolutely adored. Afterwards he said I looked so stunning I should keep them, which was naughty but much appreciated. Later I altered the frock for Sadie to wear when she was playing the May Queen's attendant – I put some ribbons around the sleeves to hike it up and trimmed it a bit. I've still got it.

Blackpool was actually a great experience. As well as my parents, Sampson had invited Ian Marter and David Maloney – I think Enterprises hoped he'd be able to keep us all in check. Brian came along as well, which gave it more of a holiday feel. He got on fabulously with Ian and Tom so it was a real party atmosphere, actually.

The plan was to have a big banquet with the Lord Mayor in the evening, spend the night in a hotel, then switch on the illuminations the next evening. *Fine*, I thought. *I'm here now, I may as well enjoy it.*

As we filed into the dining hall Tom said to me, 'Lis, lucky you – you're sitting next to the Mayor!'

Anyone else would think this was an honour. The way Tom had said it, though – I was waiting for the catch. I soon found it. The Mayor had just had an operation and for the whole duration of the meal I got a blow-by-blow account. Talk about putting you off your food! What made it worse was watching Tom up the other end of the table having the night of his life. *If he dares to laugh at me, I swear I'll throw my roll at his head!* I thought.

Still, my problems weren't as bad as Brian's. They had him down as 'Mr Sladen' so the whole night he had to put up with people calling him by my surname. Luckily he's got a grand sense of humour about these things.

When it came to the actual switching-on ceremony, it looked like all of Blackpool and the Northwest had turned out to watch the Doctor use his sonic screwdriver to illuminate the night. No pressure, then.

We got there and Tom said to Maloney, 'OK, let's have the screwdriver.'

And the look of horror on Maloney's face – 'Tom, I thought you had it!'

What a pair.

So Maloney whizzed back to the hotel and the rest of us stood up there, in full glare of the crowds, for what seemed like forever. I've no idea what we did to fill the time. When Maloney came panting back up the stairs I said, 'Where have you been?'

Apparently he'd got stuck in the hotel lift on the way back, forgetting he was holding the sonic. After a few minutes this old couple said, 'Well, are you going to use it or not?'

Eventually there was a countdown and Tom set the whole place ablaze. It was truly spectacular, he was such a hit with the masses.

I don't know what Terry, Lorne and Peter had been fussing about. The fans obviously loved him already.

Afterwards we all piled into Bessie for a tour along the promenade. If I'd thought it had been busy when Jon and I opened the exhibition, this was unbelievable. The crowds were ten deep, all yelling and waving their *Doctor Who* scarves and toys. Amazing! I just wish I'd had more than a shawl to keep me warm. Trying to smile and wave while you're absolutely freezing takes some acting, I can tell you. And it seemed to go on forever because we were crawling along behind a giant orange – the size of half a house – that carried people. Bizarre to behold! Ian lent over and said, 'Christ, Sladen, is this what it has come to, following a bloody orange along Blackpool promenade!'

Brian and I enjoyed a meal with Mum and Dad then the next day we all caught the train home. Travelling with the Enterprise boys in a first-class carriage was a bit of an eye-opener as to how the other half of the Beeb lived. Peter Dimmock said, 'Tom, Lis – do you fancy a drink?'

What a daft question after such an exhausting couple of days.

Ten minutes later he returned from the bar with a couple of boxes under each arm. He'd bought every miniature on the train! That was a journey I won't forget in a hurry – although the details are a little vague.

* * *

It was such a blast to have Ian with us in Blackpool and I was really happy to see his name down on the call sheets for the next serial, *The Android Invasion*, even though he'd be playing a 'fake' Harry for the second time running, so we wouldn't get many fun scenes together. Two other names made important comebacks on this one as well. Terry Nation was writing a rare non-Dalek story, which people were really excited about. What I could barely contain myself about, however, was the return of Barry Letts as director. As soon as I heard he'd be in charge I knew *Android* would be one to savour.

Unusually for *Who* we filmed in summer. Costume girl Barbie Lane had me in a short-sleeved pink sailor suit for this one. Very cool, although I started the story with a hat and scarf! Poor Tom was stuck in his heavy suit, cravat, overcoat, hat and scarf. A less-fit man would have sweltered to death.

We began recording in late July at the National Radiological Protection Board in Harwell, Oxfordshire. All those lung-busting running and jumping shots around the Defence Station were done there. There's an exciting scene with Tom leaping off the roof. Terry Walsh has to take credit for that one, as usual, but Barry cut it so brilliantly it's breath-taking to watch. And when Tom is confronted by an android with a gun built into his hand, he says the immortal line: 'Is that finger loaded?' so perfectly he might have been auditioning for Roger Moore's part in James Bond. Then it was off to Tubney Woods in Oxfordshire for a couple of days to capture those thrilling open-air chases. I remember Tom having to hoist me into a tree. It was like I wasn't even there; he whooshed me over his shoulder then threw me up so effortlessly. And to think Barry had cast Ian to handle all the Doctor's physical work.

We had a lot of fun in Tubney. The opening scene from Episode 1 cracks me up – it's another example of Tom and me really enjoying ourselves. He was sensational. When the Doctor chooses a route via the scientific process of 'Eeeny Meeny' he looks directly at the camera on 'Meeny', which sends a shiver down the spine of every viewer. I don't know if that was Barry's or Tom's idea but it really works.

Once we start exploring, the Doctor says, 'Mind the bramble.' A second later Sarah says, 'Ow!' Very drily, from off-camera, you hear Tom say, 'I said mind the bramble.' It's a short but tender scene, which accentuates their comfortable relationship. A second later, though, and it's a genuine effort not to stop the whole production. I'm mid-sentence when Tom releases a branch which thwacks me in the kipper. Instinctively I burst out laughing – but then continued with the line. *That branch would have to knock me out for Barry to stop shooting*, I thought. And I was right – we didn't reshoot and it's still there to this day.

If you've never tried it, I can tell you pretending to be an android version of yourself is always fun. Obviously you must convey a difference because you're playing a machine, but you still have to act like your character so as not to arouse suspicion. It was quite nice to find a level that I thought was working – and then have to fall over and be discovered. Barry was very good then, just letting me get on with my own ideas and only commenting if he disagreed.

Despite the nice weather I still felt worn down in this one. There was one shot where Barry wanted us to walk away from the camera across a cornfield – they were just filming our backs, it was a long shot. From the distance we heard a shout and Tom said, 'I think that was a "cut".'

'No, I didn't hear anything,' I said.

So we just kept walking! It was a scorching day and eventually we ended up in the village and squeezed in a cream tea before anyone found us!

When I started doing *The Sarah Jane Adventures* I had a letter from the woman at the Post Office. She said, 'Oh, you and Tom came in to hide and said, "Oh, they won't find us in here!" I've still got the photo you signed and I tell my grandchildren, "I met Sarah Jane".'

It was really magical working with Barry again, but also Ian. I had no idea this would be his last hurrah. It was never set out so formally although that's how it turned out.

Nick Courtney was too busy to take part but John Levene, one of the other regular UNIT boys, was available. I loved working with John. He was so sweet and he really made me laugh – not always intentionally. He'd drop things and he'd dry up in a scene, never a dull moment. Tom used to joke that if John's character Sergeant Benton saluted he'd poke himself in the eye. If he had a bayonet rifle, he'd stab himself in the foot.

Come *Androids*, of course, and John not only had to play himself and an android version of Benton – he also had to shoot the Doctor. Barry was so relaxed about this scene it quite threw John.

'There's no dialogue, just say what comes naturally,' Barry said.

This absolutely froze John into total traction. *Ad-libbing*? That was for other people, not him. So he came over to me and said, 'Lis, what am I going to do?'

'Just say whatever you feel, I don't want to put words into your mouth,' I told him.

'OK, OK,' he said. 'I've got it.'

So we began rehearsal then went for action. As per the script, Tom got shot. John looked at his gun and said, 'Shit, I've shot the Doctor!'

* * *

By the time we finished *Android* at the end of August, summer was well and truly upon us. Unfortunately my chances of a holiday were as remote as ever. Pre-production was already underway on the next serial and before I knew it I was standing in the Acton Hilton, script in hand, working through the latest twist in Sarah's journey. Yet again, though, I found myself thinking, *How much more is there for this character to do?*

Added to my irritation with the relentless schedule was my increasing feeling that *Who* and I were about to part company. For now, though, I was enjoying scripts for *The Brain of Morbius*.

Like *Pyramids*, *Morbius* ended up going out under a pseudonym. Having done all the legwork, Terry Dicks was sufficiently offended by Robert Holmes' rewrites to ask for his name to be taken off the credits.

'Give it some sort of bland pseudonym,' Terry huffed.

Which is how *Morbius* came to be 'written' by 'Robin Bland'.

Despite the feel of a big-budget Hammer Horror, *Morbius* was actually one of our belt-tightening exercises. The whole thing was shot in Television Centre – no locations, no puppet shoots. After the verdant feel of *Android*, the studio mountains of Karn seemed a little sterile, I admit, but I think Barry had used up all the budget!

At least I could get home at the end of each day – you need your own bed to recharge the batteries sometimes. On filming days it was different. After the pressure of a camera day, it was a relief to knock off at ten o'clock and head straight for the studio bar. You could really let your hair down in there safe in the knowledge only BBC people were around. Sometimes, on special occasions, we'd make for the Balzac Bistro on Shepherd's Bush Green for a meal. It wasn't particularly far to walk but we only seemed to venture thus far for birthdays and celebrations. The priority was always to find the nearest watering hole and pitch our tent there.

There's more than a hint of *Frankenstein* in *The Brain of Morbius*. Mad scientist Solon is trying to rebuild Morbius, an evil Time Lord, but he's short on parts. So far he's just got a brain in a jar and a body somewhere between a man and a crab. Then Tom and I stroll along and all his Christmases come at once.

Chris Barry, the 'Mad Monk', was in charge of this one. He was very professional, extremely precise and – how can I put it? – mercurial, too. Whatever mood Chris was in when he arrived at rehearsal, that was the mood you got directed in. I remember he was very excited about working with Philip Madoc, who was playing Solon. I got the impression from Chris that he was working with a proper actor for a change. *Charming*!

I see Philip now and he's a jovial man. I wish I'd known it at the time. On *Morbius* he was deadly serious, every detail had to be explored. Ad-libbing, fooling around or any of those flippant drama exercises seemed beneath him. And, I have to be honest: Chris seemed to love him for it. *Hello, Chris, you're directing* Doctor Who, *not Professor Solon*, I thought.

I'd almost forgotten the shadow Philip cast on recording until we came to do the DVD commentary. Chris and Philip were asked if they spent a lot of time rehearsing Solon's scene with the monster.

'No time at all – the whole thing was done very quickly.' They both agreed on that.

I nearly spat my coffee out. As far as I'm concerned they rehearsed that scene over and over; they were on it for hours. *We'll never get home at this rate*, I remember thinking.

John Scott Martin was also in this one (buried under the monster costume), as was Stuart Fell, so it was nice to have them around. Condo, the gormless servant, was played by an old Liverpool lad called Colin Fay. His character was a direct lift from those old horror films with the sinister servant 'Igor'. Any gap in the schedule and we'd be regaling each other with stories of the home country. That fun carried over into rehearsals. When we first arrive at Solon's castle it's raining. We knock on the door and this Lurch figure greets us. Now, just before the cameras were about to roll, Tom said, 'Do you know, Lis – when he opens the door we could be doing a tap dance like *Singin' in the Rain*.' You can imagine his face, animated and big-eyed at the idea.

'I think that might be a bit much, Tom,' I told him.

How I wish we'd done it. Perhaps it would have made Chris notice us for a change.

One person in particular needed no help in noticing us: Mary Whitehouse. If she had gone ballistic at *Genesis*, she went positively nuclear when *Morbius* was broadcast. And the offending scene? Funnily enough, it was the sight of Morbius's brain in a bell jar.

I shouldn't be too critical of her. Actually I remember Philip Hinchcliffe agonising over whether we should show that shot. To this day he still isn't sure if he should have put it in or not. Maybe it was a tad gruesome for a tea-time audience and yet, considering almost every episode has the destruction of the human or some other race at its heart, one piece of anatomy does seem rather tame to cause so much fuss.

* * *

After what was largely a cost-cutting exercise on *Morbius*, the series finale for Season Thirteen looked set to pull out all the stops. We would go out with a bang on *Hand of Fear*.

Or so we thought.

It was pretty late in the day when Philip and Robert decided the scripts were not in the right state for filming and an emergency replacement called *The Seeds of Doom* was hurriedly commissioned instead. It was a big gamble. In fact we were halfway through *Morbius* before the scripts began to trickle in. At least they were by Robert Banks Stewart – you knew it would be a good show with his name at the top of the page. Not only had his *Terror of the Zygons* been one of the better stories but he also had a pedigree, having worked on *The Sweeney*, *Callan* and various other successful series. He would later create *Shoestring* and *Bergerac*. Even more importantly, picking up the directorial gauntlet was one of my favourites, dear old Dougie Camfield. If anyone could make this rush job work, it was him.

Plotwise, an expedition in Antarctica discovers two alien pods. One takes over the base before it's destroyed. The other is taken back to England by a Bond-style villain, Harrison Chase, to add to his 'green cathedral' – a private collection of flora. There it converts a character called Keeler into a Krynoid (an alien plant creature), which grows to twice the size of a stately home.

This was a great one to film although very exhausting. There was lots of running, an unprecedented amount of shoots spilling over time and more location work than ever, even for a six-parter. In a first, as far as I know, we were allowed to have a few rehearsal days at the Acton Hilton before our initial outdoor shoot. With the later scripts arriving barely half a week before we started, it seemed the only way Dougie was going to make sense of anything.

On the plus side, at least we for once filmed in some picturesque settings. It wasn't exactly the South Pole, but luxurious private gardens in Dorset in November have their charm. Athelhampton House was owned by a Tory MP, Robert Cooke: apparently when the house is destroyed at the end of the programme he received letters of consolation from friends. He must have been used to it by then. The same house was demolished by a giant Dougal in The Goodies' 1975 Christmas Special.

We headed down to Athelhampton for filming in late October. I really think that early run-through paid dividends. The cast had only been in place a week or so and bearing in mind the Dorset shots don't really come into play until Episode 3, we all needed to get to grips with our characters. The results speak for themselves. We certainly managed to bring areas of the script to life. For example, there's a tense scene where Tom and I are captured and Tom flipped the usual villain-speak on its head: 'Get our hands up!' he yelled. 'That's right, grab us – we're very dangerous!'

After the response we got in Blackpool, I think Tom had a clearer sense of his audience and what they expected of him. I remember going through the same thing. You just have that moment of clarity where you realise, *I know this character better than this week's rent-a-writer or director-for-hire. I'm the one who plays him or her all the time.* There's a little nod to Tom's character in Episode 1 when the Doctor says he can leave immediately for the South Pole because he has his toothbrush – Tom was quite famous on set for carrying his toothbrush around with him. As an actor, you never know where you're going to end up sleeping at night!

We had some memorable scenes together. Being lowered down a wall was fun. Darting around the undergrowth is always exciting, and, of course, being confronted by the Krynoid in darkness was breathtaking. Recording so late in the year, darkness fell by 4.30 p.m. so we managed to film all the night scenes during 'day shoots'. Still, dark is dark – it doesn't matter what time it is!

Seeds of Doom was such a great story and I think it got the quality of actors it merited. Tony Beckley, who played the villain Harrison Chase, was so prim and perfect, not to mention sinister with his black gloves and smart suits. You could tell Robert Banks Stewart had written for *The Avengers* – Chase was just the sort of megalo - maniacal millionaire that Steed used to come up against all the time. (Tony has been in so many things but I think most people will remember him as Camp Freddie in *The Italian Job*.)

John Challis is another household face, if not name. There'll be barely a person in England who doesn't know him as Boycie from

Only Fools and Horses. To this day, if Tom Baker and I see him around town or at the BBC, we still say, 'Hello, Scorbes!' after his character, Scorby. John was really good in it, and so convincing as a hitman. There was a great scene in the laboratory where everything gets blown up and glass shatters everywhere. Scorbes and I are on the floor for most of it and we had a whale of a time. There's not much you can do when you've got things exploding all around you, so we simply had to cower and react a bit. That was a fun scene to do, though, especially because John is such a giggler. Nothing like his *Fools and Horses* character, you'll be pleased to hear!

You tend to flag by the end of a week away from home. Not this time. When we piled back to London for studio rehearsals there was such a bubbly atmosphere on the coach you'd have thought we were just setting off. Acton rehearsals seemed particularly inspiring as well, and Tom and I came up with a few nice line adds that pepped things up a bit. When Tom is told, at gunpoint, to turn around, I don't think anyone expected him to do a full 360-degree pirouette. How John kept a straight face in recording, I don't know. Sometimes just knowing when to leave lines out keeps a scene on the rails. There are quite a few lines that you can convey in a gesture or a look. When you live and breathe the character, you don't always need words.

Introducing us all to Chase, Tom decided unilaterally that Sarah was 'my best friend' – completely unexpected, but it gave the scene a jab of emotion. During our escape from the killer chauffeur I ad-libbed, 'Over here, cloth-eyes!' It seemed a very 'Sarah' thing to say. Another example is a scene at the Antarctic base, where the script said I had to walk along the corridor and close the external door (after the Krynoid's escape, although we didn't know that yet). *Well, that's going to be the most boring scene ever, isn't it?* I thought.

So I said, 'Dougie, what if Sarah's carrying something? Then at least I can shove it shut with my bum?'

'That's my girl!' he laughed.

So that's what we did. It's not brilliant, nobody really notices, but it adds a splash of colour to the script.

As it was a six-parter, there were three studio blocks and three pairs of filming days. Pretty standard stuff, although this was squeezed a bit because we had to pay back the rehearsal time from the start of production. You'd be amazed at how much these programmes are decided by balance sheet rather than plot.

It was budget, of course, that kept a limit on the number of retakes, although when you're working with snow machines, you have to expect the odd hitch. One scene had to be redone when there wasn't enough snow for the so-called 'blizzard'. Another was stopped when we were literally deluged in the stuff. These things happen. I remember opening a door at Chase's house when we were being attacked by the Krynoid – a giant plant monster that won't stop growing – and the trees that were meant to be blocking my exit were nowhere to be seen. 'OK, let's try that again . . .'

As I said, these things happen, but I was really proud when someone told me that I'd made the fewest mistakes of anyone on the entire shoot! I think they only had to stop once for something that was my fault. I don't know who was keeping tally of these things or why – maybe it would come out of your fee if you caused too much trouble? That's a scary thought. Of course, it would have been two stops if we'd noticed at the time how I attacked the Krynoid's tendril with an axe – hitting it with the blunt side!

Rather unusually, Dougie had arranged a further location shoot to take place during the studio block, but we had to squeeze it into a weekend. So, on Saturday, 6 December, we boarded the bus and headed out for deepest Antarctica – or Reigate, as it actually was. There was a really great atmosphere on the coach – it was extremely jolly, like an old-fashioned charabanc day out. I happened to be sitting next to Tom and as it neared five o'clock, I pointed out this would be the first episode of *Doctor Who* I'd appeared in that I wouldn't see broadcast. How would I be able to discuss it afterwards with Dad?

'Hmm,' said Tom. 'That's a shame, isn't it?' The glint in his eye told me he was already hatching something.

'You know, Elisabeth,' he said as we drove down one Surrey street, 'we could probably knock on any of these houses and ask to watch their television.'

I laughed. He was probably right, but I didn't expect him to try and prove it.

Suddenly he leapt up and staggered down the aisle towards the driver. The next thing I knew, the coach had pulled over and half a dozen of us were marching up to a random front door.

'Are you sure about this, Tom?' I giggled.

'Oh yes,' he said, his face alive with mischief.

Then he rang the bell and we waited. To this day I will never forget the look on the woman's face who answered.

'Hello, my dear,' said Tom in his most charming voice, 'I'm the Doctor and this is Sarah. We wondered if we might be able to watch ourselves on your television tonight?'

'Oh, come in, Doctor!'

And so we did. Me, Tom, John and a couple of others squeezed into a complete stranger's living room and enjoyed the third episode of *The Android Invasion*. Absolutely hysterical then and mind-boggling now – wonderful, wonderful Tom!

* * *

We were in Surrey to film the Antarctic scenes in – you guessed it – a quarry. The owners were very excited to have us there. They had all their sand pushed up into realistic snow formations by the time we arrived and had even applied the snow effect over the top.

I don't think it's ever explained why we hadn't originally flown to the South Pole in the TARDIS, but that's where we end up by the serial's final scene. I don't know if the TARDIS was offended we hadn't used her, but we went inside, closed the door – and the bloody roof fell down! Lucky I'm so much shorter than Tom – I think he caught the brunt of it. It gave me a shock, though. Funnily enough, it was only on *Android* that the Doctor had said she was due her 300-year service.

The odd time machine malfunction aside I can honestly report that the whole *Seeds of Doom* experience was a joy from start to finish. It sounds like nostalgia but it's true. If I genuinely had a TARDIS, I don't think I would have changed a thing. I really did have a simply marvellous time.

So why did I find myself knocking on Philip's door and saying, 'I'm sorry, Philip, but I've had enough. It's time for me to go'?

Chapter Eleven

Eldrad Must Live!

WORK THIS one out. I'd never been happier on *Doctor Who* – Tom was amazing, the show was reaching audience heights not enjoyed since the 60s; there was a real buzz about it, people were even recognising me on the street . . .

But it was time to go.

Mentally I'd opened the door back on Dartmoor on *The Sontaran Experiment*. After that it was only ever a case of when I would walk through it.

Of course, it was exactly because we were doing so well that the decision was so easy. What's that old comedians' mantra? *Leave 'em wanting more.*

The Seeds of Doom had seen the last appearance of UNIT – at least in the 70s. That was a conscious decision. Robert Holmes and Philip Hinchcliffe had been keen to phase out a lot of the older ties – Nick Courtney, John Levene and even Ian Marter had all been given the chop. There was even talk of a TARDIS redesign after it had collapsed on us in Surrey. That only left one remaining link with the past.

In any walk of life you want to jump before you're pushed. There was no hint from Philip that he was thinking along these lines but I thought it was only a matter of time: *He's the new boss, he wants to stamp his mark.* And the moment I broke the news to him my suspicions were confirmed.

Yes, Philip looked surprised, shocked even. Then he said, 'OK, Lis, if that's what you want.'

The moment the words left his lips I knew I'd been right. If Philip had begged me to stay, maybe I could have been persuaded. But he hadn't and that told me everything I needed to know. *I've actually helped you out by saying it first, haven't I?* I thought. Maybe he didn't want to be the person who killed Sarah Jane.

Actually, there was talk of killing her off but I didn't want that – I don't think it's fair on kids who've grown up with a character to see her die. It's bad enough seeing the Doctor disappear every few years, but at least he regenerates. Even worse, though, I really didn't want to see Sarah married off; that would have undone all the 'strong woman' messages we'd delivered over the years. I don't think it would have been respectful to Barry Letts' legacy, either.

Rushing into a hasty exit during *Seeds of Doom* would have been equally disrespectful, however.

'Stay for a little while and we'll give you a proper send-off,' Philip suggested.

That sounded fair. And in any case, rumour had it the next serial might even be shot in Italy.

* * *

On 19 March 1976 I signed up for eight more episodes of *Doctor Who*. Eight more! Then I was off. Tom was the perfect pro. He's an actor, he knows the score. It's not like other jobs – people come and go all the time. Even so, 'I'll miss you, Elisabeth,' he boomed, and we had a hug. Then it was down to business as usual.

Actually, that's not strictly true. The more Tom thought about it, the less happy he got. The next day he said, 'Christ, why have you got to leave? They'll get me some bloody girl with a stupid name like Jasemine or Jessonquin, something I can't pronounce!' (In the end, despite Tom campaigning for no new companion, 'because no one could replace Sarah', they brought in Louise Jameson as Leela.)

I don't know if the BBC were trying to squeeze in as much as they could before I left, but before we began filming on the new series a couple of other jobs were passed our way. At the end of

April we found ourselves in a BBC radio studio as the Doctor and Sarah contributing to an episode of the schools programme *Exploration Earth* called *The Time Machine*. Who better, I suppose, to talk about that? More excitingly, we also recorded a record – an actual LP! It was called *Doctor Who and the Pescatons* and I suppose it was the precursor of the audio books and those 'Big Finish' plays. Although the novels had always been popular, we had no idea back then how big a business that side of things would become. Still, it's nice to be in at the beginning.

Then it was finally time to start the day job.

It was Philip's idea to set the new serial in Renaissance Italy, Robert's idea to commission an expert on the subject (Louis Marks) and director Rodney Bennett's idea to film the whole thing on location in Tuscany. Guess which one of those three didn't get their way?

Obviously if you can't get the rolling Tuscan hills, the next best thing is Wales – specifically, Portmeirion. Actually, this wasn't so random a choice as it could have been: it was already famous as the setting for *The Prisoner*. It's a vast estate of Mediterranean-style buildings designed by Sir Bertram Clough Williams-Ellis, so perfect for capturing a hint of Italy. We actually shot in a different part of town to Patrick McGoohan's lot (*The Prisoner* looked extremely barren by comparison). Our location was meant to look very verdant and lush, rich and Italian. And it did, it really did.

There's a lot to be said for living in a mock Italian village, too. I was given a charming room in the hotel, full of character, and as soon as we arrived we had tea and cakes. It was really beautiful and so welcoming. There were lots of outbuildings on site as well, where people could stay. We were there for four nights and I think we had parties on every one.

When we turned up in Wales at the beginning of May, I couldn't help smiling at the new TARDIS. I'd been right – if they could change that, they certainly wouldn't have thought twice about losing me. It transpired, however, that the changes had gone too far. The trusty old police box was actually painted the wrong shade of blue and had to be re-sprayed – at least the roof stayed on this time!

It wasn't just the outside that had been tinkered with, though. There was even a new TARDIS control room waiting when we got back to the studio. To explain this there's a nice scene where Tom and I wander through the TARDIS and find the old console. We all just assume the old girl is infinitely huge inside so it's nice occasionally to give viewers a glimpse. And we also get to see the Doctor's boot room, I think, and of course in Matt Smith's first episode the library falls into the swimming pool. I might have stayed longer if I'd discovered that room!

Usually we only had a handful of extras and perhaps one stuntman on each serial but for *The Masque of Mandragora* (as it was eventually called after a host of earlier names), we had the full retinue. As usual, Terry Walsh led the team and then we had Max Faulkner and Stuart Fell – such an apt name for a stuntman. Terry did his usual job of doubling for Tom, but Stuart got another part: as the entertainer. I knew those circus skills would come in useful one day. But the reason we needed everybody this time was the horses. Sixteenth-century Europe bolted around on four legs – and therefore, so did we. We'd never had horses before and God, were they huge! I think it was the first time the stunt team and extras outnumbered the cast.

It was funny being there and everyone knowing I'd decided to leave. I remember one of the crew – I won't name him – said, 'Have you got anything else lined up?'

'No. Nothing.'

'Oh,' he said. 'You're very brave.'

I didn't get that attitude. 'Well, no, you know when it's time to go. You know when the time is right. You can't stick around just for the money, no one should do that,' I told him.

I could see we'd have to agree to differ on that one.

Back in London again we had a fortnight to prepare for the first studio session. Before that, however, my life was about to go under the spotlight.

The BBC were announcing my departure.

I don't know what governs the timing of these things. All I do know is that I wasn't expecting one iota of the furore it created. Phone calls, and not just from Mum and Dad, bombarded the flat (I remember Mum being very concerned about my future income: 'Oh, Elisabeth, you're not leaving, are you? Dad and I are very worried.') Strangers stopped me in the street to ask if it was true. And, most bizarre of all, the *Daily Mail* put me on their front page. Their *front page*! When Tom was announced as the Doctor he made page one of the London *Evening Standard* – I'd gone national. I even got an invite to appear on *Nationwide*, the country's daily evening news programme. It was absolutely mind-blowing.

I remember being at home before the press release went out. I was washing my hair when Brian called out, 'There's someone from the press at the door. They want to know if you're leaving.'

'I'm washing my hair, tell him to go away!' I said.

I honestly can't remember if I discussed my decision with Brian beforehand, but obviously he had heard me moaning about the show for the usual reasons for ages. He was terribly supportive – the regular income didn't matter at all, that's not what we were in acting for. We were always quite vagabond-like, moving from place to place, job to job. This was just the next step on the stones.

* * *

By the time we knuckled down to studio work on 23 May I was still a bit shell-shocked by all the attention. All I'd said was 'I'm quitting a TV show' – I was just an actress, after all. Apparently other people didn't see it so simply. Press interest was nothing like it would be today but it was still massive. Who, when, why, what? I had every conceivable question thrown at me. My agent was handling more interview enquiries than he knew what to do with. After a while of being asked the same questions, of course, you start to trot out the same rehearsed responses. For example, I remember more than once being asked what advice I'd give my successor. Remembering the scene in *The Seeds of Doom* where I was tied up and thrown into a deadly threshing machine, I joked, 'It will help if they like bondage.' That, of course, won me even more publicity. Apparently children's TV stars shouldn't talk like that.

Mandragora wrapped for me at the start of June. It had been fun. All I could think of, though, was, *Four episodes down, four more to go . . .*

* * *

The Hand of Fear, my last story, had originally been intended as the closer to Season Thirteen. But by running late and moving to the second serial of Season Fourteen it had lost two episodes. That didn't bother me – all I cared about was getting to the end.

This is the home straight, nearly there.

When I think back to how Jon soon regretted his resignation, I realise I was the opposite. I'd given as much as I could to the show; that was the best I could do. If I'd stayed, there was always the risk that it would have gone downhill. It was so exhilarating to leave on a high. Not to think, *Oh, it's not as good as it was*. It was empowering, actually. I felt in control – and you can't always say that in this profession.

Unusually, the first scenes we filmed were actually the first ones broadcast. And like a knowing nod to all the time I'd spent in one during my time on *Who*, they were set in a quarry – this time in Cromhall, Gloucestershire. From the moment I arrived to start filming, I was already aware the script asked for me to be buried under rubble. Now, depending on who the director is, this might be interpreted in a number of ways. Unfortunately for me, our director was the blood-thirsty Lennie Mayne.

And he fancied the literal interpretation.

It was quite a big deal when they blew the rocks up – it doesn't matter how often you see them, dynamite and explosives always catch the eye. But then yours truly had to be buried underneath. Lennie was all for keeping me down there for as long as possible so he could get the perfect shot. Luckily for me, our First on that one was Marion McDougall. She'd been on *Spiders*, *Ark*, *The Sontaran*

Experiment and *Android* as well. If you had Marion as your First, you knew it would be a good day at the office.

I had to lie on the ground and when Lennie called 'Action!' the rocks started to fall on top of me. Literally. They weren't huge, they weren't going to crush me to death. But it was terrifying and I felt every single one hit my body. I desperately covered my head with my hands for protection but even though I could stop the rocks hitting my face I couldn't do anything about the dust. I could feel it coating my lungs with every breath. I'd never known claustrophobia before but another minute and I would have, I'm convinced. I remember thinking, *You'd better get the shot, Lennie, because there won't be a second take*.

I'd been in there for God knows how long when I heard Marion say, 'Lennie, I think Lis should come out now.'

'What's that?' he asked, completely distracted by his camera angles. 'Nah, nah, don't you worry, Mother's all right in there, she's fine! Tell her to relax, we'll just do one more.'

'No,' Marion replied, 'I'm getting her out now, Lennie! Getting her out!'

They were a perfect match – Marion would look after you really well while Lennie was such fun. I still see Marion sometimes, always a pleasure to catch up with her. Unfortunately, Lennie died in quite tragic circumstances not long after we wrapped. He loved sailing and one day took his boat out in the fog and never came home. They found the boat but not Lennie – I think he was washed overboard. It's a tragic, terrible waste of life and my heart went out to Pidge and their two daughters.

It was only Tom and me at the quarry but the full complement had arrived by the time we made it to Oldbury-on-Severn, just up the road, a few days later. No quarries this time – just a bloody great nuclear power station. Sometimes you look at these scripts and think, *Well, it says we use it, but obviously it will all be in a studio. Think again, Sladen*.

Oldbury Power Station had been operational for nine years by the time we arrived. As far as I was concerned, it was just another location. You get driven somewhere, deliver your lines and go home; that was as complicated as I liked things to get. This one was just the same. It was only afterwards that I thought about how we were swept down with Geiger counters on the way out every day as a precaution. It sounds naïve but I had no idea that place was radioactive. What if one of the girls had been pregnant, for God's sake? I wouldn't have gone in if I'd known but we didn't have a clue. I just trolled onto the coach as usual, asking no questions, head in the clouds, la la la. Do the job, back to the hotel for a drink and a laugh afterwards.

I heard later that we got Oldbury because *Hand of Fear*'s writers, Bob Baker and Dave Martin, live nearby. They kept that quiet, the buggers! It would have been nice to pop in for a cup of tea.

One of the thrills of boarding the location bus, with your clothes case in hand, was never quite knowing who you'd find on there. For *The Hand of Fear* I was delighted to see Rex Robinson, who'd been Gebek in *Peladon*. Rex was never short of an anecdote or a kind word. Mr Versatile, Roy Skelton, was on board as well, unrecognisable as usual as King Rokon. Roy was always such fun on set – I don't know why they don't use him now. His voices just flow from him, without gizmos – and it wasn't only monsters. Sadie used to love the kids' show *Rainbow* and of course Roy would do the voices of Zippy *and* George. When they did Christmas shows with the cast's Rod, Jane and Freddie, she got to meet Zippy and still has all sorts of things signed by him.

And then there was brilliant Glyn Houston – he really enjoyed himself. If I'm honest, I don't think *Hand of Fear* was particularly well put together. In places it felt like a draft rather than a polished final script. It probably wasn't the best episode to go out on because there were one or two boring scenes, but Glyn really enlivened them. He was exceptional value.

I have to take some of the blame for the pace of the thing. This was the second serial, after *Android*, where I wasn't playing myself so you'd think I might have been used to it by then. For those who haven't seen it, the explosion at the quarry unearths the fossilised hand of Eldrad, a criminal from millennia past. Sarah's touch reignites its life and as a result, she is possessed by Eldrad. I think I should have played those scenes much more quickly; I remember toying around with it and no one said to do it differently so that's the direction I took. I don't think I'd do it that way again. That whole performance is far from one of my favourites. It's just so slow, especially those lines, 'Eldrad must live! Eldrad must live!' There were a dozen ways to take it and unfortunately I opted for the wrong one.

Despite my personal reservations, it seems to be a very popular serial. Believe it or not, the single most requested line I'm asked to quote for fans is 'Eldrad must live!'. Bizarre, isn't it? Of all the thousands of words Sarah must have said. I remember being at a convention in LA, in the lift on the way up to my room, and this guy got in. He must have been from the convention because it was clear he was nearly fainting with excitement behind me. I couldn't ignore it, so I turned round and gave him a smile.

'Please,' he begged me, 'please just say "Eldrad must live!" I won't get out until you say it.'

Absolutely true!

So I said it – in that ridiculous slow-mo delivery – and he got out at the next floor, the happiest man in California.

Apart from the exposure to radioactivity, the power station proved a challenging location in other ways. There were so many platforms and ladders running all over the place that it would have been remiss not to incorporate them, but during the final chase scene I thought my legs were going to drop off. I was going up and down, up and down this bloody metal ladder, literally quivering with exhaustion by the end of it. There was a rail all the way up but I wasn't allowed to fall on it for help and it was really steep. The next day I could barely walk, my quads were screaming in agony. You'd just make it to the top then you'd hear bloody Lennie, 'Lis, could you do it again but this time . . .' It was really horrendous.

At least they could see me coming. I still get letters today about my outfit for *The Hand of Fear* – my 'Andy Pandy' costume as I call Sarah's red top, striped dungarees and little cap.

I remember saying to our costume girl, Barbie Lane, 'Do you know what? It's the end of the road, she could wear anything. Let's just go to town on it.'

There was a shop in Kensington High Street called Bus Stop, quite small but very trendy at the time. Barbie bought these red-and-white pantaloons and I said, 'Brilliant, but how can we make them our own?' So we sewed stars onto the front, just to make them different from the rest on the hangers.

And we didn't stop there. We got this coat and tied a bandana around me. Then we found a top and socks plus a hat to match. It was pretty extraordinary but I thought, *Why not? It's Sarah's last stand. I'm going to go for gold in this episode.* Rationally, she's been with the Doctor for so long, seen so many unimaginable sights, that she's totally lost it as far as Earth clothes are concerned; that's what the Doctor's done to her. After all, space travel has very many strange effects on the human brain and form.

I wanted to underline the transformation of a Doctor's companion. By then I was no longer the Sarah Jane with the suit and the shoulder bag who had gone in – I wasn't even the Sarah Jane who'd worn that body-warmer in *Morbius*! I had experienced so much, I'd evolved, and that was reflected in my clothes.

After a busy few days we headed for our third outdoor location, a park in Thornbury. This was to be a tricky one, probably the trickiest of them all. There weren't any stunts or vast cast ensembles to rehearse with; nobody had to wear an alien costume or act against a blue screen. All of those things would have been preferable to this. Because this was the day I filmed my goodbye.

I was content that Sarah wasn't being married or killed off – the same thing, some might think. Either of those would have seemed too neat. Sarah was never neat – she was a maverick, I always thought. As close to the Doctor in her unpredictability as any human could be. So she wasn't about to go out in a blaze of laser fire or an exploding castle: she would simply open the TARDIS door and walk away.

But how to make that believable?

When I received the script, I was appalled. It was as if the writers had never watched Sarah and the Doctor before.

She can't bow out like this, it's not right, I thought.

In their defence, Bob Baker and Dave Martin, the writers, had decided the moment was too big for them so they'd simply sketched an outline and Robert had fleshed it out. But I didn't realise this at first – I just saw a clunky, monosyllabic exchange that made me see red. I was so upset that I scrawled rude words all over it. Childish, I know, but when I picked up that pen the emotion just gushed out. Maybe I was more discombobulated about my imminent departure than I was ready to admit.

Fortunately, Philip Hinchcliffe and Robert Holmes agreed.

'There are only two people who know how the Doctor and Sarah would handle this,' they said to me and Tom, 'and it's you.'

I didn't see that coming, but what an honour. And they were absolutely right: Tom and I were the keepers of these precious characters. We lived them every day, every week for nine months or more each year.

As I recall, the plot get-out Robert had come up with was that the Doctor had been summoned back to Gallifrey – home planet of the Time Lords, where no humans were allowed – so he would be forced to drop Sarah off in Croydon. That was fine. Even at the end of *The Seeds of Doom*, after all, Sarah had been angling to get home. She was after a breather from the action as well – but how to make it real?

Tom and I put a lot of thought into this. It was terribly liberating. 'What about . . . ?'

'No, he wouldn't do that. But what about . . . ?'

'No, she'd run a mile!'

It went on like that all afternoon. And then we realised what was missing . . .

The cameras rolled and we delivered the most heartfelt lines of our careers. It was two whole pages – a lot bearing in mind we filmed about eight or nine a day normally.

So what did we come up with in the end? It was quite straight-forward, actually.

Sarah said, 'Don't forget me.'

'Oh, Sarah, don't you forget *me*,' the Doctor replied.

Then: 'Until we meet again,' from him and Sarah agrees, but too emotional to speak, she just hmm-hmms. Then she scoops up her possessions – including a tennis racquet and that yellow Mac – tells a Labrador 'He blew it!' when she realises it's not Croydon and skips off, whistling 'Daddy Wouldn't Buy Me a Bow Wow'.

The dog was a last-minute addition. Maybe Lennie was looking for something for his wife to do, because Pidge was the hound-handler. You can read these things in so many ways. Some fans think the 'Bow Wow' song was put in to prepare us for K-9 – it doesn't matter that the Fourth Doctor's robotic dog hadn't even been invented yet.

Some people look for connections everywhere. I'm the other extreme. Shamefully, years later, I would perform a touching tribute to Sarah's final scene with David Tennant – and not even realise . . .

Despite the pressure on Tom and me to complete such an impassioned scene, it went very smoothly. In fact, it was great to do. Sometimes you're in a swirl, like a wave, and you just do it and it works. There's nothing I'd change – we did what we set out to.

Disappointed as I was with the overall story, I was pretty proud of my exit so I kept the script with those passages and all my rude messages. Apart from the odd costume or accessory it's the only thing I did hang onto from my *Who* days. (I know what you're thinking – and I'm sorry!) Years later, it would go to a very deserving home . . .

* * *

Recording my farewell scene in the opening week of shooting got it neatly out of the way. Going into the studio sessions after that, the pressure was off. Other problems, however, presented themselves.

All sorts of insects come out in summer, don't they, and one day we were absolutely tormented by this one bluebottle. You don't realise how loud those creatures are until you're in a silent studio, waiting to deliver your lines, and suddenly you hear this buzzing somewhere up near the lights. How can something so tiny cause so much chaos? Take after take had to be halted every time the noise started up again. There's one scene that we had to keep where you can actually see the fly walking, cool as you like, across Glyn's brow!

It turned out, Glyn got off lightly. I was repeating 'Eldrad must live!' for the hundredth time when I felt this tickle in my throat. I had to cough – and the bloody fly shot out! Still, it stopped it buzzing . . .

When my last recorded scene came I was really happy with it. Not happy with my performance or the writing or anything like that; it's just we had such fun doing it. That's how I wanted to remember *Who*.

Not everyone saw the joke, however.

We were filming a scene set on the planet Kastria. Tom and I had to climb up this craggy surface. He was carrying Eldrad, played by Judith Paris, who was covered in an unwieldy rock costume. All I had to do was get myself up, but I slipped.

I don't know if it was the tension releasing, but as soon as my foot slid from under me I couldn't help laughing. Then Tom slipped and we both started giggling.

'OK, quiet everyone, we're going again.'

So we did it again – and slipped again. Poor old Judith, she was being thrown around like a sack of potatoes and I think she got pretty pissed off.

'Look, can we just do this so I can go and have a fag?'

But we just kept on slipping and that made us laugh even more. You know when you don't know what you're laughing at but you can't stop? That was us.

Meanwhile Marion was losing her patience and Lennie was tearing his hair out.

'Look, would you stop messing about!'

But we couldn't help it. It was quite uncontrollable. And, you know what? I'm glad we couldn't. If I have to remember anything of my time on *Who*, it would be just having a blast with Tom. Me and him, Doctor and companion – us against the universe.

* * *

At least my farewell came at the end of recording. (David Tennant's took place a while before he left Cardiff.) We all piled down to the Kensington Hilton to let our hair down and party. Brian was there, and so many faces from the last few years. Usually there's a whipround when someone leaves, so I'd been asked if I wanted anything in particular. 'Oh, yes,' I said. 'I'd love some silver picture frames to put people's pictures in.' Just as well, because I posed for so many photos that night – I didn't want to forget anyone. I remember a little boy turning up and taking loads of snaps as well. Years later he sent them to me on a disc. He's not so little any more!

The frames were just what I wanted but there was something quite special still to come. George Gallaccio handed me a small box and said, 'It's in case you ever want to come back.'

Inside was a key to the TARDIS!

'Oh, George, that's so sweet.'

'Everyone should have access to the TARDIS, Lis.'

After the Hilton the party carried on at Tom's house. He was with gorgeous Marianne Ford at the time – they were such a brilliant couple. Whenever we had to go to functions for the BBC he liked her to come along and look after him. He really loved that. So, I'd met her many times, although this was the first time I'd ever seen their house. When we arrived I gasped. The garden was absolutely festooned with fairy lights. It was quite magical.

'What do you think?' Tom asked proudly.

I said, 'Tom, it's beautiful. Do you always have these lights on?'

'Of course I bloody don't,' he scowled. 'I put them up for you!'

* * *

So that was that. Three years, eighteen serials, eighty half-hour episodes. Without trying, I'd accidentally become the longest-serving companion – just pipping Katy's record. (I think Frazer Hines had appeared in more episodes, but over a shorter period.) These stats matter to some people but I was oblivious. The only statistic I cared about was the number of empty days that lay ahead of me.

Tangiers, here I come . . .

Chapter Twelve

Bippetyboo, Bippetyboo

WAKING UP that first day as a free woman was sensational. Not because I was released from the shackles of a three-year job; it was just amazing to have the whole day ahead of me and absolutely no plans. There were no calls for costume fittings; no one phoning to say a new script was in the post – I had nothing to learn and nowhere to be.

Absolute bliss.

Once I'd been on *Nationwide* and the *Daily Mail* had plastered me across their cover – and Clive James wrote in the *Observer* that I was one of the 'five best things' on television! – offers of work really did start to flood in. Some of them had nice pay cheques attached as well; they put the BBC to shame. Nothing really leapt out at me, though. Most were looking for 'another Sarah Jane Smith'. Some of them were established sci-fi projects, others were launches. The one thing they had in common, though, was that they didn't float my boat. *I've done Sarah Jane, I've put her to bed*, I thought.

You hear people say they need to put some distance between themselves and their past. Most don't mean it literally. But I did – I put two thousand miles between us.

Brian and I had been hankering for a holiday to Tangiers for what seemed like forever. Not only was it exotic and otherworldly to Europeans (especially back in 1976 when different cultures were still defined by geographical boundaries) – and not only would we enjoy weather Brits can only dream of, there was another factor, even more important: it was accessible by road. Post-Toronto, that was important.

I know bus journeys are anathema to some people but Brian and I love them. You get a completely different view of the world. It's also cheap and you're pitched in close proximity to your partner for hours at a time. When you lead the lifestyles we do, that chance to be with one another is priceless.

* * *

No one would leave something as powerful as *Who* today without an exit plan. You'd have offers lined up. Before David Tennant said goodbye to me on Bannerman Road for the final time, his forthcoming schedule was packed. But did I have a plan? Of course not, no strategy! No twelve-step programme to world domination, which is pathetic, I admit. Career suicide, really. My agent has to take a share of that blame as well – sorry, Todd! He should have been steering me a bit more. I wouldn't have appreciated it at the time, but you might have thought he'd be shaking me to accept some of those offers. After all, if you can't rely on an agent to exploit a situation, what's the world coming to?

But there you go. We can't go back, and if I had been a little bit more switched-on perhaps I wouldn't still be enjoying Sarah Jane so much now. So, as the song goes, no regrets – life's too short.

By the time we returned from Africa I was raring to go. *Right*, I thought, *what offers have we got?*

And that's how I ended up on a train to Liverpool.

Looking back it was almost certainly the wrong call. If I'd wanted to do theatre there were probably better roles from a 'career' perspective than *Mooney and His Caravans*. I only agreed because it was at the Playhouse and Brian was going to be in it as well. That was enough for me. I didn't think 'progression', I just thought, *That would be nice*.

In other words, it wasn't David Tennant's *Hamlet*. This certainly wasn't a 'vehicle' for me. If anything, I was hiding from my past.

But it was great to get back to my roots. Mum and Dad put us up, of course, and they were prouder than ever when there was a bit of interest from the *Liverpool Echo*, who ran a nice piece along the lines of 'Local Girl Makes Good'. You know the sort of thing. I think they were even more impressed when they heard about the queue of autograph hunters waiting outside the theatre for me each night.

And there were other bits of work in my other old stomping ground, Manchester. Brian and I recorded *A Bitter Almond* for BBC Radio's Afternoon Theatre segment over there. We also did *Post Mortem* for Thirty-Minute Theatre. They were both great parts but for me, the thrill was working once again with my husband.

Speaking of Brian, I have been asked how he felt being the less famous and, probably, less well-paid half of our relationship. I don't know if it ever bothered him that to the wider public I was doing better than he was for those three years – I never gave it a thought. I was probably bringing home more money than him during my *Who* years, but then he'd been the breadwinner all the time I was out of work and he was in the West End. And it's always been like that – you just pray one of you is working. Ideally both, ideally together, but one will do so long as someone is paying the bills. Remember, we had barely fifty pence between us when he bought my engagement ring in Manchester. It was always, 'Thank God one of us has got a job'.

It's true that Brian wasn't as recognisable in the street as I was – he's never been so readily associated with a single character or show. On the other hand, he never got the snide 'it's only kids' telly' comments that occasionally came my way. Yes, you knew you were popular; yes, you were in the *Radio Times* a lot, but even then, just looking at how they wrote about the show you weren't allowed to forget it was 'only a children's programme'. Even the BBC never let us forget.

More radio followed. *Laura and the Angel* and *The Hilton Boy* were both for BBC Radio. After *Mooney* at Liverpool we did *Saturday, Sunday, Monday* and *The Lion in Winter*. I have to say, I loved being back in rehearsals, working towards that opening night, learning the new play by day, performing the old one by night, and changing every three weeks. And knowing that no bugger was going to ask me to go on the book was an incredible release.

Before any of that, though, in October 1976 I had some unfinished business. The fourteenth season of *Doctor Who* – starring yours truly – exploded onto screens on 4 September and of course my swansong was just around the corner. Annoyingly I had to break off rehearsals in Liverpool and hightail it back to London for a round of promotional stunts. Contractual obligations, as they say. I managed to fit in quite a few interviews while I was down there. I'm glad my leaving wasn't a secret or it would have been horrible. Chris Eccleston must have been biting his tongue every time he was interviewed for his first series because his exit was kept secret for so long. David Tennant had the best idea, announcing it live at the Television Awards. He and Russell T Davies were so proud of pulling that one off without the press discovering it first.

My favourite event, I don't know why, was an appearance on *Multi-Coloured Swap Shop* on 2 October, the morning of *Hand of Fear*'s debut. I don't think Noel Edmonds showed himself to be the most informed *Who* fan but I had a ball. Catching up with Tom backstage and then sharing that sofa with him on-air was a genuine pleasure. Answering viewers' questions was always an honour, not a chore. And when you're not on a show anymore, you can view it from the outside. And, do you know what? I was bloody proud of what we'd achieved. Jon, Barry, Terry, Robert and Tom – I owed so much to so many. I was glad to have left but at the same time I was genuinely choked whenever I thought of *Who*'s contribution to television history. You knew it was special; even I could see that!

I managed to catch my *Mandragora* performances as they went out. By the time *The Hand of Fear* hit the screens, however, I was on stage in *Mooney*. Younger readers won't be able to comprehend this, but if you didn't catch a programme on broadcast, that was it. There were no video players, no Sky+ and certainly no YouTube or BBC iPlayer. So, while the nation was mourning my departure

– so I'm told – I was none the wiser. For all I knew, Lennie Mayne could have edited me out of all my favourite scenes.

So there I was, on stage at the Playhouse in a Saturday matinee on 23 October, knowing that the nation – well, a young proportion of it – was engrossed in my sorrowful farewell. I still spoke to my folks afterwards as usual, except this time I listened more intently to their comments. Was I any good? Did they like it? These things are more important when you don't catch it yourself.

I did see the show eventually. Do you know when? When the BBC released *The Hand of Fear* on VHS in the 90s.

It transpired that I was free to watch the debut of my successor in 1977 but – sorry about this – I didn't want to. Tom was *my* Doctor. What pleasure was there to be gained from seeing him with someone else? It would feel like watching my husband with another woman.

Bizarrely, before we set off on our African trek, Brian had been finishing up at the Orange Tree in Richmond. With time on my hands I went down to join him. Afterwards, I was sitting at the bar when this pretty young thing came up to me.

'Hello,' she said, 'You don't know me but my name is Louise.'

'Hello, Louise,' I said.

'And I'm going to be the new companion in *Doctor Who*.'

'Oh.' I was speechless. What were the odds of that meeting without a real-life TARDIS?

'So,' she continued, 'I wondered if you could give me any pointers. I mean, what's Tom like?'

We had a proper chat. I told her she was about to have the best years of her life. Well, I had, anyway.

* * *

In theatre you can be whoever you like. Audiences are very open-minded about casts, which is how I've played pensioners, teens, foreigners and sometimes even men. Television is a lot more restrictive. Producers see you doing well in one area and so they hire you to do the same thing again and again. I'd already turned down a lot of sci-fi offers but being viewed as a 'children's star' was harder to get away from. Perhaps if I'd been slightly cannier immediately my 'retirement' was announced I'd have had more choice. However, when the offer came a year later to present a show called *Merry-Go-Round* for BBC Schools, I said yes.

After all, at least I knew I could play the character!

Merry-Go-Round had actually started at the same time as *Doctor Who* and it would run for twenty years. It was essentially an educational resource for junior school teachers covering all sorts of things like science, history, geography and even the odd sex education programme. I said I'd be happy to present on any subject they threw at me.

And then they mentioned the helicopter!

The episode was called *The Fuel Fishers* and I'd have to whizz around different oil rigs. And how do you get to those? I came so close to pulling out when I heard about it but Brian and Todd kept saying helicopters were so much safer than aeroplanes – basically, anything to calm me down. But they hadn't been in *Planet of the Spiders*.

We were flying out to the Shetland Isles and from there to an operating rig. You don't need me to tell you that the weather in the Highlands in winter is not going to be great. Oblivious to the conditions, our director led us out to an airfield in the windiest, wettest conditions I could remember. Waiting for us was the largest helicopter I've ever seen in my life. It was a Sikorsky.

'Oh no,' I said, 'this thing will never get off the ground!'

The pilot laughed. 'Safer than cars, these things.'

Well, you would say that, wouldn't you? But I climbed on.

We took off with such a lurch I thought I'd left my stomach behind.

The director must have seen my face. 'It's not so bad is it?' he said cheerily.

Then the Sikorsky plummeted about a hundred feet in a second.

'He's just flying beneath the clouds,' my companion advised. 'It's safer nearer the water.'

There was a curtain between us and the pilot but I couldn't resist taking a peep through. Now, I'm no expert on flying, but watching that pilot stamp repeatedly on the floor, as though he were desperately willing the chopper back into the sky, didn't look textbook to me.

The director had noticed too. 'Perfectly normal,' he said quickly, but he wasn't smiling now.

Somehow we made it down into the middle of nowhere and went out to eat in the one available pub. I was still trying to warm up when the pilot wandered over, grinning from ear to ear.

'Well, that was a lucky escape,' he said.

'What do you mean?'

I wished I hadn't asked. There are three tanks of fuel on a Sikorsky and when one is empty, the second and third kick in; that's the theory. On our one the first tank had finished but there was a blockage in the second and third and the fuel couldn't get through. That's why he'd been stamping on the floor – he was trying to unblock it.

'Yeah,' the pilot admitted, 'I was actually preparing to land on the water!'

After that, I couldn't eat a thing. And I was still feeling sick when I heard this familiar voice.

'Hello, Lis. It's been a while.'

I stared at the man in front of me.

'Dave?'

I couldn't believe it. Dave Owen, my first boyfriend, was standing in front of me! We hadn't seen each other for fifteen years and there he was, in army gear. I always knew he'd join the forces – although what they were up to in that particular outpost I had no idea. Dave knew plenty about me, though, from interviews and newspapers. You never quite get used to strangers or people you haven't seen for ages having an endless supply of facts about your life. I always presume no one's reading anything I say!

The next morning we had to fly over to the actual oil rig. The Sikorsky was being checked over so we took another helicopter. If the other one had looked too big, this thing was so small it looked like it would be blown down by the first big gust. Somehow I was persuaded on and we made it out to the rig, safe and sound.

Or so I thought.

The moment I stepped out onto that platform in the middle of the North Sea the director announced, 'Congratulations, Lis. You are officially the first woman in history to set foot on one of these!'

I also discovered that according to old seafaring lore, it was considered bad luck if a woman boarded a vessel. I'm not one for superstitions but when I heard the helicopter we'd arrived in had somehow damaged its rotor on landing, I began to think there might be something in it. There was no way to fix it there, so we were stuck unless another one came out for us. When that chopper arrived, our bird was hogging the single landing spot so, for ten frightening minutes, our pilot had to take off with his damaged rotors and hover just long enough for the other one to put down and deliver the replacement parts. It was terrifying to watch.

Especially knowing that everyone on the rig was blaming me!

Despite their reservations, people were very kind. The food on the rig was delicious but, more importantly, I got a series of insightful interviews with some terrific characters. They took me right down to the bottom of the rig, which was even more nerve-wracking than being in the air. Every so often I get flashbacks of clinging to a post as the waves crashed around – and wonder how the hell they persuaded me!

It was such a release to just be myself for the cameras – even if you never quite do the 'real' you – and not to rehearse every last detail and learn pages of lines. Working without a script, using your wits, is very liberating. (Perhaps a little *too* liberating. I thought it hysterical to find myself talking to a man called Rex about shipping wrecks. I couldn't say his name enough. 'Now, Rex, can you tell me about these wrecks, Rex?' Very unprofessional!)

As soon as we were back on terra firma I declared, 'Right, I'm obviously jinxed. No more flying.' So, while everyone else flew down to the Scilly Isles for our next recording date, I took the sleeper train to Penzance and then a boat. The director was worried

I might run off so he sent someone with me! The train was rattling so much we didn't sleep a wink, so we both arrived a day late and miserable through lack of sleep. I'm sure they loved me!

* * *

It was while we were staying with my folks during the Playhouse run that I got quite the strangest message.

Mum had taken the call. 'Elisabeth,' she said, 'a man called Frank Kilbride wants to talk to you about landscape gardening, I think. He kept mentioning stepping stones.'

'OK . . .'

Gingerly I picked up the phone. I'd barely got 'hello' out before I was deluged by a breathy torrent of words in the thickest Yorkshire accent. I managed to pick the odd one out. Yep, he definitely said 'stepping stones', but it was nothing to do with gardening. Frank Kilbride was a producer – *Stepping Stones* was his programme for pre-schoolers.

'And I thought you would be perfect for it,' he said, 'with that lovely, warm personality.'

Now, this was before my *Merry-Go-Round* had aired. Somehow he'd decided I could front a children's show. I don't know if it was seeing me on *Swap Shop* or *Nationwide*, or if he was just taking a punt because I didn't appear to be working (out of telly, out of mind), but he was right – I was looking for something. And after a quick chat with him over at Yorkshire Television a few days later, I'd found it.

To say time was scarce on *Stepping Stones* was an understate-ment. The frenzied whirl of studio days at *Who* seemed positively luxurious by comparison. I don't think I'd received a single script before I boarded my train up to Leeds – and I was due to record the first of five episodes that afternoon!

It was chaotic but I had a good vibe about this project, right from the off. Frank was a sweetie and had sorted me out with a local landlady, May Brown, who ran a dear little guesthouse on the York Road opposite the Tadcaster Road racecourse. I had the best front room, bacon sandwiches when I got in, meals on a tray in my room if I wanted. Perfect.

Frank's mind was always whirring. It seemed like I'd barely arrived when I began receiving calls from the local press. At first I thought, *Wow, they really support their local programme-makers*. Then as soon as I did the interviews I realised they just wanted to know the inside scoop on a former *Who* girl. Bear in mind I was still amazed every time an autograph hunter popped up, I genuinely didn't think the media would still be interested in what I was up to a couple of years down the line. Luckily for *Stepping Stones*, Frank was cannier than that.

It says a lot for Frank's priorities that after coming up trumps in sorting me out with beautiful May and stirring up press interest, he then completely omitted to mention my co-star on the show.

I got to the studio for the first time and I heard a familiar voice.

'Hello, chuck, how are you? Are you going to join us?'

Keith Barron was already a highly respected actor at the time. For years, he'd worked solidly on serials and one-offs and also had a decent list of film credits to his name (and would pop up in *Who* during Peter Davison's era, a few years later). Quite why he'd chosen to present this show was unclear – maybe his agent was even less sharp than mine! – but I was suddenly glad that he had. From his opening 'Hello, chuck', I felt completely at home – but I still hadn't seen a word of script!

Somehow in two-and-a-half days we managed to film five episodes! Arrive in the morning, rehearse, record, lunch, then another rehearsal, another recording session. Bang, bang, bang! Then it was off to the bar for a drink and back to May Brown's. I liked my routine but Frank, typically, worried about me being alone.

'Come on, Lis,' he said, 'I'll take you back in my car to meet the family. We'll have a nice bit of Yorkshire ham.' So I'd meet his wife and children every time I went up and then he'd drive me back to York Road. Frank was such a chatterer and bundle of energy and so thoughtful that you felt like you were out on a jolly every night.

We had very little time in the studio but Frank made that fun as well. Always talking, always on the move, up and down those gantry steps all day . . . You couldn't go five minutes without him popping out to call encouragement or improvements, or just laughing. I think his energy must have been rubbed off on the First, because he had a nervous arm. You didn't know if he was flagging a horse down or telling you to start. His arm would be going nineteen to the dozen and Keith and I would be staring at each other: 'Was that a cue? Was *that* a cue?'

I had such fun working with Keith. On one of our first episodes we were kneeling down next to a table that had a toy train set on it. As the train chuffed round and round its track we had to sing: 'Bippetyboo, bippetyboo, I'm on a train, I'm off to loo.' Then 'zipperty zoo, zipperty zoo', and so on: it was simple but silly.

The First gave one of his funny cues, then I started singing, but all I heard from Keith was 'bippety – *whooooh*!' I looked round and he'd disappeared under the track!

Retakes were rare as hen's teeth so I had to carry on – even though I could see Keith's backside sticking out from under the table while he tried desperately to stay out of shot. I don't know how I got through it. By the time I finished I was laughing so hard the mascara was streaming down my face. Afterwards Keith said, 'Oh my God, Chucky, I'm so sorry – but as soon as you said "Bippetyboo" I thought, *What am I doing here? I can't do this any more!*'

He left shortly after that!

We did a good deal of filming outside the studio as well – nothing that required flying, thank goodness. I remember being sent to lots of farms and very quickly realised that I do not like the smell of animals. But there I was, week after week, standing in the middle of a goat herd or pig sty, saying, 'Look at these delightful creatures!' Frank decided we'd have a goat in the studio one week and of course it did the usual thing of making a mess. I thought I was going to gag. It's affected me for life. I used to take Sadie to farms when she was young and I'd have to say, 'You run through there and I'll meet you at the other end.'

Just like on *Merry-Go-Round*, there was no clothes budget so you had to wear your own things. That was OK for the first few weeks, but even when you're just putting different tops on with your jeans, you eventually start to run out. So I went to this old folks jumble sale and bought a horrendous bed jacket, which was the most incredible sickly pale green and pink, with a pink ribbon belt. I thought, *If I wear this, they'll have to get me some clothes*. So I did.

And they couldn't have been happier!

I must have done *Stepping Stones* for about two-and-a-half years (although the title changed at some point to *My World*) and – apart from the farmyard aromas – I adored every minute of it. A couple of days' work with delightful people every few weeks – what's not to love?

Looking back, though, was it a mistake to stay rooted in a kids' show for so long? Should I have been trying to do more 'serious' roles? After all, I'd just turned thirty – was I throwing my career away?

* * *

If I'd been worried about being perceived as a fluffy children's personality, two events made me grow up – fast.

The first was a happy one. Brian and I bought our first house. Strictly speaking, we bought our *only* house – because we're still there today! After looking far and wide we found a place round the corner from our flat in Ealing. When we pulled up outside I said to Brian, 'How on earth can we afford this?' Then we went inside and found out: it needed a lot of work but we just fell in love with it. It had the high ceilings and bay windows that I adore, so we bought it. Anyone who visited over the next few months was likely to find me doing a Spider-Man impression, bent double up a ladder painting, or scrubbing the ceilings and walls. I've always loved physical work in acting, but when it came to decorating I felt pain in muscles I never knew I had.

There was only so much we could do ourselves. When it came to walls being knocked down and RSJs fitted, we got the experts in. It would have been hellish to try and live there during that, so John Blackmore, Tony Colegate's assistant director at Manchester, offered us both a tour of Alan Ayckbourn's *Bedroom Farce*. We snatched at it.

Well, that was a mistake! Living in digs again was just horrendous – I would have preferred to take my chances under the dustsheets at home. The venues weren't much better. At the theatre in Middlesbrough we were told not to flush the loo backstage because it would reverberate around the auditorium. Opening night in Newcastle pretty much summed it all up. The guy playing Trevor was quite uptight, really bodily stiff, which I'd noticed when I had to swing him round in rehearsal. When we got to that part in the show, I grabbed his shoulder and heard this crack. I had dislocated his arm! He wore it in a sling for the rest of the tour. The only thing that kept us going was knowing our fees would go towards fixing up the house.

It was such a relief to finally get the place looking ship-shape but we couldn't celebrate because there was someone who was no longer around to see it. My mum had been ill since Christmas. She had been on heart tablets since I was about twenty, so any illnesses were potentially serious. I'd been popping up to Liverpool as often as I could, in between *Stepping Stones* and other bits. I kept saying to her, 'You look tired, what does your doctor say?' But she was a strong-willed woman – she wasn't going to slow down for anyone. She died of a heart-attack in March 1978. I was actually in Liverpool at the time but I'd gone out to visit cousins. When the call came I felt my world fall apart.

* * *

At times like that you really need your partner's support – that's why *Bedroom Farce* was so perfect; it meant Brian and I could be together. Then I had a small part in a telly thing called *Betzi*, which only involved a few days up in Norwich for Anglia. The cast was amazing – people like Roland Curram, Sheila Gish's husband – but the director had some funny ideas. When we got to the rehearsal room there were footprints all over the floor telling you where you should be and how you had to get there! I'm glad I didn't have a very big part – it's not at all easy to walk where someone else wants you to; it's like playing Twister.

I had more luck on my next telly. *Send in the Girls* – the story of a group of ambitious women in a high-pressured sales promotion team – was made by Granada, who had always been good to me. I auditioned for Ollie Horsburgh and won the lead part of Beverley. Then he said, 'Now, we need to find you a husband.' Guess who they hired?

I didn't even know Brian had been asked. Ollie had no idea of our relationship so it had nothing to do with that. In fact, he got himself into a terrible panic when he realised.

'Lis, are you OK with this? We had no idea – I'm not sure I can handle this!'

But I couldn't see what the problem was: I was delighted. It was also nice to have strangers think we made a good couple!

The close links didn't end there. Sadie's future godfather, Ray Lonnen, was in that one. Brian had known him longer than me, so we had lots of fun being back in Manchester together. And one of my idols, John Carson, was in it as well (I still find myself delivering lines in *The Sarah Jane Adventures* in a Carson style). He was amazingly influential on me – but on the day of the last dress rehearsal he did a wicked thing. There I was in full slap and frock when he said, 'Lis, you know my wife wrote this – and she doesn't think you're right for it.'

I could have hit him. Ollie was pleased, the producers were pleased. If his wife had a problem, she'd had months to voice it.

If this is what you have to put up with doing adult drama, then I'll take kids' telly any day! I thought.

My next 'grown-up' thing, a sitcom called *Take My Wife*, wasn't much fun either. Once again it was up in Manchester, where Brian happened to be working on something else. The director, a dour Scot called Gordon Flemyng, went up to him and said, 'I am giving your wife a hard time.'

'Thanks,' said Brian. 'I'll be looking forward to going home tonight!'

I loved Dougie Brown in it, also Joan Benham and Victor Spinetti. Victor was very funny. He rang me up afterwards and said, 'I am doing this story about D.W. Griffith the film director, and I know you adore Lillian Gish.'

'Yes,' I said, wondering where this was going.

'Can you sing?' he then asked.

'God,' I said, 'no, I can't!'

So he put the phone down. No goodbye – just hung up! I wonder what I missed out on . . .

* * *

If I'd been the sort of person to dwell on these things – and I certainly wasn't – I think I would have felt quite content with how the 1970s were ending for me. Consistent work in some high-profile television programmes, a few adverts as well, and the possibility of a role in a film coming up – that wasn't bad. And I'd done it all without stepping anywhere near a science-fiction programme. I'd managed to maintain a career and successfully put some distance between me and *Who*. Yes, I missed Tom, and Ian – although I occasionally bumped into him in Ealing – but I was actually quite proud of making a clean break. I'd never seen an episode before I joined the show and I hadn't watched one since. It wasn't exactly sour grapes because I'd never been a fan.

Which is why I surprised so many people with what I did next . . .

Chapter Thirteen

Affirmative, Mistress!

O N DAY one of filming *School Reunion* back in the summer of 2005, I found myself sitting down next to the Tenth Doctor during a break. Believe it or not, this was actually the first time David Tennant and I had had a moment to ourselves since I'd first arrived in Cardiff. On any production, there are so many people buzzing around all the time – crew, cast, friends – that private moments are genuinely rare. He was such easy company and straightaway confessed that he'd been a big fan of Sarah Jane. Wanting to keep it that way, I said, 'Whatever you do then, don't watch *K-9 and Company*.'

'Too late,' he laughed. 'I've seen it!'

'Gosh,' I said, 'you must really be a fan if you've seen that and you still want to work with me.'

Because it had been such a crushing disappointment: *K-9 and Company* should have been my first leading television role and on paper it had all the potential to become a *Sarah Jane Adventures* for the 1980s. That was the plan at the time but it didn't work out like that. In retrospect I should never have got involved, and I very nearly didn't, but John Nathan-Turner, of whom more below, could be extremely persuasive. The rotter!

* * *

The world of *Who* never stays still. JNT had replaced Philip Hinchcliffe's successor, Graham Williams, at the start of 1980. He arrived in all-guns-blazing mode and you'd hear all kinds of stories – he was thinking of dropping the sonic screwdriver, K-9, and even the TARDIS! I think he just wanted to shake things up a bit, although he eventually got his way with the dog. Not all his ideas were about breaking with the past, though. In the summer of 1980 I received a message asking if I'd go and see him. *What on earth for?* I wondered, but in the end decided, *Why not?*

So I pootled along to Threshold House: I have so many happy memories of that building, it's a shame they don't use it any more. Even the stroll up to the front door seems like a trip down memory lane, all those familiar shops and restaurants.

John's reputation was as a bit of a showman, so I was already primed for the flamboyant gestures and shirts as loud as his voice.

What I wasn't prepared for was his offer:

'Lis, I want you to come back as Sarah Jane.'

'You're *joking*!'

It was as if I was trying to talk myself out of it.

'We're deadly serious,' John said. 'You were the most popular companion. We want to put you and Tom back together. The Dream Team – the fans would love it!'

Ah, 'the fans'. How often I'd hear those words from John over the years.

I shook my head. 'I don't think so, John.'

'You don't have to make your mind up now,' he boomed, still smiling confidently. 'Take a few days. Talk to Brian, talk to your agent.'

'Look, I'm sorry, I don't need to discuss it with anyone. I had such a good innings with Tom, I can't risk going back and it not working – that would be so upsetting to me and, yes, the fans – I don't want to go there.'

Think about it from Tom's point of view, I told myself. *He's been there for years, he's in his own groove, he's moved the Doctor on, I'm sure – although I'd not seen it – I'd just be an anchor from the past.* I was genuinely worried that maybe I wouldn't fit in any more. *What if he took it the wrong way? What have they brought her back for? It's my show!*

No, I thought, *it's the right decision.*

Before I'd departed on a high – I couldn't allow anything to soil that memory.

When I left his office, I honestly thought I'd never hear from John again. Luckily, or unluckily, for me, he's not the sort of man who takes 'no' for an answer.

* * *

A year earlier I'm not sure I would even have gone in for the meeting, but by the time I saw JNT in summer 1980 I'd already been re-admitted to the Whoniverse.

And I liked it.

In late 1979 I'd received a request from my agent asking me to attend a *Who* fan event. It wasn't the first invite I'd received for something like that and usually I just responded, 'Thanks, but no thanks.' I wasn't in the show any more – to me it seemed rude to be making public appearances when there were others who were more entitled.

So what made me say 'yes' to this one?

Well, enough time had passed, I was going to be the 'star' guest and Ian Marter would also be there. Brian could come, too – if he could get out of his play in Richmond.

Oh, and the event was to be held in Los Angeles!

Lucy Chase Williams – who has written a book on Vincent Price and is such a together, organised lady – and Amy Krell, now a producer, were arranging their first *Doctor Who* American convention, 'Who1', and they wanted me as their star guest – and people say there are no female *Doctor Who* fans! I think the US Public Broadcast Service channel had recently begun to achieve good ratings for its *Who* episodes and, being a little behind the UK, I was still in the show over there. On top of that, VHS recorders had started to become more commonplace – fans were taping episodes and trading them with others. It's much easier to get a buzz going when you can all see the same thing.

Lucy and Amy couldn't have been more welcoming. They met

us at the airport and drove us to our hotel on Rodeo Drive. We got a tour of the downstairs convention rooms, dinner, and you just knew you were in safe hands. I don't know what they'd heard about Ian and me but I'd never seen so much booze around! I had a room where I would be able to relax between sessions, which was so thoughtful. 'Anything you want, Lis, you just ask,' said Lucy. Music to my ears . . .

So far it was just like a holiday – I almost forgot I was there to work.

I had genuinely no idea what to expect. Autograph hunters are one thing, but usually they're stepping into your territory. Bumping into you in the street, hanging around a location shoot or queuing at the stage door, that sort of thing. Today, though, I was stepping into *their* world.

Even as Lucy led me through towards the convention rooms I was convinced this had been a wasted journey.

I left the show in 1976. No one here will care who I am. I'm just going to be the mad aunt nobody wants to sit near at the wedding.

I couldn't have been more wrong.

It started in the morning when Lucy handed me a copy of the *Hollywood Reporter* – the movie business's trade paper. There it was, in black and white: 'Lis Sladen from *Doctor Who*, will be appearing at . . .'

Wow!

Lucy and Amy said they'd booked me as their 'star name' but I didn't expect anything like the reaction I got when I entered the room. It was incredible – the volume of applause when I was introduced blew my socks off! Just like Blackpool all over again but condensed into a far tinier space this time so it seemed even more intense. Everywhere I looked there were people laughing and smiling, whooping and cheering – it genuinely took my breath away. I was practically carried over the audience's heads just to reach the stage.

I was there to answer questions on stage, do signings, take part in discussion panels, things like that – they've all become standard events at conventions down the years and now I can do them with my eyes shut. But it was so new to me then. Being interrogated by several hundred of your most devout fans can be intimidating and mind-blowing at the same time: you're aware they know more about the show than you do but you soon learn that you can say anything and they'll consider it. There are no quick judgements, everyone in that room is on your side.

While I was doing my thing in the main room, I think there were other sessions, like workshops and screenings, going on elsewhere. It really was a packed programme. Sometimes I got to work alongside Ian, which was such a treat. Other times we were separated so they could get as many people involved as possible.

At the end of that first night there was an auction and guess what the top prize was? A dance with yours truly! An awe-struck young boy won, thanks to his father's generosity, and in fact we still keep in touch now.

The absolute highlight of the weekend for me, however, was the fancy dress competition. Ian and I were the guest stars so we were the obvious choice for judges. Unfortunately, apart from a break for lunch, we'd been sitting there for the whole day – and I have to say we were feeling a bit high by then. Possibly, alcohol may have been involved.

Anyway, they started this contest and all manner of eye-catching shapes and colours were wheeled past us. Honestly, the invention of *Who* fans will never, ever cease to impress me. Some of the monsters I recognised from my time, others were clearly pre- or post-Sarah Jane. I remember looking at Ian for help and being met with a shrug. Then we'd both nod at the entrant and say, 'Well done, very realistic.'

Most of the costumes were brilliant – obviously a lot of time and effort had gone into them. The standard had been very high when this kid walked by in what looked like a black bin liner. I just burst out laughing and slid under the table! 'What on earth is *that*?' I called out to Ian but I was giggling so much I didn't hear his answer. I literally had to dive out of view. It had been such a precious day but this costume brought out the giggles. Now I knew how Keith Barron felt with that bloody train on *Stepping Stones* – *I can't do this any more*.

We raised quite a lot of money that weekend and I've still got a photo of us presenting a cheque to the local hospital. My main memory of that convention is the American fans, though. I'd only ever met British fans before. These guys didn't have the benefit of the same historic relationship with *Who* because the programme hadn't been broadcast for as long. It might have been on loop daily but it was still years behind. You'd never have guessed it though from the noise. They were polite, they were informed and respectful – but everything was so much bigger and louder and more extreme. It was truly incredible. I loved it, I really did.

Another significant contrast between UK and US events is the *merchandise*. Shortly after I arrived, Lucy said, 'We've got a table where you can sell your tapes and photos.'

'My *what*?'

'Your merchandise – whatever you've brought to sell.'

'God, I haven't brought anything!'

'OK,' she beamed. 'That's good, too.'

We really missed a trick there. Americans, I soon learned, were so far ahead of Brits in this area.

If Lucy was surprised at my marketing naïvety, she was positively staggered by my professional ignorance. It's not just because she works in PR. Everyone I met in LA couldn't believe I hadn't come to the world's celluloid capital with the aim of finding an American agent.

Honestly, it never occurred to me.

Ian returned to London after the convention but Brian and I had bought Freddie Laker 'open' tickets. In other words, we could stay in America for a few weeks and go home when our money ran out. I was really looking forward to that – we'd had such fun in California during our Morley days. While we prepared to have the time of our lives, however, Lucy and Amy set about working on my behalf. They had loads of tapes of me from their own collections and sent these around to local agents. What an honour having people like that working for you! Through them I got an interview at Paramount and the Samuel Goldwyn Studios.

Another agent approached me direct. I'd just finished a Q&A at the convention when this older guy with silver hair shuffled up from the back of the hall. He didn't look like the usual *Who* fan, let's put it that way.

'I really enjoyed that,' he said. 'Can I give you some advice? Write to the William Morris Agency – tell them Abe Lastfogel sent you.'

I thanked him for the compliments and went backstage. When I told my hosts they were ecstatic. 'Abe's the agents' agent,' Lucy explained. 'He's been around since Lana Turner's day – you have to write to them!'

So I sent the letter, then Brian and I set off on our trip. A few weeks later I got a letter back – forwarded to our hotel in Santa Barbara. It simply said that so-and-so, the head honcho at William Morris, would like to see me the next day. I showed Brian the letter.

'Well, I can't go to that,' I said. 'We're on holiday.'

In hindsight, of course, I should have jumped in a cab, on a train or on a plane. Those offers don't come around every day, not even every year. But I was so naïve and nonchalant then. I wrote back, 'I return on this date and I'll pop in then.' So that's what I did. Of course, sod's law, on the day I turned up the main man was on vacation. I saw his second-in-command, who looked about twelve years old. There wasn't the hint of a spark between us and I wasn't surprised when I never heard from him again.

Why didn't I rush back when I was asked? I regret that, I actually do, but I didn't at the time and that was the main thing. My holiday with my husband was more important.

I had one more chance to make an impression on the city. A guy called Dave Rosen, who represented a host of international superstars, had responded to Lucy's letter. When he invited me to his office on Sunset Boulevard I was determined not to cock it up. An hour later, I was on cloud nine. He was so complimentary.

'You could achieve incredible things here, Lis,' he promised me. 'We can get you as high as you want to go.'

'What do I have to do?' I asked.

'Minimum: you have to move over here. Give me a year and I'll make you a star.'

A year in Los Angeles? What an amazing offer! With Rosen behind me, I began to believe I had a shot at Hollywood. I knew my answer.

'I'm sorry, Dave – it's got to be "no".'

There was no way I could do it. Mum had only recently died and Dad had never recovered. Every weekend I could, I caught the train up to be with him. I'd phoned him a couple of times from LA and he was anxious to see me again. There was no way I could stay away from him for a year.

Back in London Brian said I should go to the BBC and tell them about the merchandising opportunities available at 'Who1'. 'They're selling calendars, photos – all the stuff the Beeb – and *you*! – should be making money from.'

So, fire in my belly after an amazing trip I made an appointment at BBC Enterprises, the Corporation's commercial arm. 'Look, do you realise how much money they're making? We should be getting a slice of that,' I told them. They virtually laughed me out of the building – I swear it was a case of, 'Little Sarah Jane, what does she know?' That's honestly how I felt I was treated.

A year later they were knocking on my door. 'What were you saying about us selling things over there?' I could have screamed. By then the horse had bolted and the moment had gone, never to be recaptured. So long as *Who* was making money in the UK, they weren't interested in it abroad – I'm convinced of that. But in America you can be popular one minute and gone the next, so you have to harness the moment. They missed it. If they hadn't, maybe *Who* would never have been cancelled.

Despite any professional frustrations I was grateful to 'Who1' for two things: the first was magical friendships with Lucy and Amy (we're still close today). Secondly, and probably more importantly career-wise, that weekend really reignited my love for *Doctor Who*. I'd never gone off it, never become one of those people who start laughing at the wobbly sets or too-earnest acting – I just assumed my moment had passed and my connection with it, too. I thought I'd put that chapter to bed in 1976, never to be reopened. But LA changed all of that. All the love I ever had for the show or the fans came flooding back. From that moment on it stopped being something I should run away from – I needed to embrace my *Who* past *and* my *Who* future.

I'm not saying this would have been enough to influence my meeting with John Nathan-Turner, but if I were asked to take part in something else, maybe the answer would be more positive.

* * *

Adverts were still a lucrative way of making a living. I remember receiving the booking for a Dulux paint commercial and I thought, *That shouldn't take long*. Of course, I'd forgotten Dulux's mascot was an Old English Sheepdog so of course I'd be acting with him – and dogs and I just do not get on! Back then anything to do with a dog seemed to involve the celebrity trainer Barbara Woodhouse and true to form, she was all over this. She reminded me of the canine version of Mary Whitehouse.

I was meant to lie on a sofa and this dog, Digby, had to come over and wake me up by pawing my arm. *Fine*.

We did the first take and I screamed. Digby's claws had cut straight into my flesh.

'Hang on,' I said. 'This dog is drawing blood!'

Woodhouse came bustling over. 'Now, look,' she tutted, '*you* wouldn't find it very easy to balance on three legs, would you?'

'Bloody hell!' I said. 'Can't you cut its claws?'

Not one of my happier jobs.

Good times were just around the corner, though. Once again the setting was a place that had been kind to me on many an occasion. Yorkshire Television had enjoyed a successful debut year with Thora Hird and Christopher Beeney – *In Loving Memory* – and I was hired for the opening show of the second season. Thora was great pals with Keith Barron, so we had a mutual friend to laugh about. She was very funny, extremely dry and had us all in stitches when her replacement hip slowed her down.

'I'll be along in a minute, chuck,' she'd say. 'I'm sitting on steel here!'

Most of my scenes were with Christopher. I was Mary Bennett, his girlfriend, and so we found ourselves in a series of those gentle period courtship scenes. (I did panto with Chris a few years ago, so plenty of time for catching up and remembering Thora.)

It was a nice little job though not exactly lucrative. I was invited to come back for the Christmas Special but my agent said I could make more money elsewhere. I'd never really turned down parts on financial grounds before – it didn't sit well at all.

There was slightly more money to be had elsewhere on ITV. A lovely director, Bill Bain, had put together a great cast for *Name for the Day*, part of the *Play for Today* strand. I played Jo, then we had super Richard O'Callaghan as my husband, Pauline Quirke as an asylum patient, and a gorgeous actor who used to have me in hysterics – Simon Cadell (I was so pleased for him when he became so successful in *Hi-de-Hi!*). I made great pals with Pauline – we went out together quite a lot and I even got an invite to her wedding, which was beautiful. We've lost touch, which is a shame, but I was so happy working with her.

The play itself upset me quite a bit. It was extremely wearing keeping a straight face among the chaos. Afterwards Bill Bain sent me a letter. He said, 'It's very hard playing the only straight character in a humorous play when everyone else is trying to be funny. Well done!'

People like Bill are few and far between. He didn't have to send that note – he was just one of those people who are so kind and want to help others. And he reminded me so much of a certain someone else from my past – who was once again about to become very important to me.

It all began with a call from my agent.

'Are you interested in playing Lady Flimnap on TV?' he asked.

The name rang a bell. 'Can you tell me anything else about it?'

'I'm not sure what it is – it hasn't been written properly yet. All I know is it's from *Gulliver's Travels*.'

'Oh, I remember,' I said. 'She's not exactly the star of it. Maybe I'll pass on this one.'

'Fair enough,' said Todd. 'Let me see what else I can dig up on it.'

He rang back later and said, 'Barry Letts is writing and directing it.'

That's all I needed to hear.

'OK, tell them I'm in!'

I would have walked over hot coals to work with Barry again. When I left *Who* he'd told me, 'I'm going to write to some people and recommend they see you.' And he did – I saw a copy of it. He said: 'I really think you should see this person because I think she could become one of the best actresses of our generation.' I'm not sure much ever came of it – I did go to see people but perhaps I don't sell myself well enough. All I know is, he didn't have to do that. So the opportunity to work with him, however small the role, was not to be missed.

The day after I agreed to do Flimnap, Barry rang me himself and I remembered yet again why he was so special.

'I'm so pleased you're going to do it,' he told me. 'I'm going to write the part up just for you.'

What a gentleman.

* * *

Barry coming back into my life seemed like an omen and while he beavered away on the script I accepted an invite to another US *Who* convention. This one hadn't been organised by Lucy but if it was half as much fun, I'd be in for a treat. Once again Ian Marter was also on the list – as was Barry, something I was really excited about – and there was a ticket for Brian. I couldn't wait. Fort Lauderdale, here we come!

The event opened at two o'clock on 5 February 1981. At about ten past Ian and I were still standing outside the hall – it was so packed we couldn't get in. Boy, when Americans decide they like something, they really go for it! I probably hadn't thought about *Who* more than once since the LA convention – and that was during the meeting with John Nathan-Turner. I'd forgotten how massive the show had become over there. I never expected that level of attention. And I definitely didn't expect to have to be physically passed over the audience's heads just to reach the stage!

We had a brilliant time. It was blissful being with Ian and Barry again without the shadow of work hanging over us, although we weren't alone. Our hosts had pulled out all the stops and I loved meeting lots of ex-*Who* alumni for the first time. In audiences' minds we must seem like one big family but the truth is that I didn't meet most of the other Doctors and their crew until I started frequenting conventions. Even though we're strangers, we have such a rich shared history and meeting them is like having your own support network. No one else knows what you go through on that show.

A relief for me was seeing Brian fit in so easily. He and Ian really hit it off – it would have been awful if he'd felt like a spare limb. I think they both had their experiences of being at the periphery of the *Who* spectrum – even Ian – and so they bonded over that. Most of that bonding, naturally, took place at the bar way into the small hours. On one occasion it also included a drunken paddle in the surf.

Ian, Barry and the rest left after a week, then Brian and I drove down to Key West for another fortnight's amazing holiday. We'd only been there a few days when we were stopped by a policeman.

'Is everything all right, officer?' Brian asked.

'It will be if Sarah Jane will give me her autograph!'

As I've said, it's amazing where you find *Who* fans.

* * *

Filming on *Gulliver in Lilliput* began in June 1981. I was so excited to be working with Barry again, and I was even looking forward to slipping into the old rehearsal/record routine at the Acton Hilton and Television Centre.

Technically it was quite a tricky shoot. Gulliver was so much bigger than me that the actor – Andrew Burt – had to stand at one end of the studio and I was up the other end by the blue screen. Luckily the Beeb still used monitors then so I was able to position myself on Gulliver's outstretched palm. If he moved, I could react – I don't know why they ever took the screens away.

We had several weeks of filming but time was extremely tight by the end. It was touch and go whether we'd complete on time and Barry's nerves passed down to the cast. I remember at the very end of our studio time I had to blow Andrew a kiss but I just didn't do it. I was so anxious about cocking it up and making the whole production run over schedule that I just skipped it.

Costumes on the whole film were stunning – thanks to Amy Roberts – but mine was out of this world. I was scaffolded inside the narrowest corset they could find. So decadent, it felt like being in an opera – people kept wandering in just to see our underwear! (There was one marvellous scene where I had to tease my husband pulling on my stockings. Still a favourite, I believe, for some fans.) The downside is it took so bloody long to get into that outfit there was never time to take it off again. From early in the morning until ten at night, I was trussed up like a Christmas turkey. For lunch I could just about manage a hard-boiled egg and I still felt as though I'd eaten a whole chicken. When I was cut out at night, my body was covered in striations.

It was such a minxy part and there was not a minute of *Gulliver* that I did not enjoy. I know Barry felt the same. I have a letter from him in which he says that production was one of the highlights of his career. Mine too, Barry.

If only I could have said the same about my next project.

* * *

Unbeknownst to me, John Nathan-Turner had not taken my earlier 'no' for an answer. Just because I'd refused to return to the main programme to oversee the transition between Tom and the Fifth Doctor, Peter Davison, he reasoned, that didn't mean I never wanted to appear as Sarah Jane Smith in anything else. Then at the start of 1981 he discovered the perfect vehicle. Following the announcement that K-9, the Fourth Doctor's robot dog, would be phased out of *Doctor Who*, there had been uproar among the fans and in the press so, he decided to give K-9 another show – with me as the human star.

'We'll call it *Sarah and K-9!*' John enthused. 'You'll have your own show – it will be brilliant!'

I had to agree that it sounded a fabulous idea: Sarah Jane striding out into the world on her own, pursuing her journalistic instincts to solve crimes – with her trusty robot dog at her side. Even when they changed the title to *Girl's Best Friend* I was still on board. The plan was to shoot a pilot then hopefully be picked up for a full series the following year. 'That should be a formality,' John winked. 'We're all behind it here.'

I couldn't wait – I was so intrigued to discover how Sarah would operate away from the Doctor. that was the challenge. I wanted to see how she would interact with other people and how she would save the universe on her own. I didn't have a clue what K-9 was – I'd never seen him. But, I figured, if Tom Baker had worked with him then it must be all right. Of course, that was before I heard the stories of Tom booting the thing across the studio in frustration every time it ruined a scene.

I signed up in May then disappeared to work on *Gulliver*. Barry was fascinated that his creation was to get a new lease of life – I really wanted it to work for him as much as anyone. After half a decade away from it, I was suddenly more embroiled in the Whoniverse than I'd ever been. Life was good.

And then the script arrived.

I read it in between shooting as Flimnap. Sadly, it was only her corsets that took my breath away. The script was terrible. I called a meeting with John and Eric Saward, the *Who* script editor, with a list of complaints as long as my arm. First: it was now called *K-9 and Company*.

Company? Is that what I am now, John? What happened to it being my show?

More importantly, the characterisation of Sarah was totally wrong.

'Eric,' I said, 'she wouldn't do or say half these things. This hasn't been written for Sarah at all!'

Eric agreed. The writer, Terence Dudley, had his own way of doing things and was not exactly keen to bend. 'But,' John insisted, 'we'll fix it – won't we, Eric?'

They promised and, assured by their enthusiasm, I returned to Lilliput a happy bunny.

What an idiot I was. When the final script arrived shortly before rehearsals began, nothing had been changed. I think Dudley had refused Eric's changes wholesale and gone straight over his head to JNT. The politics didn't bother me – my only concern was injecting some character into my leaden lines.

Costume fittings ran for a fortnight into November. I think most of that time must have been spent on me. I can't believe how many changes I went through! Three or four different coats, jogging clothes, a journalist's Mac, a big Sherlock Holmes' autumnal three-piece suit, body warmers and lots of gloves. There was even a green silk dress bought specifically for the last scene that I seem to recall took up most of our budget. I remember seeing the Sherlock Holmes' number on a model in a magazine and thinking, *That would be good because you can just remove layers rather than keep changing*. Of course, the model was about a foot taller than me. When I stepped out of the car in my opening scene, the hem was sweeping the road.

In November we all met up for the first time at the Acton Hilton for a read-through. Delivering some of those lines still grated but I had a few solutions to try during rehearsal. They would have to wait, however. As soon as we wrapped in London it was onto the bus and down to the Cotswolds. As I sat watching the countryside blur past I realised for the first time that I was on my own. There was no Jon or Tom to soak up everyone's attention – I wasn't sure I liked it.

My mood didn't pick up on the first day of shooting. I'd been asked to bring some of my own clothes.

'Why? There's nothing in the script.'

'We're starting with opening credits,' the director John Black said.

Oh, it's nice to be told.

Unusually, JNT had come with us to Gloucestershire for the location work. As far as rallying the troops went, he was a great person to have around; always energetic and busy, busy, *busy*! I'm not sure it worked so well for the director. Sometimes you need a stronger man in charge but John Black was a bit intimidated by his boss's presence. So when JNT said, 'I want the opening credits to be like *Hart to Hart*' – all zooming cars and glamorous locations – Black should have told him to clear off. But he didn't. That's why I found myself sitting outside a country pub one minute waving a glass of wine, then posing on a rock with a newspaper, then leaning moodily in my Mac against my Mini Metro. It was already ridiculous before they asked me to jog along the country road.

OK, I thought, *it's day one, keep smiling, it will get better from here.*

They set the camera up, gave me a mark and then off I set along the road.

'That's nice, Lis,' the director said. 'But it was a bit fast for the camera.'

So I did it again and John Black said, 'Nice, but maybe a bit more slowly next time.'

'Do you have any idea how hard it is to jog slowly and not look like you're suffering from muscular dystrophy?' I said, 'Can't you move the bloody cameras back instead?' Would it have killed them to use a longshot instead of a close-up?

My favourite part of the intro was whizzing up and down the country lane in my car. I tend not to drive outside of filming requirement so it's always an adventure when I get behind the wheel. Forwards I can do – anything else takes a bit more time – and John wanted me to zoom along this road. I thought, *I can do that — just clear the road, for God's sake!* Actually I believed it would be a dynamic start to the programme so I was disappointed to see they didn't use it in the end.

John Black didn't have the best of luck. As we'd discovered on *The Seeds of Doom*, filming outdoors in November gives you the shortest possible amount of daylight to cram everything in. A few days before we set off, a second week was pulled from the schedule so that led to frantic re-jigging, which only piled on the pressure. Any hopes I had of reworking my lines while we were out there seemed to be vanishing in the rush.

The weather didn't exactly help, either. We always seemed to be waiting for a shower to pass. For the night shoots it wasn't the rain but the unbearable temperatures that were the killer. One of the things I think John and everyone got spot-on was the eerie satanic festival filmed outside a church in North Woodchester. The worshippers wore amazing goat-head masks and the whole scene really captured a bit of tension and energy, which I think was largely missing in the rest of the programme. Of course, by the time we'd been there setting up and then rehearsing and then going for takes from different angles it was two or three in the morning and absolutely freezing. Poor Ian Sears who played the sacrificial Brendan was only wearing the flimsiest of robes. In between takes his dresser would rush over with blankets, hot socks and scarves.

However bad it gets you can always rely on actors to find the black humour. There was one brilliant moment while the ring of pagans were dancing around in sub-zero temperatures calling 'Hecate! Hecate! Hecate!' when we realised it had suddenly changed to 'Equity! Equity! Equity!' – the name of the actors' union!

My only contribution to the black-magic scenes was a spot of Kung Fu, meted out to a couple of the villains. When you see something like that in a script you think, *Well, I suppose I'll be all right with training*. I got about five seconds' tuition before John called 'Action!' Let's just say I don't think I'll be getting my Black Belt in Venusian aikido any time soon.

That wasn't the only time the script promised something we couldn't deliver. There's an attempt on Sarah's life when a tractor pulls out in front of her car. I didn't even bother marking it in my script, I just assumed a stuntman would be doing it.

I remember sitting on the coach with a cup of tea when someone came on to fetch me.

'It's time to do your car crash, Lis.'

I said, 'Pardon? I'm not in this scene – it's a stuntman.'

'Oh,' he told me. 'John apologises but . . .'

It was another decision that had come down to money. Why pay a professional when you can ask your actors to risk their lives?

'We just want you to swerve the tractor, mount the embankment, then bring the car down the other side,' John explained.

'You have got to be kidding – I struggle to go in a straight line!' As far as I could see, one wrong turn of the steering wheel and that car would just flip over.

If I hadn't nearly drowned at Wookey Hole, I probably would have attempted it but it wouldn't have made the shot any better. They just wanted to economise, whether I was up to the job or not. You have to draw the line somewhere. In the end they found a stuntwoman to do the dangerous bit.

I do wonder how JNT's presence affected things. I think the director was especially cowed because the producer controls the purse strings. Nathan-Turner became a true friend over the years but we did have one spectacular falling out on set. One of the crew had been told off for something. I found John and said, 'I think you've made a mistake. I was there, that's not what happened.'

He went ballistic, storming around, throwing his arms in the air, shouting, 'Why aren't you standing up for me? It's your *job* to stand up for me!'

Well, no it's not, actually. I'm probably closer to the crew than I am the producer, I thought, but maybe it wasn't a good move tactically.

The atmosphere the next morning was frostier than usual – and it had nothing to do with the weather. Nathan-Turner needed to check something with me, but instead of coming over, I heard him say to his partner, Gary: 'Would you ask Elisabeth . . .?'

My God, it was so bloody childish. He was pretending I wasn't even there. Pathetic and unprofessional – and not what I needed on what was already a problematic shoot for me.

I think I got the cold shoulder for a couple of days. Then Gary sidled up to me one evening and said, 'Look, John is really upset about what's happening. Would you go and apologise to him?'

'No, I won't. I have nothing to apologise for,' I said. But I wasn't going to stand for this petty behaviour either, so I did go over and said, bullish as you like, 'Hello, John.'

'Oh, Lis!' he gushed, 'thank goodness you've come over. Let's just be professional, shall we?'

I said, 'Well, I thought I was being.'

That just kicked things off again! We made up later and, as I said, we were very close until he died. What a drain when you're already against the clock, though.

Hindsight's a terrible tease because so much of *K-9 and Company* seems wrong to me. In fact, it's probably just a few tweaks away from being rather good. As Eric Saward told me, 'I think if it had gone to series then all those problems would have been ironed out and we would have had a hit on our hands.'

Some of the snags just came down to bad communication. You have to bear in mind I'd never seen K-9 before, so one day in Gloucestershire I was introduced to this boxy-looking mutt and two men. Mat Irvine is K-9's operator and John Leeson supplies the voice – the team behind the dog.

Mat ran over what K-9 could do and we walked our first scene, getting our bearings. Then the director called 'Action!' and I delivered my line.

Nothing.

Have I forgotten a cue? Why isn't K-9 speaking? I wondered.

So we went again and the same thing happened. Nothing.

I looked at John Black, then John Leeson. They stared back at me expectantly.

'Well, is the dog going to answer?' I asked.

'Oh,' Leeson said, 'he can, if you like.'

I felt such a fool. Why on earth hadn't anyone told me that John adds his parts afterwards? How was I meant to know I had to leave a gap? Little things like that can really put a stick in your spokes. How to make the star of the show feel like the new girl in one easy session . . .

Forget Nathan-Turner, forget Black, forget Leeson – most of our woes originated from a single robotic sources, though.

K-9.

When I'd signed up for the show it had been such a rush, especially as I was head down in *Gulliver* world at the time. Possibly working with Barry gave me an unnaturally positive outlook towards everything BBC. I really should have paid greater attention. When I agreed to have a dog as a co-star – or *be* the co-star to a dog, as some people said! – I had no idea how unmalleable he would be. Honestly, worse than a Dalek! At least you can talk to the person inside a Dalek and get them to try to co-operate. At one point during our ritual scene, K-9 had to be attached to a fishing wire and literally dragged through the mud to save the day.

Expecting this box on wheels to negotiate a winter terrain was one thing but I thought any difficulty would iron itself out when we reached the studio. In fact it just created new problems. If you watch the show you can hear my boots clanging around on the floor. That's because carpets were vetoed – the bloody dog needed smooth, hard ground before he would budge! That meant doorways were an issue because, of course, they have a runner across them. Watching this so-called futuristic creation struggle to move from the hallway to the lounge was a joke, especially when it was trundling along so slowly.

At one point I had to flee from a room. I did a take, then John Black said, 'Lis, you need to hold the door open for K-9.'

'I'm going to save the universe but first I want to stop and open a door for a dog?' I asked.

It made no sense at all – it's amazing how that thing saves anyone.

The other problem you have with the dog is that obviously he's only about a foot tall. So if he's talking and you want more than your ankles in shot, you have to find an excuse to bend down. When you're trying to discover a way to save a sacrifice's life, this can be a slight inconvenience.

Our time in the Cotswolds ended with a photoshoot with me flanked by K-9 – and the giant Alsatian that played Commander Pollock's dog. Forget my old neighbour's Rex, I'd been scared of a Dulux dog! At least this time around there was no Barbara Woodhouse to scold me . . .

Nathan-Turner's master plan had been to shoot *K-9 and Company* during *Doctor Who*'s summer break. That didn't work with my *Gulliver* schedule so it was put back. So a lot of the problems could apparently be traced back to me . . . *Great*.

With the *Who* team tied up we were despatched to Birmingham's Pebble Mill to record there. If I'd felt sidelined on location, I was positively isolated now. Normally my closest allies on a shoot are the costume and makeup girls. Not this time. First chance they got, they disappeared to their rooms to have a Southern Comfort. I think they'd had problems in the past with London teams thinking they were superior. Whatever the reason, it just added to my mounting worry.

With the costume people ignoring me I found a new place to hide in the studio. John Leeson had the tiniest space with a curtain cutting it off from the melee. Every chance I got, I popped over.

'All right, John?'

'Oh, Lis, *do* come in!'

I was surprised by another friendly face while we were there. One afternoon I was waiting to go on when I got a tap on one shoulder and a familiar voice said, 'How's my favourite assistant?'

It was Chris Barry.

Favourite? I thought. *I wish I'd known that when I was working with you!*

He was recording in another studio, so we caught up as often as possible to mull over old times or catch up on gossip about mutual acquaintances.

It's probably quite clear by now that I was no fan of the finished show, but there were positives. I really liked the way the whole thing centred round Aunt Lavinia – who, of course, I had impersonated to gain access to UNIT back in *The Time Warrior*. So that was nice. The line that came after I unpacked K-9 gave even better continuity.

'Oh, you didn't forget!'

It meant nothing to me at the time but I now know this was a direct reference to my closing conversation with the Doctor back in *The Hand of Fear*.

Hiccoughs and hitches besieged the show right up to broadcast. It had been scheduled to go out on 23 December 1981 to the highest possible audience. Two weeks earlier it was mysteriously bumped back to 28 December – traditionally a veritable viewing wasteland. It didn't stop there. On the evening of 28 December, a failing of the Winter Hill transmitter meant the entire northwest of England was without coverage. In the event, the 8.4 million viewers scored was an incredible achievement. Despite my misgivings, it augured extremely well for a future series.

JNT rang me a few weeks later with the news. There had been a change of faces at the top of the Beeb – the new suits wanted to distance themselves from *Who*. Despite the spectacular viewing figures, the answer was therefore negative: we would not be getting a series.

It was a body blow, if I'm honest. I don't think I turned in the best performance but in the face of the problems, we did all right. The series would only have got better but the decision had been made.

So that was that, I thought. *I'd brought Sarah back and it hadn't worked. Back to the mothballs for her* . . .

On the plus side: at least I'd never have to set eyes on that bloody dog again!

Chapter Fourteen

Think Of The Fans

THE FIRST time I walked away from *Doctor Who* it was with a spring in my step. Now I was dragging my heels. I hadn't had the best time on *K-9 and Company*. On the other hand, if the show had gone to series we could have achieved some spectacular things, I was sure of it. Despite my own misgivings, I could tell from my fan mail that K-9 was a massive hit with kids. No one could explain why we weren't being commissioned for more.

I'm not one to dwell. The only way to cope with disappointment is to put your head down and work – but where? The answer, I realised, was Bristol. Brian had been there quite a lot recently under the direction of Little Theatre boss David Neilson. 'Come down,' he enthused. 'You won't be disappointed.'

If David's name seems familiar, you'll probably recognise him as Roy Cropper from *Coronation Street*. Roy's one of the comedy staples in *Corrie* and David's hysterical in real life – but in a completely different way to Roy. There's none of the pushover about him. He's utterly in control; a really, really great director and a terrific actor.

As well as being with Brian, the big draw for me in Bristol was the chance to do *Twelfth Night* again. That was the play in which we'd met. What a perfect play in which to share the stage again?

Then Brian's agent rang and said, 'You've got a part in a TV series', and all that romanticism flew out the window.

'You've got to take the telly – it's four times the money and half the work,' I conceded.

So that was the end of our little commemoration.

Brian had been slated to play Feste while I was offered Olivia or Viola. I have always wanted to play Viola. If I've got any dreams in acting, that would be one. Then I looked at the rest of the cast. If I was being honest, there was another girl in the company who was born to play her. The idea of her playing Olivia was laughable, really, whereas I could get away with either. So that was the end of another dream. I took one for the team and donned my Olivia frock. Thirty years later my chance of playing Viola has probably sailed.

I faced another casting conundrum with the next play. It was a new piece, called *Comic Cuts*, by Steven Mallatrat (who as a *Corrie* writer would go on to recommend David Neilson for the show). The advantage of being in a company is you get the pick of the parts. I would never be cast as June in an open casting and by the time *Comic Cuts* reached the West End I'd been replaced by Janine Duvitski, Angus Deayton's wife in *One Foot in the Grave*. I can't have any complaints – if she walked through the door now you'd think, *Yes, she's June*.

Then it was time for panto. Steven had written a modern-day Robin Hood update that was genuinely hysterical. I played Mrs Ross, a podgy thing with twenty children, so I was padded up to the eyeballs. It was just as well because I had to learn a fight sequence with Tim Stern, who played my husband. We rolled all over the stage in a proper slapstick wrestling match. Each night I got up covered in dirt and dust, sweating from the padding. I loved it!

Despite the high calibre of production, the Little Theatre was in financial difficulties – there was actually talk of *Robin Hood* not making it on to the stage. Then David and his backers came to us with a proposal: if we could all work unpaid for a month, that would provide enough cash to fund their next production, an adaptation of Raymond Briggs' *When the Wind Blows*. No guarantees but they were confident the show would be snapped up for the West End – and the money would start flowing in then.

So that's what happened. We worked for nothing so that the money could go into sets for *When the Wind Blows*. How many other professions are asked to do these things? Sure enough, it was quickly chosen for a London run and our cheques arrived within weeks. When you know the people involved it makes gambles like that less scary.

* * *

Occasionally, of course, knowing the people involved can evoke quite different emotions. I nearly froze when I got a message that John Nathan-Turner was trying to contact me. *Haven't you banged enough nails into Sarah Jane's coffin?*

Of course if I'd paid attention to the letters I'd been receiving, then I would have known what he wanted. For months, fans had been writing to me to ask, 'Is there going to be anything to mark the twentieth anniversary of *Doctor Who*?' and I had duly replied, 'Nothing that I'm involved with.' But I forgot how rapidly the BBC works. Almost knee-jerky, you might say! It was as though they woke up one morning and thought, *Christ, we need to do something!*

So that was what Nathan-Turner wanted to speak to me about. They were doing a Special called *The Five Doctors* – featuring all incarnations of the Doctor, with their companions, being plucked out of time to compete in the deadly game of Rassilon in the spookily named Death Zone on Gallifrey. In order to make it work they were trying to reunite as many of the main men and their sidekicks as possible. The late William Hartnell was to be replaced by Richard Hurndall, but otherwise we were all on board. Tom Baker's companion would be Lalla Ward – whom he'd recently married – and so I would tag team with Jon Pertwee.

Now that, I would be excited to do: me, Tom and Jon – my two Doctors and me onscreen at the same time – that could be special! Even so, *K-9 and Company* had left a sour taste in my mouth.

'Come on, Lis,' John urged in his usual enthusiastic manner. 'Everyone else is doing it! You don't want to be the one who said "no", do you? Think of the fans.'

That was so typical of John, playing the guilt card. 'Think of the fans' might have been his catchphrase. I thought of everything that went wrong with our shoot in the Cotswolds, but then I remembered some of the good times I'd had with Jon and Tom.

'OK, you've got me,' I said. 'When can I see a script?'

Ah, now there's a question. One of these days I'll learn to ask for a script *before* I give my answer! In the end I think that's what Tom did because by the time shooting commenced he was nowhere to be seen. They had to use clips from an unbroadcast serial instead. It didn't help, I suppose, that by then he and Lalla had separated.

Terry Dicks was given the task of writing a script that incorporated all these changing elements: myriad Doctors, companions and villains. His only stipulations were that there were to be no Daleks – and no K-9. I knew exactly how he felt.

Poor Terry got neither of his wishes. A solo Dalek does appear inside the tower, in a Benny Hill-style chase with the First Doctor and Susan. It was a welcome return for my old friend Roy Skelton as its voice. Then, to tie in with *K-9 and Company*, my part in *The Five Doctors* began with the dog warning me of danger. Obviously I then ignored him and got spirited off to Gallifrey. At least he didn't have to come as well, although it was nice to see John Leeson again so soon. There's a certain supermarket near my house where I often hear this cry of 'Mistress!' Honestly, jumping out of your skin in the frozen meats aisle isn't all that becoming.

Despite my misgivings, by the time shooting started in March 1983 I was thrilled to be part of such an illustrious cast. Only people who've been in *Who* can really know what it's like – and here they were by the TARDIS-load. Quite a few of them I'd met at the US conventions. Poor Peter Moffat, the director, really had his work cut out keeping us in check.

'Would you please stop talking!' he shouted more than once. 'I'm trying to rehearse a scene.'

It was a waste of time. As soon as they had a bunch of us in a room the gossip would start and before we knew it, lunchtime was just around the corner.

Meeting old friends was one thing, but I also made new ones. I'd never met Pat Troughton, the Second Doctor, before and what a wonder he was. I think it's fair to say we were a bit wary of each other at first, I don't know why. We would eye each other up a lot and I thought, *What's your problem?* I think actually he was very shy (he liked to surround himself with his friends), but he turned in a stand-out performance. He really brought a lot of life to it – he knew exactly what he wanted from the part and it was good to see him with Nick Courtney. At the end of the day, Pat was a bloody good actor. It would have been nice to share some scenes with him and get to know the man, though.

Pat wasn't the only one with friends. Every Doctor seemed to have his clique off-screen; some companions had their own groups as well – it's inevitable when you have so many people milling around at the same time. It was just as complicated onscreen. Everyone was paired off and at some point we all had our own villains to face. I think a few details got overlooked in the confusion so, for example, when Janet Fielding as the Fifth Doctor's companion, Tegan, enters with Peter Davison and I walk on with Jon, the men start combining forces and we're just left standing like lemons. I thought, *I'd better go and introduce myself.* How implausible would it be if we just stood there ignoring each other? Little things like that were a bit sloppy, I'd say – another sign of a rushed production.

We had some fun on 17 November – a year after I'd recorded *K-9 and Company*. A photocall was announced for the four Doctors, the Brig, Carole Ann Ford (who played Susan, the Doctor's granddaughter during William Hartnell's time), K-9 and me. Tom had also promised to put in an appearance. However, when push came to shove, he couldn't be seen for toffee – but Nathan-Turner had already thought of that. So if you look at the snaps from that day you'll notice Peter, Jon, Pat, Richard – and a waxwork of Tom, courtesy of Madame Tussauds! And if you can think of rude things to say or do to a dummy of Tom Baker, we probably did them. A rare highlight, I have to say, on an otherwise uninspiring shoot.

Location filming took place in Wales and it was bloody cold, as you can imagine in November. There was a team of people armed with hairdryers whose job it was to hide behind rocks, then rush out and give your body a resuscitating blow-dry between takes! So when the photographer requested a few snaps of Carole Ann and me, we persuaded him to come back to the warmth of the hotel. 'OK,' he agreed, 'but I haven't got long.' No sooner had we stepped inside than our faces went off the pink scale. Sweating and high-coloured is an absolutely hideous look, but the photographer snapped away regardless.

'These pictures had better not see the light of day,' I said.

'No one would be stupid enough to use them,' Carole Ann agreed.

And so we promptly forgot all about them.

* * *

Being reunited with Jon was a total buzz. He himself, though, couldn't find it in him to enjoy *The Five Doctors* for what it was. He'd never really got over watching Tom Baker regenerate into his part back in 1974. Having to sit back while Tom then went on to become the most popular and long-serving Doctor had been a hard pill to swallow. As a consequence he rarely let an opportunity slide to toss out a catty remark about his successor. Tom not taking part in *The Five Doctors* couldn't have given him more material if he'd tried.

'Oh, he's too grand for the likes of us,' he sneered. '*Who*'s not good enough for him any more! Charming, I'm sure.'

Delighted as I was to see Jon, there was only so much of this talk I could take. Some of his bitchy remarks when we were posing with the Tom mannequin had been amusing but the joke quickly wore thin. In the end I said, 'Look, if you can't say anything nice, I'm off.'

The look on Jon's face! He'd forgotten how much I loved Tom. *I'm not going to let you trample on my memories,* I thought.

A lot of Jon's venom should have been directed at the BBC. They were the ones, he felt, who had tricked him into leaving by their intransigence. More crucially, they had never hired him since – he was very sad about that. He had a proud Dickensian face. They could have used him for all sorts of things but he never got another sniff until *The Five Doctors* and nothing outside *Who* afterwards. I guess Tom might have been the easy target but in reality Jon was annoyed at the whole Corporation.

We had some fun together, of course. Jon got to trot out his catchphrase 'reverse the polarity of the neutron flow' once again, while Bessie was drafted back in to add an additional blast from the past. Annoyingly, once they'd brought her out of mothballs they needed to use her, so we had this ridiculous scene where I fall down a cliff and Jon has to winch me out using the car. All fine – except when you look at the cliff, it's about three foot deep and not steep enough to keep a toddler at bay.

Deciding where to tie the rope seemed to take an age, and all the while I was lying on this cold, damp patch of grass. In the end I called out, 'Shall we not bother?'

Shortly after that I heard Peter Moffat say, 'Why don't we just tie it around her neck?'

Jon and I just looked at each other. 'Christ,' he said, 'I could strangle you.'

I was so cold I almost said yes!

Recapturing our old onscreen relationship came pretty naturally, I think. There's a point in the show where I roll my eyes exasperatedly at Jon. That sort of thing isn't in the script but it's what I would have done – and did – back in *Peladon*. The years might have passed, I may have matured, but Sarah Jane is still there to puncture the Doctor's ego when she gets the chance.

Jon desperately wanted to make his mark on the show and despite his comments, I'm sure he had a lot more fun with Tom not being there. He revelled in being the Doctor again and you'd have to have a heart of stone not to be thrilled for him.

And I wasn't the only one pleased to see some of Jon's old pomp return. We all descended on a restaurant in Wales one night and for some reason naturally paired off in our Doctor and companion couples around the room. Jon and I both ordered trout with almonds – we always did share food tastes. Usually with that dish you got a few nuts sprinkled around the plate. When our meals arrived it looked as if they'd served the almonds with a dumper truck!

I said, 'I think they're pleased to see you, Jon!'

Bless that restaurant for trying to impress him but I still laugh when I picture him holding a knife and fork like excavation tools, saying, 'Where on earth is the bloody fish?'

I think all of the Doctors had a good time. I didn't have many scenes with Peter Davison, and it was so bloody freezing all the time that if you weren't in a scene you didn't hang around, so sadly we didn't really have much to do with each other.

Jon had a great camaraderie with Patrick Troughton. They really bounced off each other, and the marvellous Richard Hurndall was someone I immediately warmed to. The stories flowed from him and I'm such a sucker for an older actor's life story. He was such great company. It must have been intimidating playing a fake Doctor around so many originals but he didn't let it show. I heard afterwards that poor Richard had died before he got paid! I really hope that's not true but with the BBC you can never be sure . . .

The four Doctors got on surprisingly well. I suppose three of them had bumped into each other before on the convention circuit and would do so again, but it was the other companions with whom I most enjoyed spending time. Carole Ann Ford was fun to be around, and Frazer Hines, who was starring in *Emmerdale* at the time, was excellent value as well. He's the joker in the pack, one of those characters who have you in fits of giggles right up to the moment the clapperboard snaps. Then you do the scene and he has you cracking up again immediately afterwards – very naughty sometimes, but a breath of fresh air. He has been acting since he was a young boy so I suppose he doesn't know anything else.

Speaking of naughty, with John Nathan-Turner on set you were never far from a potential conflict. I'm not sure if he did this on purpose but he did like to throw the cat among the pigeons from time to time.

On one occasion I had just completed a scene. Nathan-Turner applauded and walked over to speak to Janet Fielding, who played Tegan.

'Now that's how a companion should behave.'

Oh, John, you are such a mixer! I thought. I think he'd always had a spiky relationship with Jan, but I didn't want to be drawn into it.

JNT could be a bit of a minx but I saw a new side to him on this shoot – as a director. I'm not sure how it came about but when we were at Manod Quarry he ended up taking the chair on the fight sequence with the Raston Warrior Robot – played by Keith Hodiak in a silver one-piece suit. He had all these knives and Cybermen to choreograph and I think he did it masterfully. I would have liked to see John direct more: for good or for bad, he really put his heart and soul into *Doctor Who*.

For all the large cast and big location numbers, you quickly realise the budgets haven't changed when you get the call saying, 'Can you bring some of your own clothes?' So my blouse is up there onscreen, the Mac is mine – and yes, so are the gloves on string inside it! Why they're on string I've no idea.

I didn't like the Rassilon stuff much – that whole denouement chugged along a bit too slowly for me. It was like trying to act in treacle. By contrast Jon and I had fun with Anthony Ainley as the Master in the car because those scenes zipped along. I enjoyed Sarah getting a bit tetchy with him: he's as powerful and clever as the Doctor but she stands her ground. I'd never come up against the Master before so it was good to tick off another landmark villain, something else for the fans to ask me about at the Chicago convention – where most of us were heading immediately after filming.

* * *

It's always a privilege to receive invitations to go to America. Piling onto a plane after *The Five Doctors* wrapped had an exciting end-of-term feeling. It's so nice to be among friends when you're working and, of course, after such a gruelling shoot even the people I hadn't really known before had suddenly become close.

We all gave the show a good hard sell in Chicago, which I think was fair. If you asked Janet or Frazer or any of the others what they think about *The Five Doctors*, I imagine we would all trot out pretty identikit replies. We'd been in better *Who* productions but this was ambitious and it was fun. Most importantly, it was conceived as a grand gesture, a big celebratory thank you for the fans, and I think it achieved that.

I went to the Chicago convention three years in a row. It was always fun. They were so enthusiastic, and because it fell around Thanksgiving it seemed like all of America was in party mood. I never thought I'd witness the same levels of passion in England.

But then we went to Longleat.

The Seat of the Marquis of Bath had been running a *Doctor Who* exhibition since 1973 and it had always drawn in visitors to the stately home. With the anniversary coming up, Lord Bath persuaded BBC Enterprises to up the ante and really make a feature of the place. As a result, on Easter Sunday 1983, Longleat threw open its gates to all living Doctors, as many companions as they could muster – and about a million fans!

Stately homes are never built on motorways, are they, but no one in their wildest dreams expected that level of turnout. All the roads were gridlocked and after a while the only people getting anywhere were the police deployed to sort out the mess.

I still get letters about it today. People say things like, 'I never made it' or 'I got within a couple of miles'. Some of them actually struggled through but I'm afraid there were a lot of disappointed fans that day.

Unlike the American conventions, this one was mostly outdoors so you could really appreciate the scale of the audience surging towards you. We were all looking forward to it but at times you knew how it might feel to be a castle besieged by angry villagers. My father, who had come along as my guest, couldn't help worrying. 'Is it safe, Lis? Is it safe?' he kept saying, and I had to laugh. This was a man who had ridden a motorbike through the jungles of Nigeria and now he was shaking at the sight of a horde of *Who* fans.

Just trying to cope with the vast numbers meant that standards weren't quite so high as in LA, Fort Lauderdale or Chicago. I managed to nip to the loo at one point and I suddenly heard this voice from the next cubicle: 'Lis, if I slide a photo under the door, will you sign it?'

Signings are the lifeblood of conventions – fans will queue for hours to get a signature. If Sadie ever came along she'd be asked for her autograph, too. And if Jon was around he always made sure she was spoiled by fans. Usually the organisers massively underestimate how long these things take, so I'm forever saying, 'I'll sit here signing until I've seen everyone,' which can throw the running order out completely. Sometimes you do get dragged away, because you're booked for something else but it's never my choice, I promise!

Signings at Longleat took place in a massive hall called the Orangery. The organisers had a nightmare funnelling the fans into the area but we felt quite safe cocooned in our booths as the most patient people in the world snaked slowly past. *Who* fans are always so charming and polite and interesting. Sometimes you feel as if your wrist will snap if you sign another photograph but then you see the next smiling face coming towards you and the pain vanishes.

They organised the signings in shifts so I sat down at my place next to Carole Ann Ford and before you knew it, we were engrossed in a mammoth catch-up. Then a BBC chap arrived with a huge stack of pictures for us to sign. Carole spotted them first.

'Oh my God, I never thought they'd *use* them!'

'What's wrong?' I said and grabbed a copy.

It was only the publicity shot we'd done at the hotel for *The Five Doctors*! And yes, we still looked as hideous as before.

'I'm not having this,' I said. Carole's husband and Brian were nattering away in the corner – 'Over here, boys – we've got a job for you!' Five minutes later every single photo had been submerged in one of the fire buckets of water hidden at the back.

Most fans bring their own things to be signed so it didn't matter, but every so often I'm sitting at a convention or a book signing and someone will say, 'Could you sign this, please?' and it's one of those bloody photos. God knows how they get hold of them!

It was great seeing Tom and Jon together. Funnily enough, for all Jon's waspishness, the more time they spent together at functions over the years, the more the two warmed to each other. Pat was there too, and Peter, and I met Louise Jameson again for the first time since our encounter in Richmond all those years ago. It was such fun for everyone. I remember the BBC man steering us all into the exhibition to have our photos taken with the monsters. I've got a picture of us all – Louise, Peter, Janet, Sarah, her boyfriend and me all in a line, kicking our legs up.

* * *

Longleat was incredible, and if I'm honest, it would have made a neat ending to my association with *Who*. If I had to pick a lasting memory, the sight of all those faces would be a pretty satisfying one.

The UK, however, wasn't the only place desperate to celebrate the programme's twentieth anniversary. Jon and I were booked for a summer tour of the East Coast of America, although, I confess, when the invite arrived neither of us exactly leapt for joy. Travelling for fun is one thing, but being ferried around on a tight schedule sounded distinctly unappealing. But then the organisers said that Brian and Ingeborg, Jon's wife, could come.

'*Now* they're talking!' said Jon. 'The four of us are on an all-expenses paid trip around the States.'

Suddenly we couldn't wait. If there's one thing I'd learned during those fabulous conventions in California, Chicago and Miami – the Americans really know how to spoil you.

We met Jon and Ingeborg at Heathrow. As far as I was concerned we were four friends going on holiday. A lot of our fellow passengers, however, only saw the Doctor and his companion checking in their luggage! I lost count of the number of times we were asked, 'Where's your TARDIS?', but Jon always responded as if it was the first time he'd heard it. Such an ambassador for the show – the BBC really didn't know what they'd lost in him.

The cabin crew weren't slow with the in-flight drinks and by the time we landed in Tampa, Florida the four of us were buzzing about the four weeks ahead.

'We're all in for quite an experience,' Jon observed.

And, boy, was he right.

You can never fault the passion of US *Who* fans but the word 'disorganised' doesn't really begin to cover it. Ron Katz was the President of the *Doctor Who* Fan Club of America and one of the most enthusiastic people you could ever wish to meet – but, as we soon found out, not everyone shared his zeal for the programme.

My mouth literally fell open when Ron handed over the long list of not just theatres, but agents and TV shows we were scheduled to visit in Manhattan, Chicago, Philadelphia and all points in between. Even in four weeks it looked a struggle to fit it all in. Thank God Brian was there.

Our first couple of nights were very pleasant. There was a party atmosphere as we all got to know Tampa and delivered our first talk at the town's university to hundreds of fans. Jon was in full evangelical mode, ready to spread the gospel according to *Who*. I liked that – I could hide behind his coattails, as I had for that original photo session. We weren't exactly living in the lap of luxury but, as Jon pointed out, 'It will be different when we get to Manhattan.'

And it certainly was.

After a series of bus trips we finally arrived at our hotel at three in the morning. Most places are dead at that time of night. This one was alive – and not with the type of clientele with whom you really want to share accommodation.

'Christ, it's a hooker's hotel!' said Jon.

I couldn't disagree, but all I wanted to do was eat. 'Do you think their restaurant's still open?' I asked.

Jon looked mortified. 'No, no. darling! We're not eating in this place.' And he marched us straight out and into a cab.

Where we ended up wasn't much better. Honestly, it was as if we were staying in Stalag Five. The receptionist wore all the room keys on his belt, like a jailer. It was the only place he could trust them not to be stolen. Anti-theft measures seemed to be the hotel's priority. Our pillows and all our bedding were stitched with the hotel's name in bright colours. Very chic! It really was like being in prison.

At least there was air conditioning. You were in no doubt about that because each room had a giant, noisy box above the bed.

The next morning Jon and I were being taken to record a TV programme. I opened our door just in time to see Ingeborg and Jon march past. I couldn't help noticing he had a big plaster on his nose.

'What's . . .? I began to say but Ingeborg pulled a face and mouthed, 'Don't ask.'

I got the story eventually. 'Oh, darling,' she said, 'poor Jon was so tired last night and the air conditioning was so noisy. I reached up to switch it off – and it fell on his head!'

We both burst out laughing but it must have hurt, especially with *that* nose.

Jon's day didn't get much better. We were taken in a car to what we thought would be a large Manhattan TV studio. The truth was some way short – quite an ugly building in a rather grubby area. Jon took one look and said, 'I'm not going in there.'

Ron Katz looked horrified. His big idol was upset!

'Come on, Jon,' I said. 'It will be fine, the three of us together.'

The inside, it turned out, was even worse than the exterior. Ron led us nervously to an office door and knocked. The guy inside looked like a Coen Brothers' send-up of a typical TV producer – bald, big cigar and loud. His office was tiny and crammed with scripts. Ron ushered us in. Jon shook his head, upturned a wastepaper basket, and sat indignantly on that in the hallway.

As it turned out, I don't think his behaviour hurt our chances.

'These are the actors from England I told you about,' Ron announced eagerly.

The producer stared blankly through a fug of smoke.

'*Who?*'

'I sent you a letter.'

The guy gestured to the pile of mail on his cluttered desk. Poking out near the bottom was Ron's letter – unopened.

Just when I thought it couldn't get any weirder, the producer looked at me and said, 'Do you have a Green Card?'

'No.'

'I can fix that.'

'Oh, thank you,' I said – I was just being polite.

Then he asked, 'Are you married?'

'Yes, I am.'

'Hmm, I can fix that too.'

I'd heard enough. I grabbed Jon and we headed back to the hotel. By the time we arrived, Ingeborg and Brian had moved our stuff to the nearby Ramada, which had a swimming pool on the roof. Bliss.

It wasn't entirely perfect, of course. The walls were paper-thin. In fact when I heard Jon complaining to his wife about the standard of room service I couldn't help laughing.

'Lissie, is that you?' his voice boomed from the other side of the wall. 'Can you believe they served me a paper cup? Outrageous!'

For all our trials I have to say we had a hysterical time. Brian and Jon got on famously, holding court at the bar every night, while Ingeborg and I became friends for life. You probably couldn't pick four more different people but we really gelled, especially in the face of adversity.

Which was just as well . . .

Looking back I don't know how we coped, but one of the funniest things was being turfed out of our hotel in Philadelphia. We'd started the day with Bloody Marys – hospitality was excellent, I have to say – but I think there was a problem with the bill so we had to relocate, in our drunken haze, to the Holiday Inn. Brian and I giggled our way through it but moods across the hall were more highly strung.

Ingeborg was crying, 'Oh, Jon, oh Jon!', and so out came the happy pills. Hysterical. I think I woke up at one point in the shower at three in the morning. One of my favourite conventions ever!

I seem to remember a fire alarm going off during Jon's talk in Chicago's Granada Theatre, which wasn't so bad considering the place was freezing. And somewhere along the line I was asked for a pair of knickers to auction! Apparently you're able to see a flash of my pants in *The Ark in Space* – I had no idea – so they wanted to recreate it. I foolishly handed over a red pair but I was told, 'Oh no, you were wearing *white* in the show', so I went back to my suitcase. The guy who eventually bought them – for quite a few dollars, I think – asked me to sign them. It's disturbing to think there's a pair of your pants hanging up on someone's wall.

I was sad when it was all over: Jon and I had never been closer. It turned out that a four-week bus tour was no time at all – little did I know that an even bigger commitment was just around the corner.

* * *

After such a carefree few months I thought it was time to take a step back from the Whoniverse before I got tired of it again. When I got the call from Barry Letts to appear in his new BBC production I couldn't turn it down. By then, especially after our boozy nights in Fort Lauderdale, Barry was more of a family friend than a colleague – I would do anything for him.

The show was *Alice in Wonderland*, which brought back fuzzy memories of the school production of *Through the Looking-Glass* – and of poor Edwina Currie! This time I'd be playing the Dormouse, which sounded fun. As usual Barry had surrounded himself with trusted favourites. Roy Skelton was the Mock Turtle, Linda Polan was with me again and Jonathan Cecil, who'd also been with Linda and me in *Gulliver*, returned as the White Rabbit. Best of all for me was that Brian was cast as the Gryphon – my husband and my mentor, what could be better?

As a pair of daft non-planners we dared to assume good times were just around the corner for both of us. And we were right – but not in the way we expected.

In the summer of 1984 I went along for my first costume fitting. The designer that day was Jackie Stubbs, who had worked with me on *Who*. Jackie put down her tape measure and then said, 'Lis, do you think you should have a pregnancy test?'

'A *what*?'

Jackie could tell I'd put on weight since we last met and that my bust had grown.

'It's the only explanation, Lis,' she said.

In disbelief, I went to a chemist and took three test packs home with me – they all said the same thing.

Our neighbour at the time was Mandy, a sixty-year-old Austrian who had escaped from the Nazis over the Alps. I was always round there knocking back the odd sherry with her and Arnold. That day I was so shocked by the tests I went crying next door, 'Mandy, I'm pregnant!'

Then I fainted on her kitchen floor.

Shocked as I was, I have to admit it wasn't an accident. Events over the previous couple of years seemed to have been building up to it. In 1983 Brian had gone into hospital to have a bronchial cyst removed. It wasn't in any way a life-threatening operation but I distinctly remember leaving his bedside and coming home, opening the front door and thinking, *It's so empty. So quiet. Where are the children?*

Brian got a clean bill of health soon after, as expected, and later that year we went to the Greek islands to celebrate our fifteenth wedding anniversary. What could be more romantic? Then one night we were dining in a beautiful taverna and got talking to the waiter. We explained how long we'd been together and after congratulating us, he said, 'Where are your children?'

That question again!

It sounds ridiculous, I know, but it took a complete stranger asking that to make us think: *Why don't we have children?* The answer, like so many things in our lives, was because we simply hadn't got round to it. For the first time I questioned whether our policy of not planning anything had been the way to go. And, for the first time, I decided, no. This was something that needed to be planned – and the sooner the better.

So here I was, a year later, recovering in my darling neighbour's house from the shock of it all. I couldn't wait to tell Brian when he came home. I planned a fancy meal and even lit the candles – I was going to do this properly.

Then I heard the front door open and before he'd even put his suitcase down I'd blurted it out!

Thirty-eight is pretty old to be starting a family – and it was even more unusual in the 1980s. When I went into hospital for the birth I overheard a matron say, 'Better keep an eye on this one, put her by the door.' *Thank you so much*.

I had a very healthy pregnancy, actually. So healthy that when the invite came a week later to attend a convention in Mobile, Alabama, I thought, *Why not?* I changed my mind when Brian announced he was too busy to come, but he persuaded me – 'Go, you've got to do it, you'll have fun!'

But I didn't want to travel on my own so my agent's assistant, Barbara, came along for a jolly. I warned her not to expect too much. 'When Jon and I were on tour last year half the places didn't even know we were coming, but we'll have fun,' I promised.

I have to admit, we had a terrific time. Not only did everyone in Mobile seem to know we were coming, they actually awarded me the Freedom of the City! There was a big ceremony and the Mayor of Mobile handed over a certificate.

As November drew close and the prospect of our annual trip to the Chicago convention loomed, my pregnancy seemed to kick up a gear. About ten days before we flew out, I just exploded – I simply doubled in size. Nothing would fit, so I was hurrying around for new clothes when I should have been getting ready. I remember getting in the lift at the hotel, wearing a pristine white frock, and Frazer Hines stepped in and did a double-take at my bump.

'Christ, you look like a bloody Easter egg!'

After Mobile it was nice having Brian with me again, although when the organisers paid for his ticket I wonder if they realised his own involvement with the show. In January, viewers in the UK had seen him as Dugdale in Peter Davison's *Snakedance* serial. Later, he would become the voice of the Daleks. It was nice to see him signing autographs as well.

Jon and Ingeborg were at Chicago, too. It was such a thrill to see them again and to rake over last year's fun. I loved the way Ingeborg never took any nonsense from Jon. We were having lunch in the hotel when he said, 'Inge, darling, do you want to come down and see me open the convention?'

She stared at him as if he was mad. 'Jon, why would I want to see that? I see you every day!'

There was a really good spirit around the whole event. I don't know if it was the hormones but I felt in an even sillier mood than usual, so when someone started signing fake names on the photographs, we all joined in. If you've got a photo of me from Chicago 1984, check the signature: it might just say 'Mickey Mouse'!

* * *

Workwise, a BBC strike put paid to *Alice*'s production, but for the first time in my life I didn't care. Time off with my bump was all I could think about. Brian, though, was working on a telly programme in the Midlands called, funnily enough, *Eh, Brian! It's a Whopper,* so I was alone a lot. If I wanted to see him, it meant a train up to Birmingham.

The baby's due date was 1 February – my birthday. I learned a lot about my headstrong daughter that month when she refused to budge until the 25th. By then I was so large I'd got stuck in the larder! Mandy from next door had to rescue me.

Dad came to visit in the last weeks and finally Brian finished in Birmingham. It was all looking good until he got a weekend job at Thames Television at the end of the month.

He'd been in a couple of hours on the Saturday when at five to midnight things started.

'Brian,' I said, 'the baby's coming.'

He leapt out of bed as if I'd put 10,000 volts through him and ran out the door. *Wow*, I thought, *he's practised this*! Ten minutes later I was sitting dressed on the bed, packed overnight bag next to me, and I thought, *Where the hell is he?*

'Brian!'

'Yes?' a voice came back from the bathroom.

'What are you doing?'

He said, 'I'm washing my hair – I'm recording tomorrow.'

The bastard!

I'm sitting there with my legs crossed and he's primping and preening.

'Look, I don't know how long we'll be there,' he told me. 'I might not have time to come home again.'

I was furious he was even contemplating work but that's the actor's lot. You're at the whim of the industry. Let a director down and your career might never recover. Even so . . .

We got to hospital and things went so slowly that he was still there on the Sunday morning. Barely able to stand from exhaustion, he said, 'I'm sorry, I've got to go.'

I wasn't happy but I understood.

When Brian came rushing back at eleven o'clock at night the only change was that I was now in agony. I didn't want any painkillers but by the Monday morning they recommended an epidural. My God, the relief was instant! Then I heard a doctor say, 'We need to monitor this because the baby's in a bit of distress.'

Suddenly I was on full alert.

'Hang on, *distress*? I don't mind a bit of pain but we're not risking my baby!'

After all my years on *Who* I should have realised you can't tell a doctor anything.

'We'll leave it a couple of hours then help you push.'

'*Push*?' I said. 'I can't feel anything below my neck.'

Talk turned to forceps.

I said, 'No way. The baby's in distress, I want the baby out now!'

'Look, if you have a caesarean, you will know about it tomorrow,' a nurse told me.

'If I *don't* have a caesarean, *you* will know about it tomorrow!' I insisted.

So about ten to three on the afternoon of 25 February 1985, Sadie

Isabelle Amy Miller was born. Eight pounds, but the size of a donkey, and beautiful – absolutely beautiful! I'd never been so happy in my life.

* * *

It should be obvious by now that Brian and I aren't planners. I hadn't planned to have a baby at thirty-nine – but then I hadn't *not* planned to either. I guess we both assumed it would happen one day, although neither of us appreciated that time might have been running out. Consequently I never planned to give up work – or to not give up work. When I looked in the diary at a booking for the hit cop show at the time, *Dempsey & Makepeace*, it didn't occur to me to cancel.

It was a mistake. I didn't enjoy being away from Sadie, and trying to work while you're still expressing milk simply doesn't work. I nearly knocked it all on the head but then I got a call from my agent. *Alice* was up and running again. Every instinct told me to pass but it was Barry, bless him; I didn't realise how worried he'd been about me either. 'I hadn't heard anything and she was so late arriving . . .' He admitted he'd feared the worst.

It's hard being a mother in a city with no family around to lend a hand. Mandy helped out a lot but because Brian was on *Alice* as well, we had to hire a nanny. She was nice but it wasn't like leaving Sadie with family.

Still, having the nanny gave me a ridiculous amount of confidence. Before I knew it, I'd said 'yes' to that year's Chicago convention on the proviso that the nanny had to come as well.

'No problem.'

OK, I thought, *Have baby, will travel.*

Three days before we left, the nanny announced she was pregnant (she must have known before we'd booked the tickets). We got to Chicago and she had a lie down! Pregnancy does some strange things but I was so annoyed. At nine months Sadie was crawling all over the place. I remember getting up one morning, Brian was doing a phone interview – and our daughter was trying to chew through the cables! *That's it*, I thought. *No more juggling, something's got to give*.

The final straw came a few months later. Lovely Tim Stern, who'd played my husband in *Robin Hood* at Bristol, introduced me to his wife, Paddy. She was casting director on *Emmerdale* and she said, 'We've got the perfect part for you.'

At that moment I understood exactly what Oscar Wilde meant about resisting everything but temptation. The habits of twenty years as a freelance actor are hard to give up. So while every fibre in my body was screaming, *No*, I heard myself say, 'Tell me more . . .'

I went up for a meet and greet with the producers and afterwards Paddy came over, scratching her head.

'Lis, why did you just talk yourself out of that job?'

I thought, *Yes, I did, didn't I?*

Physically I'd shown up and done what was required but subconsciously, deep inside, I really didn't want the job – and that must have shown. I had other priorities – I was now a mother and that needed to come first. And I was so grateful for Paddy picking up on it – I needed more time with my baby before I could even think of work.

* * *

Your priorities change when you're a parent – the world now revolves around your child. Some people find that easier to accept than others. When we sent out the invitations to Sadie's christening, Jon and Ingeborg came top of the list. We'd had such a blast with them in the States and Brian and I now considered them both firm friends. Sadly they couldn't come but sent a darling little dress. I took great pleasure in sending them a photo of Sadie wearing it.

Months later, when I spoke to Barry, he said, 'You haven't been in touch with Jon – I think he's quite hurt.'

You know my number, Jon – pick up the damn phone! I thought.

When you've given birth, been ill, and you're operating on no sleep and trying to spend some time with your daughter, the last thing on your mind is getting the house ready for a dinner party. But Jon had obviously taken offence – he always liked to be thought of as the leader of the pack – and we didn't speak for quite a while after that. (Once again it would be *Who* which brought us together again.)

If Jon had been so bothered about seeing Sadie he could have popped round – like Ian Marter did. It was about eight o'clock when the bell rang one night. Sadie had just gone down, Brian was working at the Bristol Old Vic and I was shattered. *Oh God, who's that?* I thought.

And it was Ian. It says a lot for how much I loved him that he didn't get the door slammed in his face. He was as happy and bubbly as ever but he'd changed quite a bit during my pregnancy. He'd bulked up a lot at the gym, which I didn't think was very healthy for an acute diabetic, but he wasn't there to talk about himself – he was just desperate to get a peep at Sadie.

'Oh, Ian, she's just gone down!'

'Let me pop up, Lis, I'd love to see her.'

You've never seen such a big man creep so silently. He was up there for quite a few minutes, just watching Sadie sleep – I loved him for that.

That was the last time Ian came to our house. In fact, I only saw him one more time. Then in 1986 I took a horrible call saying he'd died. Heart trouble. I was devastated. So was Brian – they'd been such tight friends for a while. The funeral was an incredibly sad affair but his sons were amazing, really strong for their mother. Louise Jameson leant over from the row behind me and said, 'My God, aren't they wonderful?'

Ian would have been so proud.

* * *

Ian's death put a lot of things into perspective. When I 'retired', Barry said to me, 'Don't walk too far away.' At the time I didn't think too much about what that meant.

Until I tried to get back . . .

Chapter Fifteen

Count Me In

WHEN SADIE started school at four-and-a-half, I went along to work as a teacher's helper, as you were called then. I would look after the little ones. Best of all, I got to see my daughter in the playground, on all her sports days, in all her plays. I really spent as much time as I could with her. It's not how everyone chooses to live, of course, but it suited me.

Rarely did I think of work. My agent Todd Joseph had died shortly after Ian. Had he still been around, I think I might have felt more pressure to get back into the business. Left to my own devices, I was happy to drift along outside of it, though.

We were still part of the acting community, however, and every so often a job invite would come my way. Getting a new agent helped. The problem was, casting directors expect you to jump when they say so – they didn't want to hear about my school work or having to pick Sadie up from here and take her there. I think I shut as many doors in my own face as my new agent, Claire, opened.

But the odd thing did work out. I got a part in *The Bill* – often said to be the lowest rung of any actor's professional life. If I couldn't get on there, I couldn't get on anywhere! At the time, though, the main thing was that it fitted in with my domestic life. Barely a couple of days' work in total, but at least I'd put a toe back in the water. Generally, though, I began to realise the industry can be pretty cold to women of a certain age. So, after the next door swung closed, I thought, *You know what? I'm fine without it.*

It's fair to say even Sadie had more luck than me. In fact, there was a time when she was the only Miller working! We were at Claire's agency's Christmas party and she must have been watching Sadie because she said, 'Have you ever thought of letting Sadie do something?'

I dismissed this with a laugh but of course Little Miss Big Ears heard. 'What was that, Mummy? What was that? What? *What?*'

So I said to Claire, 'I don't mind anything that involves a lot of other children. Something small – I don't want any pressure on her.'

Then *Dear Mr God, It Is Anna* turned up and Claire sent us along. Sadie got through the audition but then I bought the book and discovered it was about a little girl dying. That wasn't what I had in mind for her so we pulled out. The longer I could protect my daughter from the concept of tragedy, the better. That might have been the end of a glittering career, but when the same director was casting for *Royal Celebration* – a television play about a party to celebrate Charles and Diana's wedding – a few years later, he remembered Sadie. She went along and the next thing we knew she was playing Minnie Driver's daughter alongside Peter Howarth, Leslie Phillips (who sat Sadie on his knee and told her stories about life as a child actor), Kenneth Cranham (who'd been in *A Midsummer Night's Dream* with me all those years ago) and Rupert Graves. She needed a chaperone, of course, and I took her once, but mainly it was Brian. So, you see, she *was* the only one of us working.

The *Daily Mail* actually gave her the best review and soon Claire was back with another offer, this time to play Rik Mayall's daughter in something for Granada. Sadie was desperate to do it but I looked at the hours and the travel and thought, *No, education has to come first*. She was furious, of course, but now she's been to college, she has four A-levels and she's been to university: she still has her acting career ahead of her.

* * *

While my television career appeared to have hit the buffers, my radio career was about to spring to life – and with it an old relationship.

The last I'd heard of Jon was Barry's message that he was upset at not being invited round to dinner after Sadie was born. However, having managed to miss each other on the convention circuit for eight years, we both now agreed to take part in a *Doctor Who* radio serial for the BBC. I knew it was time to clear the air and was genuinely pleased to see him; I wondered if he'd forgotten. Then he said, 'Ingeborg is very upset with you.'

I thought, *Jon, don't play that card*. So I said, 'What do you mean?'

'Well, you know, we never got the invite to see Sadie.'

I wasn't in the mood to pull punches.

'Look, number one – you were invited to the christening and you couldn't come. Number two – after that Brian was working in Bristol, I was alone and I didn't have grandparents around to help: Brian's mother is disabled and in Birmingham, bless her, my dad was very old. I had no one down here to say, "Have a day out, Lis." Do you really think I had time to worry about dinner parties?'

He looked suitably sheepish at that.

'Get Ingeborg on the phone – *now*.'

Ten minutes later we'd had a chat, our first in almost a decade, and it was all sorted. In fact, we were giggling about how the last time we'd met she'd been appalled by me saying I was going to give birth on a bucket – apparently gravity really helps! Everything was fine. How silly to have wasted so much negative energy over the years, though.

Of course, once the seal had been broken, Jon was like an uncle to Sadie. We started bumping into each other at conventions or parties and he was so good with her. Once we were at Manchester town hall doing an event and he said to her, 'Come and help me with my signings', so she sat there drawing or colouring while he scribbled his name. Some people reading this book might actually have my daughter's first autographs! But he was such a terrible tease, too. I always think children should dress their age, not in something out of Victoria's Secret. So she'd stand there in her frocks with her little lace-trimmed socks and Jon would turn his nose up and say, 'Oh Sadie, your knickers are falling down.' Bless her, she always looked!

Our radio programme was called *The Paradise of Death* and, I was so happy to hear, it was written by Barry Letts. His son Dominic played a few minor characters, which was nice, and Nick Courtney was onboard as well. We all had a great time. It's such a treat to act without having to worry about hair and makeup. And there's zero chance that anyone will say, 'Can you bring your own clothes, Lis?'

Or so I thought.

Word came down that we were to go into the car park at Maida Vale studios in our lunch hour and have a few promotional snaps taken with the TARDIS. 'Oh, and Lis – could you wear something colourful?'

The shoot was a disaster from start to finish. Firstly, the Brigadier's costume sent for Nick came with the wrong belt. Nick's a fastidious old thing and declared, 'The Brig would not wear that and neither will I!' So, he ended up in civvies. Jon, on the other hand, was resplendent in his original *Who* coat – which was odd because I could have sworn I'd seen it at auction half a dozen times. It was almost as if he'd had a whole bunch of them run up just to sell . . .

Standing waiting in that freezing-cold car park we were aware that the TARDIS itself had yet to materialise. Suddenly a lorry pulled in. The driver hopped out and, recognising Jon, said, 'There's your TARDIS, mate.'

We all stared at it – it was completely flat-packed.

'I was rather hoping someone would assemble it,' the photographer said to the trucker.

'Not me, mate – I'm just the delivery guy!'

So there we were, me, Nick, the photographer, and the show's director, Phil Clarke, all trying to do this giant blue jigsaw puzzle. By this point, *Who* had been cancelled, ending in 1989 with Sylvester McCoy's third season, and the TARDIS had been in storage for four years. The poor old police box was covered in cobwebs and dust; that was enough for Jon to opt out. 'I can't get my coat too near that – it's too valuable!'

Of course it is, Jon, I thought. *Of course it is . . .*

And do you think we could got the thing properly erected? Of course not! Look carefully at the final shots and you can see I'm holding a wall up with my back. One step forward and it would have been on my head – and not for the first time. But the BBC used the images to promote the series anyway, so if you wonder why we look like we're being goosed in a microwave, that's the reason.

I knew he could be tricky but few things gave me more pleasure than seeing Jon at the height of his powers. He'd been back at his best on *The Five Doctors* and watching him in that radio studio, you could see he was thrilled to be the Doctor again. The difference was, when we did *The Five Doctors* he was still a big star again off the back of *Worzel Gummidge*. Ten years later, I think the good parts had all but dried up.

Jon clearly had a lot riding on it. 'Lissie, we have to get our butts out there and promote it,' he said. Which is how we came to do our first British convention – organised by Alan Langley – since Longleat.

With *Who* no longer on television, a starved fandom propelled the radio programme to number one in the charts. It was so successful a second serial was commissioned, again written by Barry and directed by Phil. When finally broadcast at the start of 1996, *The Ghosts of N-Space* was another hit, but its success proved bittersweet because by then it had been in the can for two years. When production on the *Doctor Who* television movie with Paul McGann started, the BBC held back all other *Who*-related product. Nothing was to get in the way of the Eighth Doctor's precious US-aimed adventure. (*Nothing*, that is, except the plot!)

If only they'd embargoed things before then. I might have been spared one of the least memorable experiences of my career.

* * *

Ten years after *The Five Doctors*, and with *Doctor Who* consigned, or so we thought, to the archives of television history, I never expected to receive another call from John Nathan-Turner. 'Lissie, it's thirty years – we need to do something for the fans.'

There he was again with that damn phrase and this time, as well as the stick, he held the added carrot of being part of the BBC's *Children in Need* programme. We could potentially raise a lot of money, and having dedicated the last eight years of my life to raising my own daughter it seemed churlish to say 'no'.

As befits a charity special, it was utterly preposterous. Somehow JNT had conceived of a plot involving all the Doctors – along with the cast of *EastEnders*! It was called *Dimensions in Time* and I was booked to shoot, once again, alongside the Third Doctor. After such fun times on *Paradise*, I was looking forward to it.

But once again, I was underestimating the power of Pertwee . . .

The night before the shoot, the Miller family attended a press screening of Sadie's *Royal Celebration*. All these kids were running around and it was a really enjoyable evening. Unfortunately, events ended up dragging on and all the while the buffet was sitting under the hot lights. As I was working the next day, I didn't drink. *But a couple of those prawns can't hurt . . .*

A few hours later and I'd never been sicker. As my morning pickup time of seven o'clock drew closer, it only seemed to get worse. And the thought of squeezing into my *Five Doctors* costume again after all those years made my empty stomach turn somersaults. Actors rarely have the option of cancelling and somehow I made it to Elstree in one piece, where the makeup girl took one look at me and said, 'Oh my God, you're green!'

Oh shit, I thought, *I'm really in trouble!*

I did the best I could, but Sod's law, the usually impeccable Jon chose today to keep fluffing his lines, so we were out there in Albert

Square for take after take, after take. In a bizarre echo of one of our earliest meetings, he kept calling me Lis instead of Sarah, too. Eventually I couldn't hold it back any longer. I made my excuses, then legged it round the other side of one of the market stalls and was sick all over again. Completely washed out, I stumbled back.

'Sorry, everyone,' I mumbled. 'I'm really not very well.'

I don't know what Jon was on, but he turned theatrically to someone else and nonchalantly said, 'Oh, she always does this!'

What do you mean 'always *does this'? You're the one who's always complaining he's ill!* I thought.

Any other day I would have had him on toast, but this time I was too weak. In any case, the words were barely out of his mouth when he got his karmic reward.

Wendy Richard had appeared on set. As a future Pauline Fowler she was meant to have aged an awful lot, so she was covered in grey powder. 'Oh my God, darling, Wendy looks rough!' said Jon.

And I just kept quiet. I thought, *If you haven't read the script, I'm not bloody telling you, you silly sod!*

I decided to let him go over and put his foot in it. And he did!

The end result is what it is. In the absence of anything else I think it garnered a lot of interest and fans tell me they enjoyed it. Managing so many mini-plots and myriad time travellers seemed an impossible task but JNT pulled it together. But you wonder why he bothered when nobody else at the BBC seemed to have an interest in the proper show. *Who*, to the people with the money, was a relic and so was anyone associated with it. We were only good, it appeared, for driving VHS sales – not for investing in with new programmes.

Which makes it all the more satisfying whenever I watch *EastEnders* and see that market stall. If only the BBC bosses knew . . .

* * *

Fortunately, after a few years trapped in my own version of *The Five Doctors*' Death Zone, my non-*Who* career was beginning to pick up again. I was pleased to land a small part in a series called *Men of the World*. The regular cast was very strong: David Threlfall has appeared in *Shameless* and *Harry Potter*, while Brenda Bruce was in *Paradise Towers* with Sylvester, and John Simm of course was magnificent as the recent Master. I played Lorraine in an episode called *Lost in France*. My main memory of it is of not being stuck in a quarry. Such a relief!

I have to say, that show whetted my appetite for something more. *If only* Emmerdale *hadn't been offered so early, I'm ready for it now*, I thought. The *Emmerdale* door was firmly closed at that moment but I did get the next best thing, give or take a few miles: *Peak Practice*.

I was actually a fan of the show when I was asked to audition. I'm not saying it's quite like David Tennant being a *Who* aficionado from childhood, but I had a relationship with the programme before I walked in front of the casting director. I like castings, actually, because they're usually quite near my house in London and they keep you honest – you either perform on the day or you don't. Well, I was offered two episodes as Dr Pat Hewland and as they fell across Sadie's summer holidays, we thought we'd all go up to the Peak District and enjoy a week together afterwards. It was a great idea – I loved that place. We stayed in a delightful bijou hotel, ate lamb cooked with lavender and just let our hair down. Even during filming I got to spend time with my family. We worked two days and off, three days and off, so it wasn't as full-on as it might have been.

I say I was a fan – well, I had been of the original cast of Kevin Whately and Amanda Burton. I knew there was a different line-up for Series Four but I didn't know who and I was thrown into it as soon as I arrived. At one point I was sitting at a desk, trying to establish a connection with this new actor, and I began to despair – he just wasn't having any of it. *This is going to be a long day*, I thought. I'd just about had enough when he got up and left – it turned out he was a stand-in! When the real actor came in, we got on like a house on fire but they were doing so many episodes at the same time – literally running from one scene to another – that I suppose he'd been needed elsewhere, to get the lighting right, or something.

I admit it was quite hard work getting back into the groove, especially learning how people did things outside *Who*. Some of it was quite an eye opener – and not always for bad reasons. I couldn't believe it when I was shown to my trailer.

My own trailer!

It wasn't as hi-spec as the one I have on *The Sarah Jane Adventures* – nowadays I've got my own bed, and a microwave and even a shower – but it felt like a palace compared to the old days on *Who*. Just having somewhere to take your lunch other than squatting on damp hillocks, in makeup vans or under awnings made me feel like a superstar.

I was sad when it was over so when the call came for more episodes, I didn't hesitate – 'Just tell me when.'

Two days later, I was on the train back up to the Peak District.

This sudden change of fortunes ought to have sounded warning bells. By now it was all very chaotic and they seemed extremely behind. Reshoots were going on left, right and centre and the script I was posted told its own story (every time there's a change it's printed on different coloured paper). This was pink – way down the line. By the time I arrived I'd just about got it memorised – and then the buggers handed over an amended version.

Committing two separate speeches to memory is far easier than learning two versions of the same one – you get so confused, your tongue's saying one version while your brain is remembering the other. I was still poring over it in makeup with a couple of the other actors when I heard one of them say, 'It's no good – I can't learn this.'

'Thank God for that!' I said. 'I can't make it stick either.'

Not surprisingly we had a lot of trouble that day. It didn't help that the cameramen wouldn't stop talking to me about *Doctor Who*! I was shoving rescue remedy down my throat and grabbing my script in between takes. During one seated scene all three of us had our scripts out of shot on our laps so we could snatch an emergency peek!

I had fun but it wasn't the big comeback I perhaps needed to boot me up the backside and get me back out there. In fact after that, I only took one more stab at acting, in a series called *Faith in the Future* with Lynda Bellingham – then I just thought, *Do you know what? I've had a go, I've been busy, but I haven't really enjoyed it.*

And so I retired.

Goodbye work. Goodbye acting. And goodbye *Doctor Who*.

* * *

Knowing I wouldn't be working again made it more fun to spend time with my old *Who* cohorts. In 1996 I bumped into Jon at an event organised by Nathan-Turner. Jon was in his mid-70s by then, but he looked well. He was on good form, too – cheeky, chatty and brimming with gossip as usual. We had a marvellous time reminiscing about this and that, at ease without any work pressures hanging over us. Among other things I remember he was very excited about going to stay with friends over in New England. Then at one point he leaned in and I thought, *This must be good if he's lowering his voice!* Jon was hardly discreet.

But this time the gossip was about him: 'By the way, I had a little *crie de coeur* recently.'

That floored me.

'Oh, Jon, I didn't know you had heart trouble!'

'It's nothing, darling,' he said, dismissing my concern with a wave of his hand. 'Just a little warning.'

That was the last time I saw him.

A few weeks later I got home and saw my answerphone flashing. I was still taking off my coat and unpacking my bags when I flicked 'play', but the message soon had my full attention.

I recognised the voice instantly as Stuart Money, a close friend of Jon's.

'Hello, Lissie, it's Stuey,' he said. 'I'm on my way to the airport.

It's about Jon. I will talk to you later but I think you're going to get quite a shock.'

I sat by that phone for the rest of the day – if anyone else called I just told them to get off the line. And then my worst fears were confirmed: Jon had suffered a heart attack in America.

My Doctor was dead.

I went to the funeral. Sadie sent a little something, too. But do you know who wasn't there? Barry! No one had told him. Incredible. He was devastated, of course.

The problem with being in the public eye is you're not given a chance to grieve. Every time I thought that I was over the shock another journalist would pop up asking for a comment. I don't normally mind, but I wanted to do the best by Jon and I also wanted to be alone and cry.

It wasn't until I did manage a few minutes alone with my thoughts that I appreciated just how much we'd experienced together. All the shows, obviously, but there were so many private moments, too. Even our big US trip – yes, Brian and Ingeborg were there and we all had a blast – but there were only two people up on those stages. Jon was the only one who knew what I'd gone through first hand. And now he was gone.

Jon's legacy speaks for itself, but all these years later I do get annoyed at the number of people popping out of the woodwork to tell you how Jon was, what he thought, and what he apparently said to them. There are certain DVD commentaries where the world and his wife seem to have an opinion and I find myself shouting at the screen, 'How do you know? You weren't there!' Some of them weren't even born at the time, for goodness' sake.

* * *

The older you get, the more often you have to deal with loss. When my father died, on Boxing Day 1994 – aged 94 – I thought my world had collapsed. We've always been alone down here in London but at that moment I suddenly realised it was Brian, Sadie and me against the world.

The tragedy of being associated with such a long-running show is that, inevitably, people you worked with, people you loved, will die. Some, like Jon, will be quite old. Others, like John Nathan-Turner (who died in May 2002, aged 55) are taken much too soon. Tom Baker was hilarious at JNT's memorial. It feels so unnatural attending the ceremony of a man as young as Nathan, but Gary, his partner, insisted his life should be celebrated. We were at St Paul's, the actors' church in Covent Garden. Tom gazed up at the heavens and said, 'Sorry, John – it's this St Paul's', which broke the ice. Then he brought the house down when he said: 'What would John, looking down, be thinking now? Well, I can tell you . . .

'He would be thinking, *I would rather it were Tom up here than me!*'

Chapter Sixteen

That's The Last I'll Be Hearing From Them

I ENTERED THE restaurant thinking, *I'm going to lose my agent over this!*

I was in central London, at a very swish venue, and about to meet Russell T Davies and Phil Collinson. Russell, of course, was the creative head of the newly regenerated *Doctor Who* and Phil was the show's producer. They'd asked my new agent, Roger Carey, if we could meet and I'd duly gone along with it. I wasn't hopeful. Approaching my sixtieth birthday and thoroughly enjoying my retirement, my thoughts were so far away from *Who* you'd need a telescope to spot them.

Still, it's always polite to attend these meetings and hear what people have to say. And a meal at an expensive restaurant with wonderful company is never to be sniffed at. The trick is not being afraid to turn offers down – which we, as actors, find notoriously hard to do. There's always this fear: 'What if nothing else comes along?' I'd lived with the spectre of 'what if' most my life but that was all behind me now – being a full-time wife and mother was quite enough, thank you very much.

But I wasn't daft. I knew Russell and Phil wouldn't have called just for the sake of it. They were obviously planning to propose something – just as I was planning to turn it down. It wasn't that I thought their new series with Chris Eccleston and Billie Piper didn't look amazing – because it did; it was marvellous – but my time on *Who* was so precious to me that I wasn't prepared to spoil it again for a cheap ratings-boosting, blink-and-you'll-miss-me cameo. If

Russell wanted someone from the 'classic series' to fill a few screen seconds then there would be no shortage of others who I was sure would leap at the chance.

And so, a little guilty that I was wasting my hosts' time, I decided to just relax and enjoy my afternoon.

From the moment I sat down I knew I was in the company of two men who cared more about their programme than anything else in the world. They weren't in it for the money or the ratings – although of course these would come – they truly, deeply sweated and bled *Doctor Who*. And not just *Who*. Towards me they were so warm and welcoming, and charming and funny, and . . . I could go on all day. It was a really unforgettable dinner. Russell will have anyone hooting with laughter in seconds, but he's so sharp and serious as well.

Out of the blue he placed a script on the table and said, 'We'd like you to do this story.'

* * *

It was back in 2003 that I began to hear things. Just rumours at first, idle gossip, really. At one time they were making another movie, then there was a programme about a new Time Lord. Each whisper was as fanciful as the next. Then, on 26 September 2003, the head of BBC1, Lorraine Heggessey, announced to the press one simple fact.

She was bringing back *Doctor Who*.

I remembered the ill-fated attempt to relaunch the show in 1997 with the lovely Paul McGann. *I hope they treat it better this time*, I thought, but my interest ended there. It had nothing to do with me – not as an actor or even as a fan.

'Classic' *Who* – as people started calling it – was still calling on my time, however. When I joined the show I'd just missed out on its tenth anniversary but I'd been involved in the twentieth and thirtieth celebrations. Even so, I was surprised to get an invite to the Houses of Parliament to celebrate *Who*'s fortieth. It was quite a low-key affair. Peter Davison was the only Doctor present, but there was a big cake and K-9 put in an appearance as well. It never fails to astound me how wherever you go, fans appear. I was told MPs were leaving the Commons chamber just to come over and say 'hello', before darting back in to vote.

'Hi, I'm Glasgow North! Any time you want a chat just pop up there.' Bizarre.

As usual, I was upstaged by the bloody dog! All the MPs wanted to have a word with him. Ann Widdecombe, of all people, absolutely adored him. She came running over for a hug and a photo.

The biggest celebration for the fans, of course, was the news that *Who* was being given the kiss of life by the Corporation that had killed it off in the first place. Was I bothered?

Not in the slightest, actually.

Barry always said they could never bring it back, its time had passed, and I was inclined to agree with him. I hadn't watched the programme before I joined and I'd barely seen more than a few minutes since I'd left. *Doctor Who* for me is the relationships I built up during those couple of years in the 1970s: Jon, Tom, Barry, Terry (*all* the Terrys, in fact), Robert, Chris . . . everyone who made it such a special time. Maybe the show itself had run its course.

Television had moved on since we'd run around wobbly sets with Plasticine dinosaurs. I thought, *If this show is to stand a chance it will need serious investment.* You can't skimp. Modern audiences won't stand for it. In the end, you have to say it was backed to the hilt: the money is there to see on the screen.

As soon as I get home from an event such as the Parliament party, I become Mrs Miller. Elisabeth Sladen, star of TV's *Doctor Who*, is hung up in the hallway with my coat – I'm not interested in carrying on that life unless I'm working. Even so, word from the new production occasionally filtered through; you had to be impressed with the calibre of personnel they were assembling. From what I was hearing, they had the imagination and the passion – *and* the budget. What impressed me most was they had the manners as well. Barry and Terry Dicks were both invited down to Cardiff by Russell T Davies. That just proves how much he cares – he's as much of a fan as anyone. Barry hadn't been there long when he signalled a big 'thumbs-up' to Russell (just as he had to hire me all those years ago). That would have meant everything to Russell.

There was such a buzz about the programme from people like Barry that I did find myself sitting down in March 2005 to watch *Rose*, the first episode. Five minutes later I was reaching for the 'off' button. Not that I didn't like it – I was just too nervous on their behalf. I just thought, *It's their first night, they're going to be pulling out all the stops, trying to tick so many boxes to prove it was the right thing to bring it back*. I could almost feel their anxiety from Cardiff – I've been in that position. So I decided to wait a few episodes and tune in when they'd hit their stride. I'm actually glad I did. Chris Eccleston was tremendous, magnificently dark, and it was a shame he didn't continue longer.

The revival had registered on my radar, then, but that was all. Then fans started writing in – young correspondents who'd seen the new show and gone on to discover old tapes and DVDs of my serials. They were all asking about Sarah – 'What do you think she would be doing now?' Although it was nice to know the interest was there, again this didn't impact on my life greatly. It was outside of what I was doing and thinking at the time.

When the press rang – as they did in their droves – to ask how I felt about *Who* coming back, I gave the most honest answer that I could. I said, 'Brilliant news. It's better to come back than not come back – on many levels. Actors working for a start.' Ever the pragmatist . . .

I never for a moment thought one of those actors might be me.

* * *

When Russell pushed his script across the table I instinctively did what everyone in my profession does: I checked how many lines I'd have. How else do you know if you're an important character or not? I thought I'd be rifling through for my appearance but I couldn't believe it: there I was on virtually every page! This wasn't a cameo – this was a whole story.

I started to scan the words. Toby Whithouse, now better known for having created *Being Human*, had written a beautiful, *beautiful* script and the point where Sarah realises the Doctor has returned after all those years is tear-jerking.

I didn't know what to say.

'No pressure,' said Russell. 'It's fine if you don't want to do it.'

I stared again at the pages, dumbfounded that they'd actually written it already. There I was, third on the cast list. Everything already seemed to be in place.

How could I say no?

Afterwards Russell admitted the scale of the gamble he'd taken in commissioning the script before approaching me. If I'd turned it down they wouldn't have gone to anyone else – Sarah was the one he wanted. She was the journalist, she fitted the script; they weren't prepared to shoe-horn in any old former companion just for the sake of nostalgia. What an incredible honour.

I think all that took about half an hour. Then we ordered more wine and told jokes. The perfect meeting!

Twenty-nine years after first walking away, I was going back to *Doctor Who*.

* * *

Table read-throughs are always pressured environments. It's the first time you meet a lot of the people you'll be working with. When I was on *Who*, I was firmly ensconced in the BBC family. The extras coming in had to join *our* world, not vice versa. Upon arrival at a hotel in Cardiff for the *School Reunion* table read-through in the summer of 2005, I was as nervous as I'd ever been. The train ride down had given my doubts time to fester. *What if they realise they've made a mistake? What if they think it's too much of a risk pinning so much on a near-sixty-year-old?*

But if I had a dose of the first-day nerves, imagine what it must have been like for the new Doctor. Chris Eccleston had left and

David Tennant was in the hot seat. And this was his first day at work.

Because of time limitations they were doing read-throughs for all three parts of the first recording block in one day. So whereas I expected to be met by a cast well into their stride, in fact David was even more nervous than me.

'I'm absolutely bricking it,' Billie Piper admitted. 'David is, too.'

That made me feel better so I marched over, hand out.

'Hello, Doctor.'

He couldn't have been nicer, although when he told me how honoured he felt having me on board I assumed it was just good manners. It was only when I saw him do publicity for the show that I realised how much of a fan he had been of Tom's Doctor and Sarah Jane. Everything he said about them was so heartfelt. Just like everything he said about me. *Bless!*

In my day, at a read-through, apart from the cast, there'd be someone from makeup perhaps, maybe another person from costume if they weren't busy, and the script editor. This place was heaving – so many scriptwriters, the entire makeup department, lighting, sound, cameramen. The only person not there was the tea lady – although soon enough she popped in with refreshments. There were even people standing around the edges. That was the point at which I really panicked – I knew they were there to see David's debut and not me but even so, I thought, *I'm getting terrified now* . . .

I sat next to Anthony Head (Mr Finch, the headmaster). He's got such a twinkle about him, which is why people loved him so much in those Gold Blend coffee adverts with Cherie Lunghi. Funnily enough, my daughter Googled my name recently – and a picture of Cherie came up! I don't think I mentioned that to Tony but I was so glad we were in the same episode – I knew it would be a winner with him on board.

We did the episodes in order, so Tony and I had to sit there through two other shows first. David and Billie betrayed no sign of nerves – they were tremendous. Meanwhile, I was getting more tense by the minute. *Oh God, I just want to go home!* .

I stared at the script and concentrated on summoning the spirit of Sarah Jane. Unlike David, who had a pretty blank canvas, I had a duty to honour the character they'd seen me playing on and off for more than half my life – I needed to make sure this was the woman I knew, the Sarah I remembered.

Reintroducing myself to the character was one thing. The show, I realised, was something else. I was actually shocked at how emotionally attached I felt just being back. None of the spin-offs on telly or radio had prepared me for this. Maybe I was naïve imagining I would be able to treat it like any other job. You know, come in, do the best you can, and buy something nice with the fee – that wasn't going to happen today. The nerves told me otherwise.

Come on, Sladen, I thought. *Lots of deep breaths, lots of deep breaths . . .*

Suddenly it was our turn.

Just when I thought it couldn't get any worse, the door opened and Stephen Fry strolled in. *Just what I need – a celebrity audience.*

At these sessions you literally just sit round a table and act out, as best you can, the script in front of you. Even though you're seated, they expect you to put in as close to a proper performance as possible so Russell and the director can then tweak if some of the dialogue's a bit slow, or we inspire a joke or something like that. With everyone looking on it's quite a pressured environment and some people have been known to fall apart.

Not so David and Billie, though. They were in their stride now and Tony was just as sublime. I, on the other hand, was crap! There you go. I couldn't bear to look at Russell. Despite his pledge in the restaurant, by the end I was thinking, *I wouldn't blame him if he swapped me for Jo Grant.*

Afterwards people were very kind to me and someone said, 'Russell, Phil, Billie and David are going out for a meal with Stephen. They'd love you to join them.'

'Wonderful!' I said, all the while thinking, *Will the torture never end?*

Even though I was staying overnight, for some reason I'd forgotten to bring any makeup – I must have been panicking even before I left home. I rushed over to the makeup supervisor and said, 'Have you got anything for me?' Bless her, she parcelled up a bit of blusher and a few bits and bobs then I ran up to my room and got ready.

Stephen had been going to write an episode at one point, that's why he was there – although he was also a friend of David's anyway. I'd seen David in Russell's *Casanova* and also *Blackpool*, in which he was with the only Liverpudlian who can make a Scouse accent sound sexy – David Morrissey. I must say, though, he really stood out for me in Stephen's film *Bright Young Things*. I thought then, *That boy knows how to deliver a line fast. Anyone acting with him really needs to be on their game.*

The meal was one to remember. How could it not be in such illustrious company? But throughout I felt a bit of a fraud and I'm sure I let the side down. Whenever the conversation swung round to technology I just had to sit there in silence – I didn't know how to text and I certainly didn't have an email address, so I did feel a bit at sea. For the first time I began to have doubts about how Sarah Jane would fit in. *She's from a different generation – I'm from a different generation. It's never going to work.*

But everyone was so kind, and Stephen is a sweet, gentle man. Still I couldn't help but think, *It's all going too fast. I'm not ready.*

* * *

I'd said 'no' to returning for John Nathan-Turner in 1980 because my time with Tom Baker had been so special I didn't want to reheat that soufflé. As I returned to Cardiff in August 2005 for a three-week shoot, it was to join a different set-up. Different Doctor, different era, different personnel . . . But the second I stepped into the studio I realised that the same passion was still there. The crew in the 1970s had lived and breathed *Who* – you can see what we achieved on such small budgets. I was delighted to take note that apart from the money, nothing else had changed. You will never see devotion like it – these people would sell a kidney if it improved the show!

My first day started so perfectly. I loved it, I really did. Everyone was glorious with me, and so thoughtful. They were desperate for me to have fun, and to shine and be in the spotlight. Russell gave me his mobile number and said, 'If there's anything you don't like, just call.' What an honour.

And I couldn't believe it when I was shown my trailer. On *Who* I'd only ever had an umbrella to hide under before! Waiting for me inside was a huge bunch of flowers from the producer Julie Gardner, Russell and Phil. It was a touching gesture, if I'm honest, but I wished my arrival could have been a little more low-key. I had so much to live up to. (Actually, that was the difference between now and then. Modern *Doctor Who* is massive news and a highlight of the BBC schedule, one of the Corporation's biggest hits. There was nothing low-key about it.)

The crew in Cardiff were – and still are – spectacular. There's not a weak link in the chain. Julie, Phil and Russell are so tight. But so much has to do with who your Doctor is, and David Tennant led from the front the whole time. Behind him was an incredible ensemble desperate to make the show work and he was just so pleased to be there in that moment, *every* moment. Genuinely. And that comes across. David is David as you see him in interviews – no one will say a bad word against him, nor should they. He's the consummate professional but also the loveliest, sweetest man. I remember his parents came down to see him while I was there. They were so thrilled for him and he got a kick out of them seeing him fulfilling his childhood dream.

Being back on the show was heady enough, but shooting my first lines with David proved a real goosebumps moment. Fittingly, we were in a school gym because there I was acting like a schoolgirl. I don't think I'd appreciated how much the show had stayed with me until that moment. It was a beautiful little scene in every way, my absolute favourite.

I get asked a lot, 'What was it like seeing David instead of Tom or Jon?' And I think, I've worked on *The Five Doctors*, I've been in *Dimensions* and I'm one of the lucky few who has actually witnessed a regeneration. This time I just thought, *Ah, that's what the Doctor looks like now*. I was completely cool with it – and that's how I played it.

The Doctor may have changed but another co-star proved as temperamental as ever. You can imagine how thrilled I was when I saw in the script that I'd be reunited with K-9! As usual, I was in the minority, though. It was one thing MPs being smitten but this time when the dog appeared, all those hardened professionals suddenly melted, reverting to children, oohing and ahing over K-9 like it was a new baby. Once it started moving people couldn't get enough of it. I remember Billie saying she wanted to buy one. Well, that was before it banged into her for the tenth time in rehearsal! It can actually give you quite a nasty whack. Funnily enough, Billie never mentioned it again after that.

All these years later and it was still just an inanimate box on wheels. I foresaw plenty of uncomfortable scenes delivering dialogue crouched by its side, or take after take waiting for it to surmount a particularly tricky bump in the studio floor. Actually, full marks to Russell, he'd already thought of this. As well as Mat's K-9 they found another one that a local guy had made. This model couldn't move like the original – which isn't saying much – but you could remove its side panel and see the innards. So now we had the dog on a table being fixed and all the humans in shot at the same time, without being hunched over. Genius! Why hadn't anyone thought of this on *K-9 and Company*?

Ironically, it turned out that K-9's mobility was the least of our problems.

At the end of the first day we had to film a scene where David and I run out of the school gym. *Some things never change*, I thought. *Doctor Who* has – and always had – more haring around than *Challenge Anneka*. Anyway, we just had to bolt straight forward and turn really quickly out of the door. Pretty simple stuff, really.

Unless you're on a polished parquet floor, wearing heeled boots.

We shot off on cue. In his trademark pumps, David stuck to the floor like glue. But I didn't! As I went for the turn, I felt my standing leg slip away followed by the sound of something going 'snap'.

'Christ!' I said, clutching my thigh. It felt as if I'd been shot.

'Lis, are you all right?' David asked, instinctively reverting to his natural Scottish accent.

'I'm fine, it's OK.'

But it wasn't. I struggled on but I couldn't put any weight on that side and I knew in my heart I needed to go to hospital. As soon as my scenes ended I fell into my car and was driven to A&E. When the doctors said I had destabilised my pelvis and torn my quad I just wanted to cry. Back in my hotel that night my thoughts turned as black as my leg. *They're going to hate me if I ruin this.* What choice was I leaving them? They'd written a whole show for me, gone to the trouble of making a very specific link between modern *Who* and the classic series. And now, like a silly old woman, I was about to wreck everything. You don't let people do all this for you then bleed on them!

I admit, I've had better nights.

Eventually I decided the only thing to do was to play it down – I owed it to the team. As soon as people started worrying about me, they wouldn't be focused on their own jobs (it's human nature) and then the show would suffer. David already had enough on his plate without me adding to it and the last thing anyone needed was headlines saying 'geriatric assistant ruins comeback'. So, if anyone asked I'd be just 'sore'.

Phil was great – 'if there's anything you need' – and the director, James Hawes, shuffled things as much as possible, although I'm sure he was secretly cursing me under his breath. If you look at the programme again, you can see Rose's boyfriend, Mickey, occasionally helping me around. And if you look *really* closely, you can see one of my thighs is twice the size of the other! I don't know how I got those jeans on and off.

So much of my performance has always been about body language but when it takes all your strength just to keep upright, you're bound to skimp on the details. I know I could have done an awful lot more in that episode. As it was, I struggled to do the basics. Worst of all was the shame of knowing I was less mobile than K-9!

During the final goodbye scene with David, walking up those park steps to the TARDIS, I was dying with every step. But I made it and I got my lines out. Job done!

Then I got the call from James, 'Can you go up a bit more quickly?'

The tears were seconds away. *I'll be lucky to get up them at all*.

In hindsight, if I'd been honest, maybe we could have done it differently but the script was written and I didn't want to be the one to change it. This was the team's third episode together. Billie and David were just getting established – they needed to be thinking about each other, not me.

As a result, I must have come across as a mad woman – I couldn't focus on anything apart from my leg. I remember sitting next to David between takes. He was so charming, just nattering about this and that before going on to ask about how it felt for me being there. He said, 'It must be really strange for you coming back after all the other Doctors?' And all the while I was screaming inside at the pain. Everything he threw at me I answered with a strained 'Hmm', 'Yes' or just a bit of nodding. He said he'd been a fan since he was a kid – I bet he wasn't by the end of that!

It was the same with Billie. On her first day on set we were gearing up to do some more running, or limping in my case, and she said, 'Oh, what did your character used to wear?' My head was all over the place so I managed to spit out something like, 'Oh yes, a funny skirt', but it came out a bit off, really. I'm sure Billie must have thought I was a little dim.

The leg really alienated me, I'm afraid. When I wasn't on call, I was on my own packing it with ice or resting. As a result I never really felt part of the team. Even when I was free, events conspired against me. David had a roof terrace on the top of his trailer and I remember enviously listening to him and Anthony Head enjoying themselves up there – while I was stuck downstairs, doing interview after interview. Apparently the outside world was quite excited about the return of Sarah Jane.

It was such an honour to have been chosen to return and despite everything I really did have an amazing time but the leg colours everything, even today. I know we produced a fantastic episode but it's ingrained in my head that the whole thing was a disaster. In fact, I still can't see David or anyone else from that shoot without fighting embarrassment.

At least my last day was memorable for more pleasant reasons. As we began, the First announced, 'Lis's last day', and then at the end there was a round of applause. Honestly, they couldn't have done any more to make me feel important. Even so, as I boarded the train back to London, I thought, *That's the last I'll be hearing from them.*

Chapter Seventeen

In Case The Buggers Change The Locks

THE THING about Russell T Davies is he never stops planning. My farewell in *School Reunion* was originally written as being quite a tear-jerker. Then Russell said, 'You know what, sad endings are too easy to do. Let's have her walking away into the sunset with the dog, a spring in her step and the future at her feet.' So that's what we did. (If I'd whistled 'Bow Wow' it would have been *The Hand of Fear* all over again.) Even as we filmed it you got a sense that Sarah was going on to bigger and better things. It never occurred to me that we would ever discover what.

It was shortly after New Year's Day, 2006, when I found myself back in a restaurant with Russell. This time we were joined by Julie Gardner and my agent, Roger Carey. I remember musing with Roger in the cab about what they wanted. There were whispers of an adult spin-off called *Torchwood*. Our best guess was Sarah might get a cameo in that.

'It'll be exciting for her to grow up at last,' I said.

We had a bit of a chit-chat and a glass of wine, the usual skirting around the subject – although it's never a chore sitting and skirting with Russell. The time just flies in his company.

Finally he revealed why we were there. I just stared at him, absolutely non-plussed.

'Do you think it will work?' I said.

I'm surprised Roger didn't kick me under the table. Agents can be funny about you talking yourself out of work.

But Russell didn't flinch. 'Of course it will,' he enthused, passionate as ever.

'Well, what would you call it?'

Deep breath . . . '*The Sarah Jane Adventures*!' he announced proudly.

'Why me?'

I can't help myself.

'Everyone in Cardiff loved you in *School Reunion*,' Russell explained. 'The world needs more of Sarah Jane.'

My episode hadn't even aired yet but the end result, he said, was so phenomenal he couldn't pass up the opportunity to bring me back for good.

Slowly it began to sink in. Over the next hour I got the whole pitch. Nothing had been written but Russell had all the details worked out. Sarah Jane would continue the Doctor's work of protecting Earth from alien attacks. She'd have a sonic lipstick to match his screwdriver. And, yes, K-9 would be involved. The difference this time was he wouldn't be the headline act, due to contractual issues with his creator, Bob Baker. *Oh, what a shame . . .*

Then Russell dropped the bombshell about the children.

'Oh my God, they'll be the spawn of the Devil at that age!' I exclaimed. But of course they weren't. They are truly delightful, so young but so professional. And they're very tactile, as am I – we have lots of hugs in the morning and it's one big happy family, even with Yasmin Paige (Maria) going, Anjli Mohindra (Rani) coming in and now Tommy Knight (who plays Luke) off at university. Danny Anthony (Clyde) even calls me 'Mama Lis'. If anything, it's their show – I'm sure they're just putting up with me sometimes.

The show was, in fact, everything Russell promised. He'd begun working in children's television and it was a real passion of his to produce serious, quality drama for that age group.

To say the offer was unexpected is beyond understatement. I don't think I was even coherent when I told Brian that night! It was incredible, of course, but there were serious issues. This would involve a major commitment. We'd do a pilot, then hopefully a series. That could easily eat up five or six months of the year, and I'd be working flat out, full time – away from home in Cardiff. I'd as good as retired, hadn't I? Did I really want to get back on the treadmill?

I shared a train journey with Jane Tranter, head of BBC1, shortly after *The Sarah Jane Adventures* began. We were chatting about how much her children liked it. Then she said, 'We just threw you in, didn't we?'

'Well, yes,' I said. 'I was just impressed by the quality of everything so I couldn't say no.'

'Oh,' Jane sounded surprised. 'If you hadn't liked it, wouldn't you have done it?'

'No, I wouldn't.'

'*Really?*' she said. I don't think she meets many people in this business prepared to turn down their own show.

But I was barely in the business by then. It wasn't a case of 'Where is my career going?' I'd had my career – anything work-wise was a bonus now. And there was no point in agreeing to something I wouldn't enjoy – those days were over.

Which was the frame of mind I was in when I mulled over Russell's offer. Then I remembered how much fun I'd had in Cardiff. My leg was still not 100 per cent but despite all the pain and all the problems I'd created, I also remembered how supportive everyone had been.

And then there was the BBC itself. In my day, if you want to call it that, *Doctor Who* had been very successful but you always got the impression the BBC were a bit . . . well . . . embarrassed by the programme. It was popular but the decision-makers didn't know why. 'It's only a children's show,' they seemed to say. 'We don't need to worry about it.'

Modern *Who* couldn't have been more different. A few days before I met Russell and Julie, David Tennant's first episode had gone out at peak time on Christmas Day. Imagine if they'd done that for Tom and me! We had to fight to get a picture in the *Radio Times*. Now the Corporation couldn't be more supportive and four years later they went so far as clearing the schedules for David's swansong.

Apart from the actual workload I couldn't see a downside. I wondered if Brian and Sadie could help. Aside from worrying about the travelling and the time we'd be away from each other, they both agreed it seemed too good to turn down.

'It's your own show, Mum. And look at the people behind it!'

Sadie was right. The family pow-wow was over.

'I'm going to do it.'

* * *

Of course, I had doubts. Even as I travelled to Cardiff for our first read-through I was plagued by genuine worries, 'Can she exist without the Doctor? Can you make her work?'

And the read-through was a disaster. Considering I'd played this character on and off for thirty years you'd think I'd be able to rattle off a few lines, but my tongue seemed to be twice its normal size with nerves and I couldn't get any feel for what I was saying. Afterwards, I promised Colin Teague, the director, 'I'll be better on the day.'

'Thank God for that!' he said.

When it came to recording the pilot, *Invasion of the Bane*, in October 2006, Colin did a lovely thing. I don't know if it was for the kids' benefit or mine, but we recorded everything in chronological order. That's so rare today, but it helped immensely – we really got a sense of story.

I was a bit surprised at how rusty I was. Technically, there were things I needed to get my head around as well. The biggest shock was the scripts. On old *Who* we'd learned and workshopped the script during rehearsal then shot in a studio for a couple of days. Things had changed. *The Sarah Jane Adventures*, like *Doctor Who*, was now rehearse-record. That is to say, we arrive on set, do a run-through, then film it for real a few minutes later. From the moment we turn up we're expected to have every word memorised. It's a nightmare!

When you're dealing with the amount of science-gook Sarah has to spout, there's no room for adlibbing. More importantly, Jon and I (and then Tom and I) had developed so much of our characters' relationships in those rehearsal rooms at the Acton Hilton, not on set. There's also a purely pragmatic point. Without wishing to sound too luvvy, if you've learned it one way and your co-star has learned it another, by the time you come to perform it together you might be way out of pace.

On top of every night spent pacing up and down my hotel room trying to cram for the following day's memory test, I wasn't prepared for the added pressure of being number one on the call sheet. I was the first to be picked up, the last dropped off: the whole episode revolved around my character, there was no hiding place.

But, God, how I loved it! I'd only been in Cardiff a few days when I realised just how much I had to thank Russell for. He'd let me come back to do something I adored. I didn't realise until I started how much I'd missed it, how much I'd really, really missed it.

At this point in my life it's all that matters.

* * *

I was really pleased with how *Invasion of the Bane* turned out. Russell T Davies and Gareth Roberts had written a feisty, fun adventure story where, thank goodness, the kids got to do the majority of the running. The special effects were light years ahead of anything we ever had in the 1970s – and I did enjoy being given a 'sonic lipstick'! After decades of watching the Doctor get himself out of any writer's cul-de-sac with his handy sonic screwdriver, now Sarah could do the same. (Although I still haven't got the hang of the rules yet. Every so often Sarah Jane is in a fix and I say, 'Well, why doesn't she use the lipstick?'

'It won't work on this, Lis!'

'Why not?'

And I get back, 'We're not going to open that can of beans!')

Working with Samantha Bond, as Mrs Wormwood, was great.

If this was a sign of the calibre of things to come, I couldn't wait until recording on the proper series commenced the following year.

Of course, it was all very well recording a good show: the proof would be in how the BBC treated it and how the viewers themselves reacted. Whereas *Doctor Who* bestrode the divide between kids' and adult drama, our show was pitched squarely at the children's strand. I had a nasty feeling that it might get overlooked again, just like the old *Who*. And just like *K-9 and Company*.

But then I saw the TV schedules.

If you'd told me a couple of years ago that I would be starring in a show to be broadcast on BBC1 at 4.50 p.m. on New Year's Day, I would have called for your tablets. But that's what happened. After more than thirty years, I finally felt appreciated by the BBC.

* * *

Since my first day onscreen in *The Time Warrior*, letters and notes from fans have never been in short supply. Suddenly, though, I was sure I'd be struck off the postman's Christmas card list as he began turning up with satchel after satchel of correspondence from new young Sarah Jane admirers. A lot of people have told me they've since gone back and bought the Tom and Sarah DVDs and occasionally I even receive invites to appear on the other side of the world at millionaire's children's birthday parties. That's not something I like to do, but it's nice to be asked.

The first series proper of *The Sarah Jane Adventures* went out the following autumn and I have to say we were shocked by the response. Consistently number one in its time slot and well reviewed everywhere. Lovely! Best news of all, the commission for a second series was just around the corner. Not bad for a pensioner, as my daughter kept reminding me.

I couldn't have done it if it had seemed too much like work, though. Having Russell, Phil and Julie as our executive producers was such an incredible safety net. Their notes on each episode were never short of amazing. Alice Troughton was the perfect director and Matthew Bouche was great as our producer.

That was just the behind-the-scenes talent. We had some mouthwatering guest stars, too – Phyllida Law, Chook Sibtain and Jane Asher, to name only a few – but it was with the regular cast that I really formed relationships. The kids were wonderful and juggled their acting and their educations extremely maturely. Joseph Millson, as Alan Jackson, was always a pleasure to have around, while Juliet Cowan (Chrissie Jackson) was especially lively, and Jimmy Vee and Paul Kasey are the Terry Walshes of their day, popping up in all manner of different costumes.

Even so, as an actor you're never far away from your worst nightmares. Those little voices sniping away at your confidence seem to get louder whenever you're not working. *The Sarah Jane Adventures* was doing well but there were still occasional whispers that 'it's only children's TV'. It never feels nice to be overlooked. But when I got an invite to the premiere of that year's *Doctor Who* Christmas Special I knew things at the Beeb had changed. The country's press would be there. This was their way of making our programme feel part of the main one. Little sister we might be, but important nonetheless.

It was a great event, actually, watching *The Voyage of the Damned* – the big Kylie and David double-header – on a huge screen at the Science Museum with all the great and the good – and the press – in attendance. No expense was spared, especially on the aftershow party. Angels hung from the ceiling, all the glitterati were milling about desperate for a word with David. Some of them even wanted to talk to me.

I was chatting to someone when I saw this little fella kind of duck behind a pole, occasionally looking out. I thought, *Oh, a bit of a stalker there*. It happens occasionally.

Every time I glanced over, he ducked furtively back behind the column.

A little later someone came up and said, 'There's a big fan of yours over there.'

'Oh really?'

'Yes, he'd love to meet you, if that's all right.'

I went over and it was Nick Park – my stalker!

It's amazing to think that someone who has won so many Oscars with Wallace & Gromit could be so shy but he was great fun. The whole evening, in fact, was a pleasure from beginning to end.

Our second series, recorded in spring 2008, built on everything we'd achieved in the first. I really loved the opening story. I don't know whose idea it was but Sam Bond was back – with a Sontaran. I'd been in the very first Sontaran story all those years ago, so it felt like coming full circle, working with Kaagh. I did take a quiet moment to think about dear Kevin Lindsay, though (remember, without him, we'd be saying 'Sontaran' in a completely different way).

The biggest change this time round was Anj Mohindra coming in to replace Yasmin's character. I think Yasmin, who'd played Maria, was worried even then about being typecast – showing more professional nous than I ever had – but it was sad to see her go. Moreover, I had such a good rapport with her 'dad', which left a real void. Having said that, Ace Bhatti, who came in as Rani's father, is a hoot to have around. You'd never guess from the stern character he plays, but that man only stops joking when the cameras roll. The children proved surprisingly resilient to change – they always do, I suppose. Anj was one of the team by the end of her first day. And of course Yasmin made the occasional return appearance.

We also attracted a few bigger names to guest star. Bradley Walsh was in *Day of the Clown*, Russ Abbot appeared in *Secrets of the Stars*, and Gary Beadle, as Clyde's dad, in *The Mark of the Berserker*. For me, though, none of them compared – no offence, intended – to the special guest who joined us on the season finale, *Enemy of the Bane*: the one and only Nicholas Courtney!

It was super to see Nick again. He wasn't in the best of health so we were all delighted when he announced that he could make it. Just as my relationship with Jon had blossomed after *Who*, I probably got on better with Nick during that shoot than at any time before. He was so happy for me to have my own show and absolutely chuffed to be involved. It wasn't my decision at all, but try telling him that! (We wanted him to give me away on *The Wedding of Sarah Jane Smith* but sadly he was too ill. I spoke to him about it, though. He was so disappointed not to chalk up an appearance alongside another Doctor!)

I really thought *School Reunion* would be the final word as far as Sarah's appearances in *Who* were concerned. Russell, as usual, had other ideas. David was coming to the end of his third proper season and Russell wanted him to go out with a bang. So for *The Stolen Earth* and *Journey's End* he drafted in Rose, Mickey, Torchwood and good old Sarah Jane Smith for the mother of all end-of-term parties.

I was in Cardiff anyway for *The Sarah Jane Adventures*, Series Three, but it was still a joy to be involved again. From the moment I saw the script, however, I knew I had every right to be there. Or rather, Sarah Jane had.

The villain of the piece, we soon learned, was Davros. Like the Sontarans, I'd been the first person, along with Tom and Ian, to face this monster (although this time it was Julian Bleach under the prosthetics and not Michael Wisher). Davros and Sarah had genuine history. The moment he recognises Sarah is quite enthralling and for anyone who's seen *Genesis of the Daleks*, it's guaranteed to send a shiver down the spine. It did mine, anyway, and I was in a studio surrounded by lights and wires and crew. Just think, if Sarah had got her way and the Doctor had wiped out the Daleks, this story would never have happened . . .

After the regeneration cliffhanger of *The Stolen Earth* there was massive interest in *Journey's End* and that carried us through to a funny five-minute *SJA* Comic Relief Special, starring Ronnie Corbett, and in turn to our third series. As we arrived in Cardiff the press were going crazy for David's final four 'Specials' as the Doctor. Little did they know he was actually doing *five*!

Series Three of *The Sarah Jane Adventures* was our best yet. The *Who* crossovers continued, so we got to meet the Judoon, who'd been in Freema Agyeman's debut, *Smith & Jones*, while the return of the flatulent Blathereen meant another outing for the Slitheen costumes from the parent show. The guest stars this time were really top drawer. Jeff Rawle and Suranne Jones were in *Mona Lisa's Revenge*, Miriam Margolyes and Simon Callow chipped in with voices in *The Gift*, Floella Benjamin was a hoot in *The Eternity Trap* and Nigel Havers almost stole the show in *The Wedding of Sarah Jane Smith*.

Two men, however, stand out. *The Mad Woman in the Attic* had a very special guest star from London. His name was Brian Miller!

Poor Danny had no idea. I didn't tell anyone before the read-through and it was only afterwards that he came running over embarrassed in case he'd put his foot in it. The show's schedule is so punishing that I barely got to see my husband working but it was refreshing to spend our evenings and lunchtimes together.

I'm sure he thinks I moan out of turn about my work, so when Brian nearly got swept away by hurricane conditions while filming on Barry Island beach, I couldn't help but feel a little smug – 'Now you see what I've been putting up with for thirty years!'

Apart from my real husband, it was an honour to have Nigel Havers play Sarah Jane's groom-to-be in *The Wedding of Sarah Jane Smith*. But it was our other guest who I knew would seize the headlines.

When David Tennant agreed to appear in *The Sarah Jane Adventures* I'm sure he didn't expect it to be the last thing his Doctor ever did. The poor guy had already endured his regeneration, seen Matt Smith and Steven Moffat take over, basically had run himself physically and emotionally ragged for *The End of Time* – and now he had to do it all again! He must have been completely *Who*'d out by the time he arrived with us but you never would have guessed it. And it's fitting, I suppose, that his last appearance as the Doctor is to save his former companion one more time.

The kids – I *must* stop calling them that – were obviously bowled over by the whole thing. Tommy and I had been in *Journey's End* and *The Stolen Earth* already, but having the TARDIS with us and the actual Doctor really gave the whole episode the sort of boost money can't buy. The energy of the man is utterly incredible – he's like an electrical storm arriving on set. Things just happen. Even K-9 seemed to behave for him!

The only thing about the episode that frustrates me is the ending. Sarah says, 'Until we meet again.'

'Don't forget me, Sarah Jane,' David's Doctor replies.

Loads of people wrote to congratulate me on that – 'Oh, Lis, that was a stroke of genius!' – and I didn't have a clue what they were talking about.

And then the penny dropped. It was a beautiful homage to my original farewell from *The Hand of Fear* and I hadn't even spotted it. The whole point of that scene had gone completely over my head! Gareth Roberts, who wrote the episode, is so clever – and I'm so stupid. I bet David knew – he is a proper fan. Me? Not a clue, I'm afraid – I didn't tie it in with Tom's words to me at all. If I *had* realised, I would have played it very differently. There's obviously a lot of emotional baggage you can unpack with those words. All the things I could have done . . . But no, it completely passed me by until the plaudits started to come in.

Still, at least I wasn't hiding a broken leg this time.

School Reunion had been very much me entering the Doctor's world. Now he was coming into mine. At least, that's how it should have been. But as soon as the team knew David was definitely doing it, the number of pages with his name on just seemed to go up and up. His heart must have sunk when he saw the amount of work in store for him. So he might have been forgiven if he'd served up some sort of Doctor-lite. But you never get that with David – it was a majestic performance, so alive and rat-a-tat-tat, and I'm proud to know it was his last performance as the Tenth Doctor.

* * *

I'm pretty sure my days on *Who* are over now as well – on the main programme, at least. We're just finishing the fifth series of *The Sarah Jane Adventures* now and who knows how long that will go on? As long as our passionate audiences are still there, we will be,

I suppose, although budget cuts and time constraints don't make it any easier. (Not everything has changed at the BBC . . .) And Sarah Jane can't regenerate.

Maybe one of the kids will take over, like on *Taggart*. Perhaps it will run forever.

While I knew David was coming over to us in spring 2008, I had no idea that I would be appearing in his show, too.

It would be easier to get an invite to the Royal Wedding than squeeze any information out of the *Who* team these days. I don't blame them – every single episode or piece of gossip is leaked online within seconds. So I wasn't surprised, then, to be handed two pages rather than the whole script.

We filmed it outside Sarah Jane's Bannerman Road address, so nothing out of the ordinary as far as other people were concerned. Except, of course, David had just saved Tommy from a speeding car.

Nobody told me anything. Some things don't need to be spelt out, though. The script just read: 'You come out, you see him and you're upset and you cry.'

Oh, it must be David leaving, I thought.

And so I didn't ask any questions – I took it that Sarah Jane would know that the Doctor was regenerating. But really, they might have given me a few pointers. That annoyed me, actually, not having any context. So I did it in three different ways and just hoped one of them would fit.

For me, David's real goodbye was equally disappointing. They had a no-expenses-spared party for him and emotions ran high. Russell told this brilliant story about trying to write his speech. He'd gone to a park in Cardiff, completely deserted, and sat down on one of the many benches. Then he watched a tramp enter and he just thought, *I bet he sits down next to me*.

Sure enough, he did.

The tramp said, 'What do you do?'

'I work on *Doctor Who*,' Russell replied, prepared for the inevitable conversation.

The tramp turned to study his face.

'Are you David Tennant?'

Bernard Cribbins and Timothy Dalton were at the party as well, obviously, and as Timothy left the stage, Julie said, 'My God, we've got Doctor Who and James Bond!'

Russell said, 'Ooh, is he James Bond as well?'

Everyone laughed but I heard Timothy's smile was a little forced, if you know what I mean . . .

David's father gave the best speech, revealing how the young David used to play in the garden dressed up in his mother's hat and scarf pretending to be Tom Baker! That brought the house down but it made me feel my age, I can tell you.

Afterwards I found David standing by a wall, a bit overwhelmed by it all. 'Weren't the speeches lovely?' I said.

'I was having a great time until my father let the cat out of the bag!' he laughed.

In hindsight, this was the perfect moment to say goodbye properly. I'd thought long and hard about the perfect gift for him and had wrapped up the old TARDIS key that George had given me when I left. Knowing David was such a fan I thought it would mean something to him and because the TARDIS is now opened by a simple Yale, I wrote, 'In case the buggers ever change the locks.'

I was pretty pleased with it, I have to say, especially after David's dad's revelations but when I came to hand it over, David had gone. The night was young but I think the emotions had caught up with him and he'd slunk away without fanfare. I sent the gift to his assistant and I hope he got it: he deserved it.

* * *

It wasn't just goodbye to David, though. The whole team was handing over the reins and Russell and Julie were relocating to Hollywood. I wondered how this would affect my little programme. Russell put me straight at the party – 'Never forget, I'm only a phone call away.' In fact, it works perfectly. We speak and text now more than ever and it doesn't matter what time of night or day, he's always on. I was anguishing over an awards show outfit recently so I texted, 'Blue or pink?'

A second later: 'Blue.'

He just *knows*.

It's unprecedented, in my experience, to have that level of access to the execs but *The Sarah Jane Adventures* is Russell's baby. He looks over all the scripts, looks at the edits and fires off notes left, right and centre. It's as if he's in the next room.

But it wasn't just the show I was worried about when Russell announced he was leaving the UK – I also needed to give him the best farewell gift, but what? When I'd left *Who*, I bought Tom an engraved gin glass, which he claims to still have to this day – but what for Russell?

Then I realised I had the perfect thing at home. *Russell's leaving, the Doctor's leaving – just as I once left*, I thought. So I rooted around in my cuttings box and there it was: my original script complete with my own deliciously inconsiderate comments in the margins!

Russell being Russell, he knew exactly what it was the moment I handed it over. There's no one else I would rather have given it to, actually. He has been so important in my life and totally deserving of something truly unique as a thank-you present.

* * *

Russell's generosity didn't only extend to me, though. I'll never forget how thoughtful he was in inviting Barry and Terry to Cardiff to give their opinions on what he was doing. Poor Barry died unexpectedly in 2009. That shook me more than even Jon's death, I think. He was my mentor, my inspiration in so many ways, and my friend. It was a dark few days in the Miller household after that. It was a very private family funeral so we didn't attend, but we sent a card and I spoke to his daughter. I'm just so glad Barry lived to see the heights his Sarah Jane had achieved. I owe him so much. It's fair to say, not even Russell could have rejuvenated *Who* if Barry hadn't lain such solid foundations.

A few months after Barry's passing, on New Year's Day 2010, I sat down with my family to watch part two of *The End of Time*. My scene at the end is one of those blink-and-you'll-miss-it numbers but I think it works. It's nice, actually, and says all it needs to. Matt Smith is the Doctor now and even joined us on the fourth series of *The Sarah Jane Adventures*. He was brilliant – so young and so tall! But I think my time on the main programme passed with David: his Doctor brought me back. So now – thirty-seven years after I first stepped inside the TARDIS, after I encountered my initial alien encounter, after having my life turned upside down by the wonderful team on *Who* and the fans who made it all worthwhile – we were leaving together.

As the credits on *The End of Time* rolled I realised it was three years to the day since the pilot episode of *The Sarah Jane Adventures* premiered on the same channel. Who saw that coming, back in 1973 when Brian and I sat down to watch my fledgling appearance on *The Time Warrior*?

Who indeed.

Epilogue

Who On Earth Would Want To Read About Me?

Lis – precious mum to one of us, dear wife to the other – worked on this book throughout 2010 with her co-writer, Jeff. In December of that year, she received a printout of the final draft from her publisher and put it in a drawer. Christmas and New Year with the family were more important to her than anything work related. Weeks passed and the book stayed in her desk. When her editor, Sam, rang to ask about progress, Lis said she was struggling to find the time to go through it. New scripts for Series Five of *The Sarah Jane Adventures* were beginning to arrive; they had to take priority. More importantly, she wanted to be fully focused before adding the finishing touches to her book. She didn't want to give it anything less than her best. If only she wasn't always so tired . . .

And then in February 2011 Lis's world, and ours, changed forever.

She was diagnosed with cancer. She had probably been suffering its effects for two years – that accounted for the tiredness. Worst of all, she was informed the disease was already quite far along. Her doctor said, 'We can't cure it, but we're going to throw everything we can at you to fight it as long as possible.'

That fight lasted no more than two months. Lis died at the Meadow House Hospice in the early hours of Tuesday, 19 April 2011. She was 65 years old.

* * *

The first person Lis told about her diagnosis was Russell T Davies. She actually rang him on the way back from the doctor's in February. She loved hearing his voice. He was always so positive, always instinctively knew what to do, but even he couldn't help this time.

Lis owed Russell so much. She had just attained pensioner status when he'd plucked her out of retirement to appear once again in *Doctor Who*. It's fair to say none of us saw that coming. And as for then creating an entire TV show for her to star in – that was just magical.

Lis was so proud of *The Sarah Jane Adventures*. It was playing a character she'd always loved and had protected so strongly for decades. Plenty of writers or directors in the past hadn't really understood Sarah Jane, but Russell *knew*. In his hands, Sarah Jane got to have the life she deserved.

Lis loved having her own show. She used to say it was such an honour, and such an unexpected one at her time of life. But she really gave it her all. She never did anything at less than 100 per cent effort – you can see that on the screen.

She played a surrogate mum in the show and she felt like one as well, because it was such a loving relationship between herself and the cast and crew. Lis loved fussing around the kids and being part of such a big, dedicated team. (She would have made a wonderful grandmother.) Decades after her theatre training she was still an ensemble player at heart and it gave her such a thrill to think all those lovely people around her had employment at that moment because of her. She was so happy that her good fortune could be shared with as many others as possible.

Of course, with that realisation came great pressure. In her final days and weeks, Lis was at her most despondent when she thought about her dozens of good friends in Cardiff, and many more unseen champions of Sarah Jane in London, who would be out of work because of her. And then there were the fans, hundreds of thousands of disappointed children, who would be left with unfinished adventures. 'All these people are depending on me,' she would say.

'I'm letting everyone down.' It was typical of her – worrying about everyone else when really, she should have been thinking of herself.

* * *

Lis was very stubborn, extremely motivated and quietly ambitious. Once she'd recovered from the shock of being given her own show she determined to do everything she could to make it succeed. If that meant leaving her home and family to live in Cardiff for six months a year, then so be it.

The BBC provided a wonderful apartment in the Bay area that Lis transformed into her home from home. But more than anything she loved coming back to her real home – and to us.

In the early days she would return virtually every weekend. Being driven all the way to London was her one luxury, but while it was Elisabeth Sladen who left Cardiff, the woman who climbed out of the car in Ealing was unmistakably Lis Miller. She had no problem separating her two lives. Perhaps the long journey helped her adjust. Seconds after entering our house she'd find some little job to do, often in her beloved garden. You couldn't stop her.

'Mum, *I'll* do that.'

'It's all right, I won't be a minute.'

The idea of relaxing never occurred to her. If she wasn't pinned down with coffee and a flapjack, she would never have stopped.

From being the centre of a creative maelstrom one minute to running around fussing and clucking over us like a mother hen the next, Lis took it all in her stride. Or so we thought. As the programme became more successful and the schedule more punishing, Lis's trips home became less practical and we began to visit her instead. That was when she confessed, 'Every time the car taking me back to Cardiff pulled away from our house, I cried. Every time.' As much as she adored being Sarah Jane, she loved being Mrs Miller.

Lis kept that secret to herself for several years, but that was her way. She was intensely private. In fact, you know she would have hated us revealing any of this!

She was an actress, she was famous and she was often recognised, especially in the last few years, but she wasn't a celebrity. That wasn't the life she led, or the lifestyle she wanted. Lis only wore dark glasses if it was sunny.

So then, you might ask, why did she write her autobiography? The simple answer is because she was asked: again and again and again. But even at her first meeting with Jeff, her co-writer, she admitted, 'You're going to hate working with me. Most actors put on a mask when they take on a role – *I* put on a mask when I'm talking about myself.'

She wasn't joking, but over the course of 18 months she confided more and more. But still, after every session she did for the book, she'd fret, 'What am I doing? Who on earth would want to read about me?' She didn't believe she was at all interesting – 'It's Sarah Jane people want to hear about, not Mrs Miller.'

She was also terrified of offending someone in print. The idea of getting an old colleague's name wrong, forgetting them or mis-remembering an incident filled her with dread. But her biggest worry was upsetting the fans of her shows (she could never bring herself to admit they were fans of *hers*!). Even though she was no devotee of science fiction, she owed so much to people who were. Lis loved going to conventions, being made to feel so welcome by thousands of children – or children at heart – and being welcomed into their world. Her greatest fear in writing this book was that she'd get her *Who* facts wrong. She was devastated by the idea that fans would think she didn't care. Despite being assured, 'It's a book of your memories. It's how *you* saw the world – it's not a *Who* encyclopaedia,' she never fully believed it. The idea of just one child being disappointed in her was almost too much to bear. For that reason alone she nearly pulled the plug on the project at least half a dozen times.

* * *

Watching the news reports and the tribute programmes the night Lis died was surreal. We couldn't believe she wasn't there any more. There she was on the TV screen, smiling and laughing and looking beautiful. How could she be gone?

It probably still hasn't sunk in yet. Over the last five years we've grown accustomed to Lis being away all summer. We're used to not having her in the house all the time, but she always returned. Now, whole hours or even days can pass and then you suddenly realise all over again: this time she's not coming back. Our cat, Chyna, is still looking for her. Every time the front door opens, she's disappointed.

Lis died early in the morning, just before we arrived at Meadow House. A nurse brought us a cup of tea and sat with us. Later, she said, 'My son will be devastated. He loved her.'

It was the first clue that we wouldn't be the only ones grieving.

We had cards from so many friends and family, some real blasts from the past. We had many more from strangers, people whose lives had been touched by Lis at some point. There were heartfelt messages from fans of her original *Doctor Who* appearances and others from kids who only knew her from *The Sarah Jane Adventures*. Young or old, it doesn't matter. She reached out to them all, as she reached out to us.

Some of the tributes were very nice. Tom, David and Russell all said such lovely things on television and in the papers. And wonderful Ed Russell, who worked with Lis as a BBC brand manager, embarked on a walk from Cardiff to Television Centre in White City in her memory. The money is still coming in, but as we write nearly £20,000 has been raised for Meadow House Hospice in Lis's honour.

* * *

It was thinking about all these people, mostly strangers, who had been moved by Lis that brings us here, to this book. For weeks her desk had remained untouched. We knew the manuscript was there but neither of us wanted to pick it up. It was too personal and we weren't ready. Not yet.

But then one day we did.

We read page one and we were hooked. Lis's voice rang out from every line. It was just black text on white paper but it was indisputably her – her way with words, her little phrases, her love of life and of people poured out. Sam, her editor, was very kind and offered the opportunity to cancel the project but we both agreed we had to share this with her fans. After all, they – *you* – are the people it was written for. You are the reason it was written.

Words, of course, will never bring Lis back but we are luckier than most: we have her book, we have her face in magazines and we have her voice ringing out, seemingly on loop, from the repeats of *The Sarah Jane Adventures*. It's of some comfort hearing those episodes in the background as we get through each day.

Everywhere we turn there are reminders that the world lost Elisabeth Sladen, but we lost Elisabeth Miller. This book, hopefully, is a fitting tribute to both.

Brian Miller & Sadie Miller
London, September 2011